ONE GEAR
NO BREAKS

ONE GEAR
NO BREAKS

Lori-Ann Muenzer's Ride to Belief,
Belonging, and a Gold Medal

LORI-ANN MUENZER
with KARL R. WILBERG

KEY PORTER BOOKS

Library and Archives Canada Cataloguing in Publication

Muenzer, Lori-Ann
One gear, no breaks : Lori-Ann Muenzer's ride to belief, belonging, and a gold medal / as told to Karl R. Wilberg.

ISBN 1-55263-757-3

1. Muenzer, Lori-Ann.   2. Cyclists—Canada—Biography.   3. Bicycle racing—Training.
1. Wilberg, Karl R.   11. Title.

GV1051.M84A3 2006   796.6'2'092   C2005-906488-9

The publisher gratefully acknowledges the support of the Canada Council for the Arts and the Ontario Arts Council for its publishing program. We acknowledge the support of the Government of Ontario through the Ontario Media Development Corporation's Ontario Book Initiative.

We acknowledge the financial support of the Government of Canada through the Book Publishing Industry Development Program (BPIDP) for our publishing activities.

Key Porter Books Limited
Six Adelaide Street East, Tenth Floor
Toronto, Ontario
Canada M5C 1H6

www.keyporter.com

Text design: Marijke Friesen
Electronic formatting: Jean Lightfoot Peters

All photos courtesy Lori-Ann Muenzer except those with a credit line indicating source.

Printed and bound in Canada

06 07 08 09 10 6 5 4 3 2 1

To R.J. Childerhose,
Fighter Pilot, Writer, Mentor

CONTENTS

Preface 9
Prologue 11

1 Hunger 15
2 Apprentice 21
3 Breaks 31
4 The Deep End 41
5 Monster 49
6 Fall 63
7 Rich and Strange 73
8 Mystery 85
9 Coach 101
10 Odyssey 111
11 Rocket 121
12 Lighting the Fuse 133
13 Buried Treasure 145
14 Rocket Ride 155
15 Waiting for Dirndl Girl 161
16 Bike Monster 169
17 Playing with Fire 175
17 ½ El Toro 185
18 School and the Seventh Sense 197
19 Here Be Dragons 205
20 Athena 215

Epilogue 243
Acknowledgements 247
Glossary 251

PREFACE

one gear, no breaks /wun geer no brakz/ *n.* **1** *idiomatic phrase.* Describes the track bicycle, a fixed gear machine evolved for speed, with no means for speed reduction. **2** describes the journey of the aspiring competitive cyclist. Ambition is limitless, so too is adversity.
—From the *Cyclists' Listing of Words and Phrases (Cyc.L.O.W.Ps.)*

Lori-Ann's story is a true one. However, when she related to me her story, with all of its agonizing reversals of fortune, I wondered what language, what words, could best explain her almost invulnerable cycle of success followed by disaster?

Was there a dictionary—a code book—that could define the language of competitive cycling? As I soon discovered, my authorial colleagues have left the shelves bare of a sufficient dictionary. Therefore, the task is mine.

Competitive cycling is about suffering and speed. Its contradictions include participants seeking fulfilment through mind-bursting, soul-roasting difficulty. Of the cycling disciplines, match sprinting is an arcane sport of codified duelling, where diabolical suffering and danger are meted out, not in a Wild West free for all, but in an indirect, Old World way. Pain, panic, and punishment would certainly be among the most commonly used words in this language.

Creating the word list to encompass these contradictions would be a tall order. Yet this was the easy part.

Like an archaeologist unravelling an ancient mystery, I leafed through Lori-Ann's training diaries—hundreds of meticulously maintained pages—and interpreted the entries. She and I spent months in digitally recorded interviews. I played and re-played the recordings, searching for the essence of this language. Her coach, Steen Madsen, was interviewed, and these results, too, were sifted through. Also, my own much less successful cycling career had to be reviewed to find the correct meanings.

Months followed, and it became clear that for those who seek the summit, those who want to win and win big, there's a special language hammered out through the triumphs and catastrophes that inevitably follow. Never mind the difficulty of describing the journey, try to explain *why* it is so. Words do not only describe, they also explain.

Fate and time conspire against all of us, including Lori-Ann. The difference with her is that she beat the system.

Explaining this is, indeed, the hard part. Eventually, I found the language of ambition, of adversity, and of triumph, and incorporated it in the *Cyclists Listing of Words and Phrases*—the *Cyc.L.O.W.Ps.*

This language is spoken well only by a few, and I am pleased to share it with you. Of course, Lori-Ann is, *with one exception*, the most eloquent speaker of this tongue. The commentaries by her coach, Steen Madsen, reveal his fluency in this language. Others are not so capable. However, this language sees no need for personal criticism, and so I have altered the names, and personas of certain officials, in order to speak truly.

The exception, though?

It's not really a person, it's a . . . thing—an old thing. But more of that later.

Take your time looking for this anomaly, and while you're conducting your search, you'll run across Lori-Ann's story about finding belief, belonging, and, of course, one other item: an Olympic gold medal. Commence reading. The story begins.

PROLOGUE

Write off

August 18, 2004, Athens Olympic Velodrome, 10:30 AM, Velodrome Parking Lot

Help me. Somebody.

I swore this would never happen again. You'd think that here, in Athens, where I'm a contender for an Olympic medal and Canada's only track-cycling athlete, I would not be a castaway, jettisoned by my team like so much ballast.

But, here I am; on the bus to the velodrome, anxious, alone, and heartsick for home. Maybe I'm unique, but disdain and abandonment have a poor effect on me.

Team Canada staff? Gone. Assistants, managers and helpers? Gone.

They've wandered off to watch riders that have youth, sponsors, and no need for a day job—everything I don't have. Today is a critical training session. All I needed was one person to time my practice sprints, but I've been written off.

I'm thirty-eight years old, and my competitors are young enough to be my daughters. Maybe the officials don't think I can hack it. Little do they know that the workouts I've done—700-pound leg presses—would crush twenty-year-olds, and the next day leave them hobbling.

I've survived those, and a lot more too.

I've put family, friends, and a home life on hold. I've abandoned any hope of leisure, and anything new. My back is held together with scar tissue, and I've been patched up by chiropractors and physios around the globe. Yet, it's not age or pain that will stop me. Only one thing has *ever* stopped me.

It's the leering dragon of loneliness, a scaly beast with a hyena's sick smirk.

I thought I'd left it behind, but now? It's that voice in my head, the one I've heard for two decades, saying, "You'll never win, you'll never belong."

It's a loneliness with a knife to my soul. A chain around my heart. A gun holding my dreams hostage—and I'm not at an event that permits frailty.

The bus stops. Other athletes spring to their feet. The driver stares into his mirror at me.

What kind of person would keep going? Not a person, maybe a monster; one so driven by ambition that she's lost all care for the risks. Duelling at seventy kilometres per hour. Playing chicken on a forty-five-degree banked track while wearing an overgrown Speedo.

Is that me? An ambitious monster hooked on high-speed conflict?

My eyes scrunch together. I can't break down, not four days before the finals, but I know what my team thinks: *she's too old.*

I have one last ride for an Olympic medal, and one last shot at vindicating the costs. This is Lori-Ann's Athens Alamo, and it's a one-woman fight. Has my inner Muenster—the distilled firewater of concentrated competitor—gone fishing too?

On every front, it seems impossible.

I can't time myself and sprint at over seventy kilometres per hour. I could just give up, I think, and go home.

Home! The thought washes over me, a soothing, warm wave of comfort. Home pulls on my heart from across half a world. Home is a sleepy neighbourhood, a green backyard, and phone calls to my sister. Home is a red-trimmed house, an antique rocking chair, and people who love me.

Home is my coach, training partner, and friend, Steen Madsen.

Yet, he's on the other side of the world, and I'm in an empty bus about to face the race of my life. I'm facing a bigger opponent than a mere dragon. I look away, not wanting to name her. And I know her name well—she's always the last one to believe in me.

My heart wants me to close my eyes, and imagine I'm home. My brain says, "Get moving."

Seventeen years of training take over. Home pulls me back, and yet everything it means is pushing me on.

If home is a million miles away, so too is my goal—an Olympic gold medal.

I stare at the velodrome on the horizon. My mind is quivering like a car trying to claw its way backwards out of the ditch. The motor's revving, like the whole thing's going to blow. My feet scrape on the pavement. Why do I keep trying? Fighting?

I could take my foot off the gas pedal, but, at age thirty-eight, I wouldn't want to develop a bad habit. Besides, it's the only way to get home.

CHAPTER 1

HUNGER

AND THE 1976 MORLAND ROAD, TORONTO, GRAND PRIX

hunger /hun gur/ *n.* **1** intense desire, often for food, sometimes for success. For competitive cyclists, a continual state. **2** (*variant*) a troubling condition. Victories take place, but the hunger remains unsatisfied. Appetite expands and increases the want.

—From the *Cyc.L.O.W.Ps.*

There were a lot of reasons why, even twenty-eight years ago, I would never back off. Some reasons were hidden, discovered only recently, and others were obvious from the beginning. Fast things are fun things. Slow things are boring. Boredom is the enemy.

Of course, like all love affairs, there is a cost. Speed is your friend until you crash. That's when you learn the relationship can be painful—until it whispers in your ear, "Feeling better? Bet you can pull it off this time."

The voice whispered in a little girl's ear twenty-eight years ago.

I can see her now: a blonde-haired missile, rocketing on her black bike, working the frame with her thin arms, leading a line of children, snaking past parked cars on Morland Road in Toronto, Ontario.

The ten-year–old girl turns to look back.

I clench my fists. She's gonna hit an AMC Gremlin right in the bumper.

The girl looks forward, and arcs away from the car. The boy behind her, his mouth a dark "O," careens into the curb, and vaults out of sight, his body thrust forward like Superman.

The girl's blonde hair swings back as she accelerates for the finish line, a stop sign. The other kids aren't even close, but she shoots her left hand in the air, claiming victory, and jams on the brake, leaving a black tire mark at the stop sign.

She was glad she won. I was glad she was alive.

The others wobbled to the finish. They had lost to her—again. The other kids shrugged and went home. It was suppertime anyway. The girl went into her house at 22 Morland Road, and asked her mom if she could stay out and play baseball. I recognized the two-storey brick house, the front flower bed with tulips, and the green door. And I recognized the girl.

The house was my house and the girl was me, twenty-eight years ago.

That day was a good day, like so many others I had as a child. I had loving parents, and good schools.

So, where did it come off the rails? Why did I have to leave on a twenty-year adventure to become the fastest woman in the world? How did home become a prison? How did a child become a stranger, one hungering for challenge and recognition?

Yet, the same causes for the rift were also the seeds of my Olympic success, and ultimately for reconciliation. I'm on good terms with my parents now. But *now* is a long time from *then*.

Then?

The world, according to my parents, was to be a stable and ordered world. One with Peter Pan collars, skirts, and limits. "Lori-Ann, wear this dress," says Mom. "Lori-Ann, don't wear a black top with black bottoms. Lori-Ann, why won't you sit still? Lori-Ann, why don't..." On the other hand, my world—the world of my childhood and adolescence—was one where risk reigned, and limits were made to be exceeded.

I don't know where it comes from, but I've been blessed with an extraordinary amount of energy. I wore out the kids on Morland Road. My tormented back tire blew out after countless skidding-stop finishes. If the racing was too dull, we'd play a version of follow the leader. The leader would weave between cars, skimming the car doors, side mirrors, and bumpers, daring the rest of the pack to follow. Go faster, close the critical rider-bike-car gap and lose your opponents. I didn't think of this as training myself to make critical judgements. To me, this was pure and simple fun.

After the bike races there would be baseball. When the ball players caved, I'd find the tennis players at the courts near the wall of James Culnan Catholic School.

"Hi," I'd say. "Mind if I hit off the wall?"

They shrug and ignore me.

Wackawackawacka, goes the threadbare tennis ball as it careens off the bricks.

My hand is waving the racquet like it's a fan on a hot summer day. *Wackawacka...pop!*

I pick up the split sphere, stare at it, and wonder why it broke.

I'd get back on my bike and rip around the neighbourhood. When the street lights went on, I'd sprint home, disappointed to call it a day.

My mother couldn't understand why her daughter was a wind-up doll that clattered, chattered, and never ran down. Demure, understated clothes were demolished. Knees were covered in bruises. Hands were dirty with bike chain grease. I had no interest in the ordered, stable world Mom tried to build.

Everybody envies my abundant energy, but it comes with a price. Ask my mom. She'd say I have a tendency to become easily bored; restless with others who aren't trying hard, refusing to take no for an answer. And, perhaps the hardest thing: I'm different than everybody else, and don't easily fit in. Still, like everyone else, I wanted to belong in a community that I respected, and to be accepted on my terms. Some people are lucky to be born into that community; I had to ride my way into it.

Then, my family was no more interested in my exploration of adventures, sport and otherwise, than I was in a traditional, middle-class Canadian existence. Their lack of interest created a hunger, a gnawing, empty feeling, and it became another reason why I was hooked on pushing every activity to the limit, hoping to be recognized for succeeding at what I felt was important. The net result was familial conflict and a growing, but nameless hunger.

While at home, I had some early successes, and many of the attributes that my family taught me—persistence, perseverance, and pride—were essential to my ultimate triumph. Ironically, they combined with the nameless hunger and led to an Olympic gold medal. But that is *now*. Let me tell you about *then*.

It's a myth that successful Olympic athletes are sped on their way by sponsorships or a wealthy sport administration. Also, there is the legend of the successful athlete who starts out as a promising child, and builds on each success in a continuous progression to the top. Maybe that's the way it is for some lucky athletes, but I don't know any whose lives live up to that ideal.

In my case there *was* a promising start. In grade eight, at Humbercrest Public School, I made Athlete of the Year. A big factor in my success was the encouragement of our coach, Mrs. Jenkins. She believed in me, and helped me channel my vast enthusiasm. Even if I didn't understand the hunger, there was a simple clue to my success: if just one person helped or cared, I blossomed like a sunflower.

Later, in high school, I was lost in the large school population, and, without direct encouragement, I left sport behind. After grade twelve I trained as a legal secretary at Retter Business College in Toronto, and began to make my way through the working world.

At eighteen, there was a final showdown with my parents. I wanted to live by my rules. I was given a choice: live their way, or hit the highway.

I chose the highway.

My parents had, I felt, written me off. As I moved out, I thought, if they wouldn't believe in me, then I would have to. The problem was I didn't.

Some results of moving out were surprising, others not. Loneliness I expected. Privation was anticipated. But the hunger, the primitive need to prove myself? At the time I couldn't explain it, but being cast out transformed the mouse of loneliness, nibbling at my adolescent soul, into a psychic dragon, undermining my spirit and demanding to be fed.

Over the next twenty years, I learned a few things about dragons. One, you can feed them forever, but they're never satisfied. Second, I like to kill them. Third, it takes a monster, an ambitious monster, to kill a dragon.

Everyone thinks their adult life starts when they leave home. In my case, the real beginning started on a bike.

It was not the black one with the bald back tire, and not the $8000 carbon-fibre model I ride today, but a forty-four-pound mountain bike with squishy tires and reflectors on the spokes. This generic bike, the key to my beginning, was designed to ride from the garage to the corner store. At this time, 1987, I was twenty-two-years-old, working the day shift, doing aerobics in my Reeboks, but still not feeling that I fit in.

Unfortunately, this boat anchor of a bike's fate was to be ridden by me three times a week, from 5 AM to 7 AM, and for up to eight hours on weekends. I was its worst nightmare: someone who loved to ride for the joy of it, for riding puts you closer to the adventures that you dream of. It's hard to say why this is so, but the French author and pilot Antoine de Saint-Exupéry said, "The machine does not isolate us from the problems of nature, but plunges us more deeply in them."

In my case, the bike was the machine that plunged me deeply into life. Here was a machine that would take sweat and turn it into speed. Your speed, your limits are up to you. And so, my apprenticeship began, but I had no idea how tortuous it would be. Throughout it all, the hunger to succeed kept me churning through not one apprenticeship, but two.

CHAPTER 2

APPRENTICE

apprentice /a'prentis/ *n. & v.* **1** (*typ.*) a person learning a trade. Material rewards are *small*. **2** a new cyclist. Goals are unrealistic. Pain is ever present. Material rewards are *nonexistent*. **3** ordinarily, cyclists *under* the age of eighteen. After adulthood, the human body is less able to ignore intense physical pain.

—From the *Cyc.L.O.W.Ps.*

"A $1000 consumer loan, for a bike?"

The loans clerk at Toronto's Main Street branch of the TD Bank held her ballpoint pen over my application form. If she didn't sign it, I wouldn't be able to buy the bike, a real racing bike. The owner of Toronto's LocalMotion bike store said he had one for me. They had the bike, the TD had the money, and I had the ambition. It was a perfect solution. However, if she turned me down, I'd be doomed to pedalling the forty-four-pound boat anchor, my legs beating its lethargic pedals in ponderous circles.

The clerk's eyes, glaring through the expansive glass of her ovoid spectacles, pin me to the wall. I stare back, trying to appear as though, in 1987, it's perfectly normal to take out a loan for a bike.

"It's a racing bike. A Bianchi."

"A Bonkey?"

"Beeonkay," I say, slowly, trying to speak like an Italian.

"I'm not deaf," she says, and adjusts her glasses. "This Beeankey is only $600. Why do you need $1000?"

"For a helmet, a jersey and shorts, and some shoes."

"Shoes?"

"Special bike shoes. They have cleats in the bottom that fit the pedals. The special shorts have a leather pad in the crotch."

"Figures," she says. "What do you want with this Beeankey?"

"I want to race."

The pen moves closer to the approval line. I will the pen to become like a lawn dart, to plunge to the paper, and press through all four copies and their carbons. The pen stops.

"Race?" she says.

"The bike," I say. "I want to bike race."

"Have you raced before?"

"No," I say as though it's perfectly normal to risk one's credit on a sport you've had no experience with.

"Do you belong to a team?"

"No."

"A bike club?"

"No."

She pulls the application towards her, guarding the precious form. The pen is raised to her teeth. She taps them. On behalf of the board of directors and shareholders of the bank, she has to carefully weigh the miniscule benefit of extending credit to this misguided dreamer. I have, she thinks, been working for the same boss, in the same law office, for three years. On the other hand, no one's ever asked her for a loan for a bike, let alone a $600 bike.

"Why do you want to race?" she asks.

It's the critical question. A philosophical answer will confirm that I am unbalanced. A practical answer will cinch the loan.

"If I wanted a car, a stereo, or a holiday, I'd get the loan, right?"

She nods.

"I don't need a car. I don't want to sit around my apartment listening to music and dreaming about what could be. I don't want to sit at work waiting for the only two weeks of my life I'll enjoy living."

She stares.

Years ago, I had glimpses of bike racing. In 1984 I saw Canadian Steve Bauer sprinting for Olympic gold against American Alexi Grewal. At that time, a TV commercial was playing, the story of a farm-boy cyclist whose father did the boy's chores so the aspiring athlete could train for the games. Bauer's performance and the fictional farm boy's dream had tantalized me.

"It's all I dream of," I say. "I want to be the best."

She looks at me over the top of her glasses.

"I want to be really good at something exciting," I say, throwing up my hands. "I don't know why."

The pen descends. She's scratching at the form, checking boxes that no doubt say: "application declined for other reasons," or some other euphemism for "crazy idea, crazy person."

The application is thrust towards me. She frowns. "Take it to new accounts."

"I don't need an account."

"You do for a new loan."

There is a smile, a thin and lopsided smile. I stare at the form and the word "approved."

I look up to thank her, but she's gone.

Loan in hand, I return to the bike store—LocalMotion. I had seen its ad in the Toronto phone book and liked their logo. Did I check their references? Shop around? No. I liked their logo.

The owner, Leo Petrus, said he had a bike for $300. Petrus is surprised when he sees me. I'm five feet ten inches and 170 pounds; most male road riders are slight, and female riders are petite. My legs are too long for the $300 bike. He is a good salesman. I end up with a $600 Bianchi Brava, shorts, shoes, jersey and helmet. Petrus ends up with $1000.

He does a good fit. A poorly fitting bike will numb your pelvis, cramp your arms, and cripple your back. While he sizes me up, Petrus asks my intentions. I restrain myself. I don't say, "I have this poorly understood need to be really good—a champion, in fact." I just tell him I want to race.

"Join the club," he says. Petrus tells me that to get a racing license, I need to qualify. He said a lot more, but all I remember is, "Get three top-three placings in the novice races."

I leave the store, riding the bike, my street clothes in a bag, feeling like an apprentice on the first day of work. The clothes are new, the tools sparkling, and the beginner excited. And, like any apprentice, I have no idea what it's really going to be like. But I have a good feeling. I can sense a dream becoming a reality in my work-a-day world. Of course, I have no idea that a bike race and "a good feeling" are seldom experienced simultaneously.

My friend, the Bianchi, is a traitor. It's torturing me.

I'm hanging my head over the handlebars, tromping on the pedals of the Bianchi. The air is roaring in my ears, and sweat rivulets are tickling my nose. I wipe my face with one gloved hand, the crusted goop on the glove's terry cloth thumb scraping my cheek. My front wheel swerves for the ditch. I wrest it back, and straighten my course.

"How long will this take?" I wonder, as I strain against the pedals in the forty-kilometer LocalMotion club time trial. Riders are started at one-minute intervals, and speed down a quiet countryside road, trying to hold a winning pace for the distance.

A time trial is indeed a trial. It's not just against the clock—it's against your pain threshold and your ability to suffer in the absence of external motivations. There's only you, the heartless clock, and a world of suffering.

Suffering? Did I say suffering? The bike has the ability to inflict more pain than any other device intended for human enjoyment. The bike supports your weight, freeing up energy for riding. It's why you can ride faster and longer than you can run. Ever seen runners collapse? If they were on bikes, they could keep going.

In the distance, through the late August haze, I see the dark speck of my *minute-man*, the person who started ahead of me. Finally, there's something to focus on. I feel a surge of competitive fire. Two things are growing, the apprentice and her helpful assistant, a monster. Competitive instinct is like a hungry monster. Suffering? What suffering?

The monster needs to be fed. The minute-man is mine.

The minute-man was mine, but a top three was not.

My first mass-start race was another matter. Our club travelled to York University in Toronto for a *criterium*. A criterium, or *crit* for short, is a multi-lap race on an urban circuit of a kilometre or so. Cornering, sprinting for lap prizes, and speed are the keynote features of the criterium. It was, compared to the lonely suffering of the time trial, an event made for me.

The novice race is first. The LocalMotion team, all ten of us, with me being the only woman, ride to the course. The Bianchi is clean, the chain oiled, and the tires filled to the point they hum on the pavement. My teammates prop themselves against trees, waiting for me and a handful of other novice women to complete our few laps. We're the warm-up event for the category races.

I'm on the line, looking at my competitors. Their jerseys, bright blues, reds and yellows, contrast with our black shorts. The officials, called *commissaires*, are dressed like hockey referees in black-and-white striped shirts. One stands at the line and holds a starting pistol in the air.

I have no idea how good the other women are. Similarly, I don't have any strategy. There are only two knowns: I want to go fast and I want to win. Do you need anything more? The answer is yes, but the gun fires off, and so do I.

The road flows beneath my wheels and I churn into the first turn. The bike sweeps through the turns, I complete the first lap, in the lead, and pass our club. Their yells of encouragement are distorted by wind noise.

A spectator standing on the first turn is shouting something, but I'm too wound up to understand.

"Up five," I think he says. Up five? I shake my head and line up for the next turn. The next lap he says, "Up three." I look back and see the small pack of women, their group stretching back in a pace line, closing.

The pain I feel is rewarded by the sight of my competitors struggling to catch me. I pull up on the bars, and ignore the build up of lactic acid that is threatening to turn my legs into sacks of sand.

Next lap, the man yells, "Up five." I look over my shoulder and see I've put distance on the pack. Finally, I understand the man's mysterious shouts. He's telling me how many seconds I am ahead of the pack. I've got an ally, almost a coach, who's cluing me in.

I wonder what I've gotten myself into. I have only a few laps to go, but I'm dying. This is worse, I think, than time trialling. Worst of all, I may be caught. The idea of being defeated trips a switch.

Get caught? I'd rather die.

A roaring, almost an animal-like growling, fuels my riding. I can't explain it, but I love being at the front, suffering like never before, but taking charge of the event.

"Up six," yells my impromptu coach.

Later I meet him and learn his name is Fred Garriques. Like many other long-time cyclists, he's happy to help out a novice. My willingness to tough it out, not withstanding a total lack of cycling knowledge, won me a foothold in this community, one that would take me around the world, and to the top of the athletic ladder. It also won me the race at York University.

Over the next two years, 1988 and 1989, I continued my apprentice-ship. These years were ones of training, racing, and as much of both as I could handle. Yet, without effective coaching, my results were hit and miss. At the club level there was a bewildering mix of homespun advice and training myths imported decades ago from Europe. Still, sheer determination helped me collect scores of road-race medals.

A sense that I wasn't progressing enough after two years prompted me to move to Quebec. Provincial medals were not enough to quell the dragon, the one lurking in the periphery and goading me to push beyond local success. Quebec riders had good coaches. Maybe, I rea-soned, I could get the help to move onto the national stage.

I found myself working in Montreal at the law firm of Stikeman Elliot. The culture of blue-blood and blue-chip companies grated on me: I did not take well to their dictate that I wear a skirt. The antediluvian atmosphere drove me to apply to Oerlikon Aerospace, and was I hired as a desktop publisher.

My apprenticeship progressed. I joined Club Cycliste Monteregie, and then Espoir de Laval, Canada's top club, and immersed myself in eighty races a season. I won tons of medals, but fixated on the need to get to the next stage: the National Road Team.

Part of my desire was fuelled by the stories I read in cycling magazines. *Bicycling*, *Winning*, *Pedal*, and especially *VeloNews*, the industry newspa-per, were windows on the world I wanted to inhabit. Every month I bought a stack of these periodicals and pored over them, memorizing the riders' names and their results. I admired their sponsored clothes and the latest gear they were given. Occasionly, an interview with a top coach would appear, and I would scan it, trying to glean training tips.

"*Motorpacing*," I said to myself, reading an article describing the technique. "No problem," and toss the magazine on the stack. "Why isn't everyone doing it?"

Next day, I explain the technique to my friend and teammate, Veronica. "We'll use the Honda Civic," I say and explain the protocol. It sounded simple: follow a car at race speeds, using the reduced wind resistance behind the car to suck you along.

I lived in St. Jean, south of Montreal, on the broad St. Lawrence River Plain, and we decided to use the local roads. I know motorpacing is illegal, but it's supposed to work. The trick was well known, but, for reasons I soon discovered, little used.

Of course, no one told me what it would be like.

The first time, I follow Veronica onto the road, and expect a smooth acceleration and an easy ride in the pocket of quiet air behind the Honda. Instead, Veronica guns the Honda, and I'm sprinting to get to the target zone—two inches from the bumper—and into the calm air burbling behind the open hatchback. I'm straining to close the gap, and craning my neck to see where we're going, the base of my skull pressing into my shoulder blades.

My neck is throbbing as I peer into the open hatch, past Veronica's seat, and through the windshield. I want to get close, but not too close. If my front tire, a paper thin tube of rubber, hits the back bumper, there will be a puff of smoke, and I'll be launched onto the road at fifty kilometres per hour. On the other hand, if I lag behind, the wind envelops me, and I'm flailing to push back into the slipstream.

Veronica swerves, avoiding a pothole, and I hit the brakes. The Honda darts ahead. I'm out of its shelter and out of the saddle, chasing it down. The wind outside the slipstream of the Honda is like a hurricane and I'm buffeted for minutes until I can fight my way into the draft. My legs are burning, and I feel my eyes bursting with the exertion as I fight my way to the bumper. Another swerve and my hands clamp the brake levers.

"Jeez Louise!" I shout. What now? A wooden two-by-four: Bad for a car. Lethal for a rider. I feel like I've worked an eight-hour day, but we're barely out of town.

The increased speed increases the risk, not to mention the potential for death. Surely Mr. Honda would shake his head: one of his creations being used as a motorized rabbit for a human greyhound.

But I stick with it, and eventually adapt to tormenting my neck, breathing half-burned fuel and dodging potholes. The increased training speeds flowed into my legs. By 1992 I was Quebec Road Champion. Same for 1993. For two years running, I was the Quebec Cycling Federation's Rider of the Year. At this point, most riders would have said, "I've made it."

Not me.

Nothing short of making the National Team was sufficient. I knew I was capable of more, but sensed there was a missing ingredient. Support from my club was also an ongoing problem. I knew then that I was an exception: a developing rider, at twenty-seven, when most riders retire at twenty-five. I trained more than anyone else. I risked my hide motor-pacing when few others would. My results were better than the men's, yet they continued to receive more support. It was as if, because I was a woman—an older woman—I had been written off.

Written off? At twenty-seven? Preposterous. I didn't want to think it, and filed the misgivings away.

The lack of support had one good result. The situation spurred me to keep a day job and to round up my own sponsorship. My parents had taught me to be responsible and to pay my way. Speaking engagements, appearances, and product promotions were the other side of the coin, and I never failed to live up to the letter of the deal. In fact, I would bombard my sponsors with the press clippings and photos featuring my results. Good public relations? Yes, but these efforts ensured continued sponsorship.

Not that racing was a money-making exercise. I had a good salary with Oerlikon and later with jet-engine manufacturer Pratt & Whitney. But racing and its extensive travel costs burned through my paycheque. In 1993 a fully equipped road bike cost $4000. Wheels were $600 a pair, and a minimum of two pairs were necessary.

By the end of the 1993 season, I took silver at the National Criterium Championships, and bested a number of National Team members. Nothing turned on it. The National Road Team remained aloof. My apprenticeship, it seemed, would continue forever.

I knew I had to do something drastic. The stories I'd read in *VeloNews* triggered a wild scheme. Veronica and I would stuff the Honda with bike gear and head off to the States as freelance racers. The big prize at the peak of the 1993 season was a US series called Super Week. The event featured ten days of racing and good cash prizes. Good results, in the toughest racing on the continent, could not be ignored.

For once, I was heading for a road trip, short on luggage space, but long on sponsorship. A cold call to Super C grocery stores in Quebec had netted $6000. It was perfect. I wouldn't go in the hole, and I'd prove myself to the National Road Team.

My apprenticeship, I thought, was about to end.

I won the first race, a crit in Chicago, and in the races that followed racked up plenty of top-three placings. We travelled like knight-errant Amazons, jousting on the streets and avenues of the American Mid

West. Americans loved the series, and thousands of spectators lined the courses.

Day after day, I slugged it out with the best on the continent. Short lap racing gives you mere seconds, between turns, to move up and place yourself for a lap sprint or the finish. Wheels touch and sometimes tangle. The race goes to the fastest and the boldest.

Want to know what it's like? Here's how to do your own crit race simulation. Tell your partner, late one Sunday night, that you have to get some milk. Find a quiet street in an industrial area with no cars parked on either side of the road. Locate a ninety-degree right-hand turn: this will be your simulated criterium turn. Circle back, and drive through the turn. Start on the left side of the road. Sweep across, hit the apex of the right-hand turn, and drift out to the left side again. Do it at fifty kilometres per hour and don't brake as you go through the turn. Now pretend it's a sprint lap. Do it again at sixty kilometres per hour.

You'll learn two things: First, you can barely make the turn on four wheels, let alone two. Second, it's hard enough on your own; imagine there are fifty other cars on the circuit, all trying to be first.

Get the picture? Good. Now don't try it.

And so, lap after lap, you fight into the corner, your bike leans, the pedal scrapes, and you sprint out of the turn, bumping elbows and straining for the line. With luck, the lap prize is yours, and you do it again every five, three, or, in some cases, each lap.

By the end of the race, the timid are chewed up, spat out, and, in racing terms, "off the back." Only the hard core of daring riders remain, a tight pack of gladiators in a feeding frenzy for lap prizes.

These were days when my helpful assistant, the competitive monster, came out to play. By the end of Super Week, I was fourth overall, and garnered more trophies, medals, gift certificates, and cash than any other Canadian. I had even made the results page of *VeloNews*. Truly, fortune favours the brave. I expected two payoffs: my prize money for the overall fourth place and a call from the National Road Team. Ten years later, I'm still waiting for both.

I went back to work, the winningest road rider to have a day job. Every day after work I checked my answering machine. Nothing. The silence was the loudest thing I heard that season.

I could imagine nameless bureaucrats at the Canadian Cycling Association (CCA) headquarters in Ottawa, considering if I should get a break:

"What about Lori-Ann? She's won more than any other Canadian at Super Week."

"Yes, but after all, she is..."

"Old?"

"Quite."

I did not dwell on the official silence. Yet, I did yearn for someone to believe in my potential. *That* was the break to hope for. In the meantime, the dragon of unfulfilled expectations was not happy. However, there was little to be done. All she could do was thrash her tail and taunt me.

CHAPTER 3

BREAKS

break(s) /breik(z)/ *v. & n.* **1** a gap created by cyclists that leave their competitors behind. **2** *informal* an unexpected stroke of good luck. **3** separate under strain, to fracture and fail, to fall apart. **4** changes in fortune, coming in groups of three (applies to **2** and **3**).

—From the *Cyc.L.O.W.Ps.*

September in Toronto is a beautiful time of year, and the fall of 1993 was no exception. The wind drops, the hot days moderate, and tree leaves turn red and amber. For riders, it's a time for leisurely rides with your teammates, and sprinting for signposts and imaginary finish lines. It's the bike racing equivalent of summer hockey.

For bike industry companies it's also the time when manufacturers, suppliers and distributors promote their business at the Toronto Bike Show. Riders, like me, tag along to meet potential sponsors. Although I'm disappointed at the lack of National Team interest, I'm not quitting.

This year Veronica and I catch a ride with Pete Ryffranck, a bike builder. He is a master builder. I refuse to part with the road and crit bikes he made for me. The difference between a good and a bad racing bike is like the difference between a pair of sharp skates and a pair of street shoes.

We enter the Canadian National Exhibition Automotive Pavilion, and I walk from booth to booth, greeting and meeting. I plan to meet Winnipeg's Tanya Dubnicoff, 1993 World Sprint Cycling Champion, and get her autograph.

Before I meet Dubnicoff, I bump into Clara Hughes, Canadian National Road Team rider, and also National Speedskating Team member. Later, she'll become one of only four people ever to win medals in the Summer and Winter Olympics.

Dubnicoff joins us and is surprised to see Hughes talking to me. I'm an unknown. Track stars like Dubinicoff seldom enter road races. Similarly, roadies like me never go to the track. Once, in 1988, I had been to the Montreal velodrome, but shortly thereafter the city deliberately punched a hole in the costly African hardwood surface of the track and destroyed it.

Hughes excuses herself. This gives me a chance to meet Dubinicoff. She signs a poster, and I wave goodbye. I'm on the way out when Veronica rushes over; Desmond Dickie, the National Team track coach, wants to meet me. To this day I have no idea what Hughes said to Desmond. Whatever it was, it led him to seek out this drifting, dejected dreamer.

Desmond talks to me. He's an affable man, tall for a rider, and with the easy manner of a native Trinidadian. I've heard about Desmond, and how he's got a sharp eye for new talent. After a brief discussion I hand him my sponsorship profile.

I leave the pavilion, with no sponsors and no money.

I don't care—and I can't stop talking. The return trip to Montreal is a six-hour drive, and the passengers in Pete's car hear, repeatedly, that Desmond is interested in me.

Road racing? It was something that I'd finished. I was trying out for the Canadian National Track Team. The concept resonated in my soul. It sounded good. Almost as good as knowing that at age twenty-seven I hadn't been written off.

What did I know about track racing? Nothing. Aside from the one trip four years earlier, I'd never put a bike wheel on a velodrome. I didn't appreciate that a track bike has one gear and no brakes. Also, the gear— the rear cog—is fixed. Fixed means you can't coast. In other words, if the bike is moving, so are your legs. You can't stop pedalling, at least not without catastrophic results, and there are only two ways to slow down: apply back pressure to the pedals or hit something.

Did I know any track riders?

I knew Dubinicoff, a previous world champion, and Curt Harnett, Canadian champion and Olympic medallist. I had seen Harnett's Pert Plus shampoo commercial on TV, but Harnett and Dubinicoff were familiar faces, not friends. Except for Hughes, I had never spoken to a real track rider.

So, why my excitement? Part of it was the opportunity to make it to the National Team. Part of it was my natural enthusiasm for an ambitious adventure, for throwing myself off the deep end, hoping to survive. Another part included the speed and confrontation. Track racing was similar to crit riding. You went fast and you fought for position.

There were other reasons too, but I wasn't thinking of my underlying motivations that fall of 1993. The beast of ambition was a blur, a being sensed and not seen. Ambition to what end? To be recognized, of course, but recognized by whom? My parents? I still wasn't speaking to them. In any event, I would throw myself off the deep end. Later, I would find out what it's like to drown.

But that moment was over a year away. In the meantime, the new apprentice had some learning to do. First thing on the curriculum was learning to ride a track bike. A minor point, I know.

At the Toronto trade show, Desmond promised to courier track equipment to me. A few days later, large boxes arrived at my home in Montreal. Assembly of the track equipment took hours.

First, I didn't know how to put together a track bike. You have to install the rear wheel's axle in the bike drop outs—slots cut in the back of the frame—and line it up precisely. This process must be done by eye, and the side-to-side alignment has to be performed at the same time as a top-to-bottom alignment. Complicating this process is the need to simultaneously adjust the tension of the chain. Simply installing a wheel becomes a three-dimensional process.

Good track riders could change a wheel in two minutes. I would struggle for half an hour, and still manage to let the wheel rub against the frame and ruin a $60 training tire.

Then there was the matter of the Gizmo indoor training bike. There are many gizmos in the world, but in the track world, there is only one. The Gizmo, a device developed in the secret labs of the East German sports machine, is a track-rider mainstay. It looks like an old-style exercise bike, one with a chain-driven front wheel and bull-horn handlebars. There the resemblance ends. The drive uses a gearing system designed to increase the speed of the wheel. Flat, metal paddles, attached to the spokes, provide aerodynamic resistance, and make turning the pedals an eye-popping exercise.

Air is a strange medium. Wave your hand, and you barely feel the drag. Stick your hand out the car window at 100 kilometres per hour and the air tugs with a mighty force. Air resistance increases log-arithmically, which is to say that once you pick up speed, every 2 percent increase in speed takes a 4 percent increase in power. A 3 per-cent increase requires 9 percent more power, and so on.

The Gizmo draws its fearsome ability to sap your legs from a com-bination of wheel speed and aerodynamic resistance. Desmond knew this, and built my indoor workouts around the Gizmo. His program had me riding from one to three hours in my log cabin. The setting was a Canadian stereotype: a log cabin in the woods, buried in snow, but the scene indoors was straight from Dante's "Inferno."

It's hard to ride your brains out in the sweaty confines of a small log cabin, and to stare at the same point on the wall while your legs are seared with pain. The Gizmo would whir, stirring fetid air past my damp skin. Every kink in my back, every crick in my neck, would stop time and prolonged the suffering. My legs would beat the pedals, my lungs would heave, but the Gizmo would never relent. As bad as any-thing else was the total lack of distraction. At least if I had been riding on a road there would be scenery, sights, and the need to pilot the bike to distract me.

On the Gizmo? There was only pain: Lung pain. Leg pain. Pain, pain, pain. And suffering. Still I knew the Gizmo would work, and work quickly. Good thing, too. The first National Team project, a seven-week trip to Cuba for the Cuban Track Championship, was only five months away.

Warm up, curse the Gizmo, warm down, and do it all again, day after day, from October to February. That was the formula for what I hoped would be success in my new apprenticeship: Lori-Ann Muenzer, ex-road rider, now track rider, and international competitor. The fact that I had already paid my dues, with five years of road racing, was irrelevant. The cost was minor.

Five years put in? How can this be minor? It is when your life depends on it.

Without this goal, without this chance, I felt that life would have been a hollow exercise. Being hunched over the Gizmo, black spots dancing in front of my eyes, tongue hanging from my mouth, was nothing.

I had been to Europe, and an all-expenses-paid resort in the Bahamas, but I had never been exposed to a third-world country like Cuba. It struggles in its isolation from the US. However, Canada has a good relationship with the country, and Desmond exploited this by taking his track team there for early season training.

We're lucky in Canada.

Cubans have to make do with dilapidated public structures and outmoded equipment. Their airline flies creaky Soviet-built aircraft, and the terminal is teeming with bugs. The roads are cratered, and the supermarket shelves are vast, empty expanses. As a result, the basic diet is beans, beans, and more beans.

In spite of deprivation, Cubans are fanatical about supporting their athletes. Government-sponsored athletes are given incentives to perform: much as in the old Soviet system, they are rewarded with apartments, cars, and other luxuries. Combine this with the general Cuban zest for living, and track racing becomes a reckless melee.

My introduction to the track begins with our dorm accommodation. We're lodged in rooms at the velodrome. Three bunk beds and six people to a room. At least, I think as I throw my bags onto my bed, there are showers.

I throw the shower taps wide open and wait for the water to warm up. I step in and leap back, gasping. There's no hot water. In fact, sometimes there's no water at all. Once I was lathered up and about to rinse off when the taps ran dry. In our dorms, there *may* be water, but there are *never* toilet seats. As a result, using the toilet is a strength-testing event.

Also, there are bugs. Big bugs. Bugs so big you can mistake them for small mammals.

The weight room is like something out of a movie about soldiers training in a Soviet commando camp. The equipment is rusting, dirty and made from plumbing pipe. It is, however, like many things about the old Soviet sport system, effective.

The track riding and racing is frenetic. In Cuba, I am in the deep end of track racing. The Cubans are aggressive, and will do anything to win. I'm intimidated in the mass-start events, and have trouble riding to my potential. Unlike everyone else on the track, I'm not only competing, I'm learning to ride a track.

A bike track is a surface that continually undulates. All tracks are bowl-like. The *straights* slope to the inside, or the *apron*. As you ride from the straights, the banked turns flare up and sweep you around to the next straight. The banking, which keeps you on line when speeds increase, is anywhere from thirty-five to forty-five degrees on most tracks. If you go too slowly on the bank, your tires slip because there's not enough centrifugal force to overcome gravity pulling you down the bank. When travelling quickly, it can be easier to turn uphill—up the bank—than to swoop down. On the other hand, if you're travelling slowly, and turn too sharply up the bank, you'll catch an uphill pedal and crash.

At this time I had trouble riding a straight line, much less a curved one. Racing against twenty race-hardened Cubans was a test of survival. Every time I entered a group race, the seconds passed like hours. Afterwards, I was relieved just to survive each frantic event.

On the other hand, if it was just me and another opponent in the *match sprint*, I did better. It was easier for me to track one competitor instead of twenty. The match sprint is a duel—a rider-to-rider confrontation covering three laps. A head-to-head fight against a single opponent was something I could fathom. For some reason, a duel, the gunfight at dawn, was my kind of showdown—elemental, brutal, and final. It was a clear and certain judgment of the winner and the loser.

There actually was a *code duello*: the rules of duelling, formed centuries ago, when duelling was legal. So, too, is there a code in match sprinting. The rules are simple: two riders (usually) start. One is assigned the lead and must maintain a walking pace for the first lap. Thereafter? First one to the line wins.

In Cuba, I learned the typical match-sprint pattern that would play out for the rest of my career: a lap or so of two riders toying, testing, and probing, sometimes barely moving, and then, without warning, one rider unleashes the sprint. Only the last 200 metres are timed and only the winner advances. There are no points for style or artistic impression.

After weeks of practice, my second apprenticeship was progressing, but the Cuban Championship was fast approaching. However, before the championship took place, I rode in one of my last road events. It was billed as a major international event, complete with opening ceremonies and presentations.

For the first time I was selected to carry the Canadian flag into the streets. The honour was overwhelming. Spectators line the route and cheer, their faces bright with expectation.

The last ten kilometres of the road race was unforgettable. A fastening pin under my bike seat, shaken by the patchwork road, worked loose, and my saddle flopped about. It's like playing hockey with the top laces of your skates undone. In spite of this I won. Desmond had given me a National Team jersey to wear, and as I stand on the podium, it's hard to believe I'm not dreaming.

Finally, when the Cuban Championships arrive and I take the gold, I quit trying to separate my reality from the dream. I had a log cabin full of medals, but for this apprentice there was no sweeter reward than the Cuban title. I wasn't a raw apprentice anymore, and I wasn't just a rider. I was a track champion. For a moment, the dragon was happy.

It was a hard road I'd travelled. After meeting Desmond in Toronto, this was my second big break. However, it's true that things happen in threes. And, there are two kinds of breaks.

Why can't I move? I'm lying on the track, unable to budge. I can see my teammate Sue Hall, her motionless body lying ahead of mine. A big guy, his bike crumpled in half like a twist tie, is staggering to his feet. It's the day after the championship, and I had been in a pace line with fifteen other riders when a young rider from Alberta pulls up from the front and decides to stop pedalling. Predictably, he slips and skids down the track in front of the pace line. The line slams into him and folds up like an accordion—rider, bike, rider, bike, rider, bike.

Lying there, I am just another body struggling to get out of my pedals. I'm on my right side, and the left pedal is out of reach. I can't reach far enough with my left hand to loosen the strap, and am trapped.

Someone comes by, hunches over and releases the toe straps that bind my shoes to the pedals. They move on to the next victim and I try to push up. Pain, like angry bolts of lightning, pulses through my shoulders. I can't move. I'm used to pain, but this is more intense than anything I've inflicted on myself.

Eventually I'm helped up. I can't move my right arm. Hall and I are carted off to the hospital. The trip is hard on my battered right shoulder, and every bump produces a jolt that makes me gasp. Hall, suffering from a serious head blow, has closed her eyes. Her head wobbles like a doll's.

At the hospital, I am told they will cut off my *skinsuit*, a one-piece Lycra racing outfit. "No way," I say, not wanting to buy a new suit. The staff shrugs, and I wince as they peel the sweaty fabric off my clammy skin. I am wheeled into the X-ray room and a shot, from the front, is taken.

"It's just a hairline crack of the clavicle," the doctor says.

"Okay," I reply. Although I'm feeling nauseous, I am relieved.

"It will heal by itself, and soon you will race again."

Nurses bind my right shoulder with rough, brown paper towel. Cuba is subject to a trade embargo, and paper towel is the Cuban equivalent of a tensor bandage. Painkillers are also hard to find. Desmond is used to the shortage of medicine in Cuba and gives me some Tylenol. An hour later I'm back at the track spectating.

Two days later I return to the hospital. The pain has continued. I can't ride, and I'm worried. This time an X-ray is taken from overhead. This new image shows the bone to be completely severed, and one half has slid in front of the other. The first X-ray produced a misleading image. By now, my well-trained shoulder muscles are knotted like steel cables, pulling the broken ends of my collarbone past one another and preventing it from reconnecting. Healing, without the correct treatment, will be impossible.

My third-world experience takes on an added dimension. Two big male nurses, looking like Saturday afternoon TV wrestlers in white shirts, lumber into the examining room. The English-speaking doctor tells me what they're here to do.

"They're going to do what?" I say.

"They will attempt a relaxation of your muscles, and allow the bone to reattach."

In other words, they will haul on my pulsating arm and pull the muscles loose. Their theory is that, once pulled apart, everything will snap into place. One wrestler pins me to the chair. I am not encouraged by this measure. His partner inhales, grunts, and pulls my arm.

Pain blinds me like a camera flash. There are no thoughts, only jagged stabs of pain. I gasp, and, like a monstrous animal whose arm is in a trap, I fight against the pain. I hate it and retaliate, trying to send it back, but I'm overwhelmed. The hurt overpowers my anger and leaves me resigned.

My goal becomes simple: do not scream.

If you scream, it wins. If you grind your teeth, tense every muscle, you might not, must not scream. At some point, I think, the pain will stop. Until then? Don't scream. In a way, it's a compressed version of my life thus far.

I stare at the ceiling. I do not scream.

Minutes pass. The arm puller hisses and wheezes.

The wrestlers can't pull my cramped muscles apart. Even if they could, the muscles would indeed snap back into their last position and pull the jagged bone ends past one another. The wrestlers reel back, sweating and gasping. My mind is numb, all thought erased by the pain, and I am carted back to the velodrome.

Desmond tries to ease my anxiety. "It's just like what happened to Curt," he says, referring to a crash Curt Harnett had in Germany. "He got a pin put in," says Desmond, "and was on the bike the next day." He explains that a doctor here, a Dr. Quintanero, can do the same for me.

Colin Hearth, Desmond's assistant coach, takes me back to the hospital. I'm dropped off and wait, alone, in an examining room. I don't know where this hospital is. I don't even know its name. Dr. Quintanero walks into the room, and a throng of other white-coated doctors follow.

Dr. Quintanero explains the upcoming procedure. "We will make a cut from your neck to the edge of your shoulder," he says, tracing a long line across my upper chest. "Then we will insert a steel rod through the collarbone." He shrugs. "A few centimetres of the rod will protrude through your skin on the other side of your shoulder."

I imagine a bolt end, fit for Frankenstein's monster, sticking out of the top of my shoulder. This is not the procedure Desmond had described.

"Who will be doing the operation?" I say, forcing the words out of my dry throat. All the doctors hold up their hands. "No," I say, "which *one* of you will be doing it?" All the hands rise. I push myself up out of the bed and look for my shoes.

"Sorry," I say, "I am not going through with it."

It takes me hours to find a working phone. "Please pick me up," I say to Desmond. "I'm going home."

My teammates help me pack, and at four in the morning I'm waiting at the airport, watching the cockroaches scuttle in the darkened hallways. The flight is long, and Sue Hall and I sit, leaning against one another, exhausted by our injuries. The plane lands, and like sleepers waking from a bad dream, we stumble into Toronto's Lester B. Pearson airport.

My bags are left to sit outside the house, the better to freeze any travelling *cucarachas*. The next day I'm taken to the hospital. More X-rays are taken, and a figure-eight bandage is applied. First, however, the mouldering paper towel is removed from my skin. Underneath, the skin is breaking down, and its acrid odour is added to the days of accumulated sweat.

The new, clean bandage does the job and relieves the pain. That's all it took. No sliced neck, no steel pin hammered into my bone, and no protruding bolt.

I'm at the gym the next day, riding the exercise bike. I have never been so happy to be back in Canada. As I thump the pedals I dwell on Desmond's announcement. At the Cuban hospital, the day of the crash, Desmond gives me some news: First the good: I am on the Canadian National Track Cycling Team.

Then the bad: the first World Cup, in Denmark, is only six weeks away.

CHAPTER 4

THE DEEP END

deep end /diːp end/ *n. informal.* **1** *in the sense of:* (going off of the). Implied drowning is metaphor for self-destruction. Common result, for cyclists, of excessive training and work stress. **2** losing one's sanity. **3** for riders, the act is frequently associated with inflexible, lofty ambition.

—From the *Cyc.L.O.W.Ps.*

The figure-eight bandage keeps my bones together, and I return to my urgent training regime. April arrives, and I am on the road, piling on the miles. It's not just the collarbone setback that spurs me on: I'm playing catch-up for the late start of my second apprenticeship. I'm nearly twenty-eight, three years past the age when most cycling athletes have finished their careers. I have six weeks before the World Cup to accomplish what even the most talented riders take four years to do. As a result, I feel an urgency to push myself through Desmond's punishing training regime.

The collarbone has not healed, but I continue weight training. I do front raises, hoisting a barbell from my waist to the horizontal until the whispered warnings from my collarbone become screams.

The collarbone is a critical part of your upper body's framework. For a sprinter, the upper body is the anchor for the legs. Sprinters' legs provide the explosive power that drives the pedals. If they had no handlebar to grasp, their legs would simply propel their bodies into the air. In my case, the anchor was broken. I could bench press a broom handle, nothing more, but I ignored my disability. No broken bone, I vowed, was going to stop me.

At this point, my flaring ambitions are impatient with any obstacle to progress. Broken bone? No problem. I'll take any measure except rest. I have my chiropractor, Dr. Marc Potvin, use a special electro-magnetism machine that casts an electrical field around my upper body. I can't feel anything, unless I'm wearing a metal necklace. *Zap, zap, zap* goes the necklace as it absorbs the current and shocks me.

Work too, is another hurdle, so I take a leave of absence from Pratt & Whitney. I'm scraping by, but Desmond has confidence in me. He says, "I'm not worried about the broken bone. You're going to Copenhagen." I abandon my previous rules—to keep a day job and to raise money—and go into the hole.

However, there are continual reminders of my flimsy collarbone. One morning, I'm out for a training ride and puncture my rear tire. My grip is so weak that I can't peel the tire off the rim. I push my bike to a cycle shop in Chambly. I have no money for a spare, and have to explain to the owner that I'm a National Team athlete, but can't change my tire. He fixes the tire, and I ride fifteen kilometres home, get the money, and ride another thirty kilometres round trip to repay him.

The desperation of my situation should be obvious, but I'm still glorying in my new status as a National Team rider.

Before leaving for Europe, Desmond took us to Victoria, where we would familiarise ourselves with the track, warm up for Europe, and be in good shape for the 1994 Commonwealth Games, also in Victoria.

One afternoon, I'm in a local convenience store. I see Commonwealth Games pins at the checkout. I know my friends would like some games souvenirs, but I hesitate. The cut won't be made until after Europe, and I don't want to jinx my chances of making the games team. I leave without the pins. I don't want more bad luck to interfere. Why let my woozy willingness to get in over my head, tempt fate and risk disaster, like another broken bone? Sometimes fate needs no encouragement. And the worst breaks are the mental ones.

The passengers are sleeping. Some are wearing eyeshades, but my eyes are dry from staring out the plane window. There's a six-hour time difference between Quebec and Europe, but it's not the only thing that's disorienting. I'm en route to my first World Cup in Copenhagen.

The World Cup features the world's best track riders. World champions and Olympic champions will be here. It's the meeting ground for pitiless competition. Careers are built and ended in these events. Europe is bike crazy, and track racing is well supported. Thousands of spectators will come out, and national prestige is on the line.

Disoriented? Cockeyed would be the best description of my state. I was happy to be representing Canada, but fully aware that I was little more than an absolute beginner. And in a few hours, this beginner will be on the expert slope.

Expert slope? I'd be on the avalanche chute. When you're riding along the track's top rail, and looking down the banking, you're looking down the equivalent of a double-black diamond expert run. Many tracks have banks of forty-five degrees or more. In ski areas, a forty-five-degree slope is off limits and subject to lethal avalanches.

My first ride is frightening. Seventy riders whir past me, swooping over and under my line. I'm in the middle of a multicoloured tornado, and don't know where it's safe to ride. What's the protocol for warming up? For practising your sprint? I don't have the answers, and try to not to crash into anyone.

Also, my knees are sore, but I chalk this up to the raw wind blowing off the frigid North Sea.

Frequent rain delays reduce the time we have to warm up. The pre-event rides become dangerous melees. The crash in Cuba has left me with a fear of mass start events. Too soon, the 200-metre qualifying ride takes place.

Although I'm a sprinter, the 200-metre event is a mandatory ride, where your last 200 metres are timed to establish the seeding. The top finisher is seeded against the slowest. Once in the pool, however, sprinting is a second-chance sport. Each round is the best of three. Losers of the first round go into the *repechage* round in which they may be pooled with up to five riders in an unpredictable free-for-all race.

First, though, everyone has to qualify. In my case, I ride the 200 metres scared. The aftermath of Cuba, the setting, and the difficulty in warming up all contribute to my failure. I don't make the cut.

"What," I ask myself as I ride around the track after failing to qualify, "have I got myself into?" Twenty riders swoosh by, and the officials flag me off the track. I knew I was in the deep end, but wondered if it had a bottom.

Next stop is a misshapen track in St. Denis, France. The track has dead flat straights and sharp transitions to the steep banks. Every track is different, but this one has no equal. A jarring transition, from straight to bank, makes it hard to ride a straight line into and out of the turn.

Track smoothness is important. The tire of your generic garage bike has a contact patch of several square inches. The tire's footprint is half as large as your foot. My skinny track tire, pumped up to 160 pounds per square inch, is another matter. The contact patch is the size of your big toe.

Imagine sprinting in your runners on a banked concrete turn. Now do it again, but on your tiptoes. Finally, try this at over sixty kilometres per hour. Now, if you've mastered that, try it on a rough or poorly designed track.

At St. Denis, and the following event at Reims, I'm shaken, not sturried; and fail again to qualify.

My troubles don't end on the track. I call home and stave off my creditors. I hang up and know that upon my return to Montreal, a mountain of debt will be one of my well-wishers.

After a brief rest we travel to Dudenhofen, Germany. The 250-metre track at Dudenhofen is a jewel. It's designed by a third-generation track architect and rides like a dream. The smooth surface and the easy transitions from straight to bank inspire confidence. Instead of fighting the banking, I'm spinning through the turns. Finally, I am able to unleash my strength, and my 200-metre time qualifies me for the competition round. Dubinicoff takes first, and a wily Estonian, Erika Salumaee, takes second. I am a surprised bronze medallist and stand on the podium, looking at the spectators, realizing that they're cheering, this time for me.

Not that it was an easy ride. Salumaee, a one-time World Champion, is crafty and ruthless. We meet in the quarter finals. Salumaee, a lithe, dark-haired woman, is like a cat with well-honed claws. In the final sprint for the line, she *hooks* me.

In rider terminology, a hook is a swerve thrown at your opponent. At the very least it's a feint that strikes terror in the overtaking cyclist. At worst, the hook knocks the other rider's front wheel sideways. A sideways front wheel, at over sixty kilometres per hour, is guaranteed to launch you headlong into the planking. With luck, you might recover for the next season.

My only counter to her experience is to ride at the front. Riding at the front has the advantage of a clear path for the sprint, the final blast down the last 200 metres of the track.

On the other hand, riding at the front means having to watch your opponent's every move. For those with eyes in the back of their heads, this is easy. For me and the rest of the population, it means riding forward, on a continually curving track, and watching over your shoulder. Experienced sprinters can ride while looking over their shoulder like a barn owl. They're able to accelerate, move up and down the track, all the while looking backwards.

Don't try this at home.

Just imagine driving down a curving street and continually watching a car behind you. If the car speeds up to overtake, you speed up too, but you can't look forward. If you do, the car will take advantage of your lapse and burst past you.

And that's what a cagey rider like Salumaee will do. As soon as you look forward, a slight rise in the crowd noise is your only clue that she's attacking. You look back and it's too late—the track behind you is empty and you're in second place.

There's one other disadvantage of taking the front. The rider who shelters in the pocket of reduced air resistance behind another rider has a 25 percent energy advantage by *drafting*. NASCAR drivers, CART drivers, and Formula One racers draft. So, too, do bike racers. Riding at the front is tactically simple. It's also a recipe for being taken by surprise and for towing your opponent to the finishing line. For me, the roadie who's apprenticing as a track racer, riding at the front is my only choice. I'm so busy playing catch-up that Desmond and I don't consider any other strategy. After all, the main job for any apprentice is to survive.

Off track, my reception was warmer. The race at Dudenhofen introduced me to Europeans' fondness for cyclists and Canadians. At the Dudenhofen track, a man approaches me.

"Are you Lori-Ann Muenzer?" He's German, but his English is good. "Yes."

"I am Karl Heinz Münzer. I saw your name on the track program, and invite you to dine at my house with my family."

I check with Desmond. He says that in Europe, invitations like this are common, so I call Karl Heinz and accept. On leaving the track that day, I pass a young boy riding into the velodrome. We greet one another like old training partners and go our separate ways.

Hours later, I arrived at the Münzers of Dudenhofen. Karl Heinz and his family stood in the doorway and I recognized one of his sons: he was the boy at track. Karl's family entertain me, and he shows me the Münzer coat of arms. We joke about my grandfather Münzer being a distant relative. He takes me on a tour of the area, and I learn that the track in this tiny, quiet town was built for a local rider. It amazed me that an entire town built and supported a track for one rider. This was a town to love.

To this day, I wonder if I was born to ride the track. Is there something in our genes that leads us to these pursuits? For a moment, I think that my existence, as an international competitor, is meant to be.

We head to Hyeres, France. Hyeres, pronounced "e-air," is on the Mediterranean coast. The warm sea air is soothing, and so is the knowledge that at Dudenhofen I have made the time-qualifying standard for the Commonwealth Games. Although my disorientation should be dissipating, I still feel uneasy. I shrug off the sensation and immerse myself in pre-meet training.

The lodgings in the Agelond Hotel are simple, but clean. The velodrome is set into a large hill, and the daily routine involves a climb to the track. Trees cover the hillside, and the sound of locusts, their wings clacking and buzzing, permeates the air.

We settle into a daily routine. After our track workouts we eat, and stumble to our rooms, hitting the switch as we fall into bed. Although I'm with world-class colleagues, everyone's got their own concerns. Harnett and Dubinicoff are facing the pressures of trying to turn top-three results into World Championship titles. Unlike other teams, who have mechanics, masseuses, physiotherapists, and other assistants, we're on our own.

Equipment problem? Fix it yourself. Health issue? Go find a doctor and hope you can find one who speaks English. Broken wheel? Find a bike store and buy the parts. By the end of each day, we're exhausted. We're too dedicated to jeopardize our training by wandering into town and nightclubbing. Instead, recreation becomes phoning home and trying to stave off creditors.

Finally, on my last day in Hyeres, the isolation wears me down. After our last meal, I head to my room and close the door, staring at the clock on the desk. "Is this what life on the National Team is like?" I ask the bare walls.

Guts, determination, obsession: doesn't matter what you call it. If you have it, the result is the same—you're confident and a stranger to doubt, except, for the first time in years, doubt is no stranger to me.

"Is this what I really want?" I say, flopping onto the narrow bed. I've gone off the deep end. Alone and in debt, I feel like a kid who's trying to join the club, but always gets the same answer: "You don't belong here. Get lost."

This is my second apprenticeship, and I feel a huge pressure to produce results. I stare at the ceiling, and list the things I've put on the line: my job, my car, my house—my life. At twenty-eight most women are working on a career and serious relationships: two things I've given up. I am afraid to count the cost.

I need more time, but because of my late start, time is not my friend. I've been playing catch-up for nine months. My confidence is crumbling. Part of me had already failed. It wasn't the cold that was bothering my knees. That morning, the day before the 200-metre qualifying, I asked the French team physiotherapist if he would check my knees.

"What is it?" I ask, hoping he'll say, "*De rien.*" (Nothing.) We're sitting in the infield.

"Allow me," he says, and kneels on the infield grass, pressing his hands around my knees. He's squishing the muscles and tendons. Hot shards of pain shoot through the joint. The physiotherapist frowns. He moves to the other knee.

"Stop! It's really hurting."

He continues, as though making a fascinating new discovery. Finally, he nods and looks up. "What have you been doing?" he asks, sitting on his haunches. I recall the last lap when I couldn't develop full power for a practice sprint. Sharp pain, almost electric shock, had shot through my knees.

"Training."

"Of course," he says, and shakes his head. "What *development* are you using?"

Development is the French term for a rider's gear ratio. Riders pick gear ratios based on their ability and strategy. There are two ways to make a wheel go fast. Use a big gear, or spin a smaller gear faster. The second method takes years of practice. The first one, my choice, is the quick way to speed. It's also, I'm learning, the fast track to injury.

I tell him my gear ratio. I know my big gear is making up for my inexperience. So does he.

"It is tendonitis. You must rest." He stands up. There is no further discussion, and no question of racing. I was paying for all the months of trying to push the pedals instead of spinning them. My knees were saying, "Enough." My mind? It too had caved in.

Nobody imagines that once you're on the National Team there will be problems. It's viewed as a goal in itself. Plus, for me, it was a step toward being the best in the world. Never mind the dimly seen reasons why. Achievement had been replaced by disillusionment and debt—a mountain of both. No one warns you that the achievement of your dreams may become the weight that drags you to the bottom and drowns you.

If only we had a team physiotherapist. If only I didn't have any debt. If only I hadn't been lonely. The what-ifs wear a groove in my mind.

"If this is what it's like," I say, "I don't want any part of it."

I lever myself up from the bed, and try to ignore the pain in my knees and my heart. The French telecard is in my hand, and I trudge to the phone booth in the courtyard lobby. I feel like a snitch turning in my best friend.

The call is made.

I fly to Toronto, and instead of connecting to Calgary for the Canadian National Championships, I drive the wrong way, straight to Montreal. It's July, and the Nationals are the last warm-up for the Commonwealth Games.

I never quit, but I've quit.

"Write off," says the inner voice.

I don't care anymore.

CHAPTER 5

MONSTER

monster /mons tur/ *n*. **1** an imaginary being, big and scary. **2** a state of inhuman determination, theorized by some, that a winning cyclist must become in order to overcome pain and adversity thresholds: the inevitable state of the champion cyclist.

—From the *Cyc.L.O.W.Ps.*

Swoosh, whap, whap, whap, booom. The bike magazines, sliding down the garbage chute of my condo in Mississauga, make satisfying noises as they plunge to the garbage bin, several floors down.

"Whooo," I say, chuckling as I hoist another handful of *VeloNews* magazines into the chute. I turn around, and see a tenant staring at me, his eyes goggling behind thick glasses. He's holding his plastic garbage bag like it's a prize. I bow, and open the chute door for him. He stuffs the bag in, and speeds away, looking at me over his shoulder.

"Was it something I said?"

I lift another bundle of *Bicycling* magazines. "Remember," I say, "lift with the legs and not with the back." The magazines flutter to the pit. To me, they're not keepsakes of a sacred dream; they're junk to be heaved out. I am never, I vow, going to ride a bike again.

Every time a bundle of mags went down the chute, so did a piece of my heart. I had come home, dejected and deadened. The aftermath of failed ambition is despair, pain, and disdain—disdain for your previous dreams, and disdain for yourself.

I am so desperate for help that I even make the call that I have been waiting to make for years. The phone burns my hand like a hot coal, but I dial the number. "We're always here," Dad says, even though we haven't seen one another for ten years. They are pleased to hear from me, and allow me to use their cottage at Bay Lake.

I return to the woods of my childhood summers. As the days wash over me, I try to focus on my situation. Without my dreams, my goals, I'm like a zombie. My life revolved around cycling. I had sacrificed everything, and now had nothing but lost hopes.

Eliminating every trace of cycling in my life seemed to be a solution. No painful reminders and, therefore, no pain. Right? Wrong, of course. But I sent every magazine down the chute.

The pinpricks continued. I return to my old job. My temporary replacement has, I am advised, become permanent.

"Good for him," I say, standing in the personnel manager's office at Pratt & Whitney.

"Ah, Lori-Ann," says the personnel manager, "he's got your job, and he's staying there." The manager shrugs. "We couldn't keep holding it for you."

I drive to Oerlikon. My old job there now pays 30 percent less. I shrug, and drive to Toronto. Within two days I have a position at Nabisco Brands Ltd. Soon after, the log cabin in Quebec, the place of so many dreams and accomplishments, is traded for an ordinary condo in the strip mall wilderness of Greater Toronto.

Did the Commonwealth Games take place in 1994? Of course they did, but I couldn't tell you what happened. At the time, if I saw coverage on TV I would turn it off. My disillusionment was too great to bear. I was angry and lost.

No one thinks of being saved by a monster. Most of us run from them. I, on the other hand, ran to one. One day, driving home from Nabisco's head office, a sign catches my eye: "Monster Gym." It's a weight room and fitness centre. I am feeling perverse, like the gym's namesake. I turn my car around, and wander in.

It's perfect. A bare-bones, high-ceilinged, concrete-block cavern. The monster's belly is filled with free weights, machines, and the clang of metal. It's desperate, like me. The Monster is open every day of the year, twenty-four hours a day, even Christmas Day, Boxing Day, and New Year's Eve.

I know. I was there all three days.

Clang, thump, clang, thump. I look up at the ceiling, catch my breath, and return to beating the leg press into submission. My workouts at the

Monster begin at 5 AM, the hour when the most desperate measures take place. Hopeless adventures, last-ditch stands, counterattacks, all take place in the early morning. Every day I stagger from the condo, fumble my way in the pre-dawn void, and visit my buddy, the Monster.

I move from machine to machine, in a tour de sweat. If some poor soul happens to be on the next machine and socializes with a colleague, he's pushed on his way.

"Are you talking?" I say, glaring at the trifler.

"Uh, yeah," he replies, glancing at his friend. Who is this woman?

"Keep talking, but I'm coming through."

I adjust his plate stack. By this point, I don't have to tell him to get moving.

Clang. Thump. Clang. Thump. The banging and crashing continue until 7 AM, and then I head to work. The day's started, and the weights have been battered. Now I'm off to work, with the same urgency, to earn a paycheque, and apply it to my debt. Month by month, I'm working the weights and restoring my credit. The days pass, a blur of training and typing.

Every day I'm in the gym. Every day I stare at the computer screen, tapping memos and letters. There's no problem at work, and nothing special at home. Dawn breaks over the grey sprawl of Toronto, and it's back to the gym, and back to work. I'm part of the everyday world, and it's part of me.

A goal always helps focus my training. My old teammate Veronica, a bodybuilder before she was a cyclist, enlists me in her plan to return to body building. I will be her training partner and enter a competition, not to bulk up like some mutant, but to have a toned and sleek body like an Amazon. I decide that I can use the training to fill the void in my life. Never mind why there's a void. I ignore my own history, and what seemed to be my destiny.

I enter the Monster, and along its gullet, on the way to the locker room, I pass Polaroids of previous champions. Yeah, I'd like to look like that, I say, admiring the ripped physiques. The discipline of weight train- ing and the demanding dietary regime is a harness that I wear lightly. Like the disillusioned climber who's stopped short of the summit, I would rather distract myself with lesser climbs than confront the earlier failure.

Every time I remember my slinking exit from cycling, bitterness almost paralyses me. I breathe deep and push the weights. Heaven help anyone if they get in my way.

"Are you talking?" I ask another dawdler chit chatting with his buddy. "Huh?"

"Good," I say, and pull the pin, "I'm coming through." I'm almost disappointed if the startled trifler leaps up and scurries away. Maybe I need a confrontation. Maybe someone needs to challenge me and what I'm doing. Or what I'm not doing. Maybe, I need to confront myself.

I shrug off the thought and don't ask why the nameless hunger won't leave. I distract myself by moving mountains of iron.

A year and five months pass. It's now December 1995. My body is stronger, and hardened. It's ready for something: a body-building competition? I sit down and push the huge stack of iron. The wall, as I stare at the whitewashed concrete blocks in front of the leg press, is the same as yesterday's. Riding gave me an ever-changing point of view. I actually had to watch what I was doing.

I look at the ceiling, at the grey metal fans spinning and sending the musty air in sluggish currents. The air of the Monster smells the same in December as it did in June. Cycling down country roads, I could smell the good and the bad. Blooming apple trees, blossoming goldenrod, rancid pig pens, manure on the fields, sweet hay in June, and a sharp nostril-clearing tang in October.

I remember how my bike would whistle into the home straight turn, and the entire frame would settle down under the g-force. I remember how the field of vision narrowed, and the pole line was reeling me in, leading me to the finish.

I remember straining, eyes popping, to follow the motorbike, the exhaust floating in the draft as we whirr around the track's banking.

I remember the crowd noise, rising like a wave, and melding with the wind roaring through my helmet as the last 200 metres swept beneath me.

I remember riding in the raw air of spring, winds gusting and buffeting my bike. I remember the ends of my blonde hair turning white in the searing summer sun. I remember, best of all, knowing I was setting my limits, reaching for the sky. All of these things, the successes and the failures, I remember. This time the failures are not a separate part of the story: they are essential to it.

I walk out of the Monster, gym bag in hand, and sit in my car. My mind is blank, and I can't remember the drive to work. There, sitting at my desk, I remember the last thing, the final matter. I remember myself, and who I was meant to be. Dare I say it: champion?

My hands leave the keyboard, and I dial the number.

"Desmond?"

"Hello?"

"It's Lori-Ann," I say. "Are you sitting or are you standing?"

"Standing."

"I want you to sit down for what I want to tell you."

"Okay."

"Sitting down?"

"Sitting down."

"I'm coming back to racing. And I want you to coach me."

Desmond is ecstatic. He no longer works for the CCA. At this time he needs a rider, and I need a coach. I know I can't do this on my own.

"I need to balance riding with my job," I say. "It's taken me a year and a half to get out of debt. I won't go into debt again. One other thing—it has to be fun. I won't race unless it's fun."

"Okay."

"You tell me what I need to do to get to the World Championships," I add.

The World Championships? Could I have set a more difficult goal? Of course not, but it was the goal that intoxicated me. It was a ticket from the unsatisfying routine my life had become. I felt released.

Like the refrain in "Amazing Grace," I once was lost, but now I was found. I walked out of the Nabisco office, across from their subsidiary, Christie's bakery. The warm yeasty aromas issuing from the bakery weren't the only fresh smells in the air. I could smell, in the December chill, the hope and excitement of a new dream.

Speed and confrontation, the chess-on-wheels of the match sprint, would be in my life. The chance to exceed normal expectations would be mine. Again. How could I have left it behind? I keyed the ignition, and drove home. This was not the time for introspection. It was time to get on my bike.

Two days later the program and the Gizmo appear. How could I have forgotten the Gizmo? There were times—when the black spots swam in front of my eyes, and my body was saturated with Gizmo-induced fatigue toxins—that I wondered if I should have stuck to body building.

Still, the moment the spots cleared, I would let my legs spin and tilt my head back, the sweat draining away from my eyes. There was suffering, to be sure, but no doubt.

Desmond and I had made a comeback plan. I would compete in local events that would allow me to keep my day job. These events would culminate in the 1996 National Championships. In the meantime, I returned to the training that he had set for me in 1994. Gizmo, whirling head, black spots, dry heaves. It's a lot of work, but I know it's critical to build the base for a comeback.

Also, it's possible that even without my crisis and spiritual exhaustion that I had needed the year and a half off. All the pressure to catch up in 1994 had left me with a deficit that had to be paid, and paid it was with tendonitis. At eighteen, I might have recovered in six months. I was verging on twenty-nine, and already realized that recovery now took more of the precious time I had so little of.

After riding the 1996 Nationals, I would aim for the 1997 World Cup circuit. In the meantime, I had to retrace my steps, and take up the apprentice's tools. There was a race in Hamilton, an indoor track race, said Desmond. It was in February, only weeks away.

Indoor racing is commonplace in Europe, and fills the track rider's winter schedule. Aspiring Canadian track builder, Peter Junek, from Ontario, was promoting an indoor track revival for Canada, and had set one up in the Copps Coliseum in Hamilton. Indoor track means a minuscule 165-metre circuit, and lap times of ten seconds. It also means fifty-nine-degree wood banking and no room for error.

Was I interested? The race couldn't take place soon enough.

The day arrives, and I am on a bike borrowed from a junior rider. I can tell this bike is poorly maintained, and I am not sure the tires are properly glued on. The tires will be under a tremendous strain in the steep turns. There will be no slow laps on this track. The only thing keeping me glued to the track will be centrifugal force generated by my own speed. Unfortunately, this factor may also separate the tires from the rims. For a moment, standing at the edge of the track, I hesitate. Riders hiss by, their tires drumming on the plywood banking. It's been a year and a half since I last rode the track.

I shrug. It's just more incentive for me to ride smoothly.

I push the bike onto the apron and shoulder check. My pedal straps are done up on the fly. Remember, when the bike's moving, so are the pedals. Immediately, I'm accelerating to gain enough speed to stay on the bank.

I spin around the tiny track, and think it's like riding inside the drum of a large washing machine. No, I correct myself; it's the "Wall of Death." The Wall of Death was the tiny wooden cylinder I had seen daredevil motorcyclists ride when I had gone to Toronto's Canadian National Exhibition. The riders zoomed into the cylinder, a wooden barrel really, and after gunning the motor, they'd climb onto the vertical wall, and keep their speed high enough to ride at ninety degrees to the vertical. I had never expected to join their exclusive club.

I finish my warm up, and am on the apron warming down. The men's racing has started, and I have to clear off. There's a shout.

Crunch, craaack, aieeee!

Two men, Alain Boucher and another rider, collide at the top of the banking and splinter the two-by-four railing. Boucher spins through it and into space. It's a long drop to the concrete floor. The racing is halted, and he is carted away, his pelvis broken. The incident does not inspire confidence.

After this, the racing is anticlimactic. I win the match sprints. The tires stay on, and I haven't smashed through the railing.

I walk through the infield, and hear my competitors whispering:

"Lori-Ann is back. What was she doing over the last year?"

Good question.

Over the next few months, I win local races and feed the hunger. This is 1996, an Olympic year. I've tried to keep my ambition in check, but it's hard for me not to yearn to be at the Olympics. Finally, at the end of July, the Nationals arrive. I arrive in Victoria, and look forward to competing against Dubinicoff.

Dubinicoff doesn't show.

I collect a sheaf of gold medals and winner's jerseys, but I'm not happy. I wanted someone to challenge my limited tactical ability.

Back home, I half expect the National Team to notice my results, but the phone maintains its usual silence. A breakthrough occurs in early 1997, and it's not at National Team headquarters in Ottawa. My employer, Nabisco, agrees with my pitch for a sponsorship. The $30,000 budget is astronomical for a cyclist. The money allows me to take on the world, literally. My modest plans expand, and I contact the National Team. If they won't call me, I'll call them.

"Can I take part in the 1997 World Cup program?" I ask.

"You have to pay your own way."

"No problem," I reply. "I'm working with Desmond. Can you get him accreditation?"

"Sure."

"Great. I can hardly wait to get to the first World Cup this May in Trexlertown."

"Just one thing," I'm told. It's about Desmond.

"Yes?" I say.

"You'll have to pay his way too."

Pay for your own coach? But so strong is my hunger that I'll use my own sponsorship money to get Desmond to Trexlertown, Pennsylvania.

At T-town, Desmond and I set up at the track. The pits, the recessed booths in the infield, are for the riders and coaches. I set up amidst the national teams and their entourages. I am surrounded by a sea of other national teams. Their equipment is sponsored. Their clothes are sponsored. Their coaches are paid for. I bet I'm the only rider here with a day job.

I'm an intruder, but I'm an intruder who wants in. This time I am not intimidated. With Desmond's support and no doubts dampening my spirit, the competitive monster inside is ready to rumble.

I win the sprint for fifth through eighth. It's a photo finish. The photo shows my wheel, edging across the line, besting American Jennie Reed. It's not a World Championship medal, but it's proof. Proof that I'm not a has-been, and that all the sacrifice might, for once, pay off.

I'm nearly afraid to believe it.

Finally, at the 1997 Canadian National Championships in Calgary, I go up against Dubinicoff. She's got the golden touch, but I'm trying to learn, not just how to ride fast, but to ride smart. The rides start the same way. Dubinicoff and I sit on the start-line bench. We're like kids in the front row of a church, hands folded, staring straight ahead, behaving well before trying to kill each other. I'm visualizing my ride. My thoughts go something like this: I'll lead out, and watch her. I'll keep the speed high—to take away her jump—and when we hit the 200-metre line, I'll pour it on. It's a good theory. However, against the 1993 World Champion, it's just a theory. I'm beaten two straight.

Dubinicoff is pleased to receive my sincere congratulations. It's first nature for me to be gracious. But why can't I make tactical prowess my second nature?

Even so, Desmond and I don't spend much time on tactics. It's rumoured that he will be hired by the United States Cycling Federation (USCF), and he is busy with the Americans. I'm lucky that he still has some time for me, his lonely Canadian sprinter, the thirty-one-year-old who is on her second sports apprenticeship when most women her age are starting a family.

The first sign that my ambitions were dreams, and not delusions, was in Adelaide, Australia, at the August World Cup in the Adelaide Superdrome. There, I beat a host of top-ranked cyclists, and faced Dubinicoff in the gold-silver ride.

Before the final race, I'm sitting on the bench, stunned to be there, but certain that I can win. I plan to ride at the front: it's my only plan after all, but I know I can execute it. It doesn't work. She plays with me like a cat with its toy.

Still, I'm ecstatic. I've got my first World Cup medal, and know I've come a long way from the timid rider who, three years ago, crept onto the Copenhagen track. The Adelaide World Cup leads to the World Championships in Perth, Australia, and for once, the CCA is paying the travel bills.

Even though I'm out of the medals in Perth, I'm pleased. I've had two seasons of solid results, and one spectacular World Cup medal finish. Plus, I now have a Sport Canada monthly stipend, termed a *C-card*. And, a good thing too.

I return to Toronto and the Nabisco legal department. They can't keep me on. I leave with a small payout, and no budget for 1998.

At least, now that I am over thirty, I can compete in the World Masters Games. It's ironic that I'm old enough to qualify for the "senior citizens'" event for athletes. I tap out my budget, and plunk down the money for the airline tickets for Desmond and me. A good performance will help me gain a new sponsor for 1998. It's only after I buy the tickets that I learn the Masters Games rules have recently been changed.

Yes, I am old enough to compete. No, I have now been issued a Category One Elite racing license, which makes me ineligible. You can be an Elite rider or a Masters athlete, but apparently not both. It's a sign that no one expects you to be one of the world's best at age thirty-one. The airline tickets were not refundable. Thus ends the 1997 season.

At home, I clutch the World Cup silver medal, tangible proof that I can be... something.

Who is this clown? It's now 1998, and I'm at the World Championships in Bordeaux, France. His name is Steen Madsen, younger brother of Lars Madsen, both of whom are Canadian National Team track sprinters. But here in Bordeaux, Steen's playing tourist. I'm in my hotel room, gathering my gear and stuffing it into a gym bag.

"Hey," says Steen, video camera pressed to his eye. "I can sit on the toilet and touch all four walls."

"Good for you," I mutter, and hope that he goes away.

Steen persists and, like a kid discovering a new toy, he shoots the room and anything that is remotely unusual. At the track he's no different. Everywhere I look it's Steen, hanging over railings, peering into corners, always with the video cam poking its glass eye into everything.

"Lighten up, Lori-Ann," he says when I try to shoo him away. He saunters away, his flip-flops flapping.

"Tourist," I say.

I'm not in a joking mood.

Desmond now works for the USCF. The change deprives me of the only coach who had the expertise and gave the emotional support I required.

At the Worlds, I observe the reality of coaching in this sport. In my case, I respect the principle that here at the Worlds we have to put aside our personal coaches and work with the staff sent by our cycling organizations. I need someone to coach me, but Desmond is working with the Americans. As a result, I don't call on Desmond for help. However, not everyone feels this obligation.

I am in the basement of the Bordeaux velodrome, heading for the washroom. I walk down the dim hallway, the cleats on my shoes tapping on the concrete floor. I head for the women's washroom, but see two figures in the gloom, their voices indistinct and echoing off the concrete walls. I recognize one figure. She's one of my competitors, from the United States, and she's speaking to her personal coach. We've been neck and neck for years.

I push the door open and sigh. Too bad a Canadian coach is giving her advice. I wish the coach was speaking to me. Perhaps a younger woman is a more promising prospect for the advancement of one's career.

The Bordeaux 1998 World Championships are a write-off.

I watch the team sprint finals with Steen. I note that he's recording all the best competitors. Steen's not just a jester. However, I'm too absorbed in my own dilemma to ask for his help. Without Desmond's encouragement, I'm lost. The monster of competitive drive, the revived beast, has been deflated. The lofty goals—the ambitious comeback—only mock me.

After the Worlds, Desmond is free again to help. He thinks I can regroup for the Commonwealth Games, three weeks from now, in Kuala Lumpur, Malaysia.

He believes in me, so why shouldn't I?

The monkeys in the trees watch me as I ride to the Cheras Velodrome in Kuala Lumpur. The sky is a milky blue, and cumulus clouds tower in the midday heat. I'm part of the Canadian Team at the 1998 Commonwealth Games, and our team is having no problem staying loose—quite the opposite; pulling ourselves together for an event is an effort.

Kuala Lumpur is surrounded by ocean and is near the equator. Riding here is like riding your bike in a steam cabinet. In a few minutes I'll be sweltering in the open-air velodrome.

The air is not the only thing here that is hot. The games 200-metre record has been broken three times. I'm proud that my qualifying sprint was the first to smash the record. After I ride, Australia's Michelle Ferris and Dubinicoff best my record-setting time.

For some sport disciplines, the Commonwealth Games are not world-class events. Not so for cycling. The Brits and Aussies, not to mention the Kiwis, Scots, and Canadians, are at the top of the world standings. This year Ferris and Dubnicoff will be silver and bronze at the World Championships. Ditto for 1999. They're at the top of the game, and I'm fighting for a medal. But it's not just the heat or the competition that I'm fighting.

Today, I joined the usual warm-up pace line, a snaking multi-national collection of riders circling the track. After every half lap, the lead rider swings up and dives down onto the tail of the snake. It's the same at any track meet—provincial, national, or international. There's a camaraderie and cooperation amongst riders that would be unheard of in other sports. Imagine rival hockey teams practising their passes, or taking shots on the other team's goalie during the pre-game skate.

In any case, I'm sweating and struggling as I try to keep my place in line. For a sprinter, the speed of the pace line is never a problem. We take it for granted that we'll match anything the endurance riders can put down.

Not today, though.

In fact, every time I've pushed my bike onto the track, I've wondered if I've got legs or just overstuffed sausages attached to my hips. Could it be the heat? Maybe I have a stomach bug? I always maintain a positive and confident approach to life. As my grandmother said, "Stand tall, and be proud of yourself." In spite of what happened in Bordeaux, I am looking forward to a match with the world's best.

But this strange resistance is almost like riding in glue. I slide out of the pace line. I know, after years of world-level competition, that the slightest hindrance will scotch your chances. Here, five or six riders could be in the top three.

My bike coasts into the pits. I remove my helmet, and squeeze the sweat out of the foam padding. My legs don't have the capable feeling that is supposed to follow a warm-up. Instead, they feel like I've climbed the CN Tower.

The plastic chair creaks as I thump down and put my head in my hands. I take a swig from a plastic water bottle. The warm water, flavoured by the hot plastic container, doesn't help. The heat is inescapable. Panic rises.

"Lori-Ann." It's our manager, Eric Van den Eynde. "Change to your race wheels. Your ride is coming up."

I smile and pretend to be confident. I remove a training wheel, and spin it to see if the bearings are running freely. The ball bearings inside the hub are seized, and are growling like a noisy coffee grinder. No wonder it felt like I was riding in glue. I put on the race wheels, and hurtle out to the track. My bike seems propelled by angels. I can't stop smiling.

A medal could still be mine.

I win my quarter-final, and in the semi-final I confront Michelle Ferris. She is last year's silver medallist at the Worlds. She takes advantage of my tactical naïveté, and toys with me. Ferris goes on to ride against Dubinicoff, who will later take the gold.

No one will be surprised that I haven't got the gold, but the bronze is another matter. I know I can win this medal, and that brings its own pressures. I'm riding against Lyndelle Higginson. She's only twenty, and has been riding a bike since she was four. Higginson also has the benefits of attending the Australian Institute of Sport, a full-time, all-expenses-paid training facility.

I am thirty-two, have less experience and a day job.

The comparison is daunting. I sit on the riders' bench and, for the first time, feel the constricting hand of public expectation clutch my heart. Added to this is my overwhelming desire to win, and its expectations. Somehow I have to convert this to speed, to tactical skill.

"I can win this," I tell myself. "And, if I lose it," I add, "heaven help me."

Canadian team manager Van den Eynde calms me. "Just one race at a time, Lori-Ann," he says. It's good advice. He leads me to the straightaway, and helps me mount the bike. I let myself settle on the bike, and do up the straps.

"What," I ask myself, "would Desmond tell me?" Ride at the front, of course.

I beat Higginson two straight, and the bronze medal is mine. It's especially sweet to be one of two Canadians on the victory podium.

With this medal I've made it to the next level, and a world title is in sight. I'm strong enough to be here. I'm smart enough to choose the right plan, and I am tough enough to bear up under the pressure.

There's more to it than being on the podium and having a pretty medallion around your neck. I look around at the other athletes and the coaches. They're happy to see me here. For once, I realize that I'm somewhere I belong: I love being a competitor and a member of this community. And for a moment, the dragon is quiet, and I can love that other being who is so seldom satisfied—myself. It means as much as the medal. I don't ever want to leave this place and its people.

One year from now, I'll receive my eviction notice. And the signature on it? Mine.

CHAPTER 6

FALL

fall / *n. & v.* **1** a plunge to a low level. **2** lapse into a pathetic state. **3** *see also*, **fallen**: *typ.* leaving a state of grace. A rider who has quit, the result of cycling-related torments. Ironically, after leaving the sport, torments continue; they merely change their guise.

—From the *Cyc.L.O.W.Ps.*

August 18, 2004, Athens Olympic Velodrome, 10:30 AM

I've trudged into the velodrome, slinking like a kid who's late for final exams. The other teams, their mechanics bustling, their coaches hustling, are bursting with confidence and purpose. I'm sitting alone on a plastic chair in the pits.

I need someone to time me. I need...someone. After all these years, and everything I've survived, I thought I could tough it out. Even after being cheated of my gold medal at the 2002 Commonwealth Games, I didn't feel this lost.

Death stole someone special that year too. Someone who let me know I wasn't alone. I wear her medal around my neck whenever I travel. I touch the medal now, and remember her belief in me. This remembrance brings another one: when was the last time I felt this isolated? It was 1999.

In 1999 I had been sent halfway across the country, alone, to train. "You'll have to time yourself," they said then too. The lack of support, and the isolation triggered an accelerating slide into aimlessness. And, as the fates seemed to dictate, the mental lapse was followed by a physical plunge, a fall off a cliff in which I landed on my back onto jagged rocks. The physical scars are still there. I hear them when my overtaxed back blows out, and the joints pop like walnuts crunching in a nutcracker.

The events leading to the back-busting crash of 1999 were so ordinary. Back in 1998: it's $12 a day to park in downtown Toronto and I'm working at the law firm of Minden, Gross, Grafstein, Greenstein on Richmond Street West. It's the early fall after the Commonwealth Games, and for now Desmond will work with me. For how much longer, I don't know. My employers allow me to work flex-time hours. I start at 6:30 AM and finish at 2:30 PM so I can evade rush hour en route to Desmond's in Brampton. There was no other way to do it. The alternative? There was no alternative. Steve McQueen, in the movie *LeMans*, said, "Racing is life...everything else is waiting."

The late actor and I agree on this. In the fall of 1998, it was clear that Desmond's involvement was tenuous. Still, racing was my life, and I ignored the inevitable.

Not everything was shaky. Even though my bronze medal at the Commonwealth Games hadn't garnered a lot of attention, it did help me maintain my C-card status. I made my usual rounds of calls trying to garner sponsorships, but rely as ever on forgiving employers who allow me to indulge my dreams.

At the end of 1998, Desmond gets the news he's been hoping for, and I get the news I'm dreading. Desmond is now the United States Cycling Federation coach. I wish him well, but feel like a kid whose favourite teacher has transferred to another school.

The next training ride should have told me.

I'm riding in the countryside, passing the usual mileposts that every rider uses to gauge progress. "By Simcoe's farm, by this bridge," you say, as you churn the pedals, "I should be at thirty-eight kilometres per hour." The road flows beneath your bike. Checkpoint by checkpoint you are riding according to plan and expectation.

But not today and not this time. I don't know it yet, but I'm spiritually lost. I'm wandering my usual routes, my pedals dragging on the ground, just slightly above the level of my heart.

What do you do? Admit that there has to be a change? Realize that you need help?

No. You keep a brave face. You're thirty-three years old, and your family's traditional values have always seen you through: stay positive and never give up. Besides, you've invested so much, and can see the top of the podium. The workouts hurt more than ever, and it's hard to be coach-less, but you have that dragon to best and that ambition to satisfy.

You arrive at work and beam at colleagues and bosses. They're always happy to see you: your perennially sunny outlook perks them up. And why not be positive? Nothing's to be gained by slumping around, eyes downcast. Yet, I needed help. Were there any clues? I didn't see them at the time.

First there was the move out of the house I was renting. Home? Who needs that? If I'm homeless, it will be easier to manage my cycling career. Besides, I have friends I can split room and board with. It seems to work out well at first, and I head to Mexico City, and then to Fort Lauderdale, to take part in National Team projects.

Mexico City is not only one of the largest urbanized areas in the world, but it's one of the most polluted. The Olympic velodrome is near the airport and ranks of jets, lined up on the taxiways, spew black soot from their exhausts. Looking across the track I can see riders on the other straight, but their outlines are blurred. There's a brown filter of pollution over the sun that sucks the colour out of the landscape.

After one day on the track the riders are hacking and clearing their throats. The corrosive murk does not promote world-class perform-ance. I fail to get past the fifth through eighth rounds. However, I do acquire a persistent lung infection. Our next event, I say, consoling myself, is in Plano, Texas, at the Electronic Data Systems (EDS) track. The air in Plano will be clean and I'll beat this lung bug.

Upon arrival, the team goes to a Mexican restaurant. The fiery taste of the local food is a welcome contrast to the usual hotel fare. During the meal my tongue starts tingling. By the end of the meal my tongue is blue, and itchy red bumps have blossomed all over my body. Less than twenty-four hours later it happens again.

My lungs are getting worse. My riding follows suit. I send myself home.

Home? I forgot. I don't have one.

A friend of mine, doing a post-graduate degree and living on the poverty line, has a four-hundred square-foot apartment. She takes pity on me and, like Mother Teresa with the homeless, she takes me in.

Clues that something's wrong? I've had plenty, but I persist. When racing is your life, and your life has been racing, there's nothing else to turn to, not unless you want to admit failure, which is, of course, the very thing that the elite athlete fears most.

By May, I'm struggling, but still managing to train. It's ironic, but this is the first time that the CCA gives me the call. The years when I've been raring to go have come and gone, but now of all times comes the miracle call.

"We'll pay for you to go to the World Cup in Berlin."

"Great," I say, imitating the ever-confident and enthusiastic athlete. "Do I fly direct?"

"Funny you should ask, Tanya doesn't want to go. You'll have to fly to her town, Calgary, and catch the plane from there. You're on her ticket. Same thing coming back."

I hang up and realize why I got the call. Dubinicoff couldn't go.

Berlin is not only the site of the World Cup race, but will later be the venue for the 1999 World Championships. This first trip to Berlin is an eye-opener. The Germans have built the track below ground level. Stands, filled with beer-drinking and chain-smoking fans, surround the velodrome. Again, I fail to pass the fifth through eighth barriers and I am still labouring with the lung infection. I return home to the postage-stamp apartment.

"Welcome to Edmonton," reads the sign in the airport terminal. There's time to kill, waiting at the oversize baggage counter for the bike box.

I've come here for a National Team training project. Ottawa still plans to enter me in the World Championships in Berlin. The Berlin track is 333 metres like the one at Edmonton's Argyll Velodrome. Hence, I am here to prepare and am waiting for my gear. But I don't have to wait for the rest of the team, for this project is a project for one. Coach, trainer, mechanic, and athlete share the same name: mine.

The Argyll Velodrome is in a park next to Mill Creek ravine's south end. It's a pastoral setting, and I am struck by the silence when I haul my bike out of the hatchback. It's mid-morning, and there's no traffic noise. A lone car, the custodian's, joins mine in the parking lot. The custodian is a young woman and a track rider herself. She shows me where to change and prepare my bike.

I pump up my training tires, and wheel the bike out of the clubhouse. My feet crunch on the gravel path, and I breathe in great lungfuls of

clean air. A faint balsam tang, from the aspen groves on the west side of
the track perfumes the air. Magpies chatter and hop across the infield.

Before I start the workout, I sit up on my bike and gaze at the sky.
It's a huge dome of clean blue, not the hazy, milky sky of Toronto. It is
hard to believe that thousands of spectators, at the 1978 Commonwealth Games and the 1983 Universiade Games, watched riders duel on
this track. Today it's just me, the magpies, and the track.

A breeze riffles the papers I have left on the bleachers by the track
railing. My street shoes weight the pages of Desmond's program. "Go
out and do the intervals," the pages say, chiding me for my lack of
enthusiasm. "Go ahead, Lori-Ann," I say, "beat your brains out."

I hold onto the track railing, staring at my pedals. I gaze at them the
way a monk meditates: no thoughts, no emotions—just slow breathing
and a steady gaze. The pages rustle, and I hear the same breeze whisk
through the aspens. The air here, on the high plains, is thin and dry. The
wind brushes my face, like a warm shroud.

A thought pushes through. I lift my head, and ignore the thought.
The setting is elemental, beautiful. I try to focus on the job. "There are
no distractions here," I muse. Yet.

"I can't do it," I say to the track, the woods and the magpies. I slide
off the saddle, my cleats clacking on the banking, and gather the papers.
The papers thump into the garbage can.

This season, I fought against the strength-sapping effects of a lung
infection. I succeeded in working, scrimping, and paying my way. All
of this I did alone. These obstacles I could wrestle to the ground. But
the feeling of isolation? The lack of encouragement? I trudge to the
clubhouse.

I have lost touch with my family, and I've lost track of the friends
who have gone on to careers, serious relationships, and children. In the
meantime, I kept riding. Riding the track, and riding in circles. What
has this cost me? Plenty.

The fear that I've made a terrible mistake, that the sacrifice has been
in vain, nearly sends me to the ground. I clench my teeth, and remind
myself that at least I have a job. At work I have colleagues, friends. I'm
going back to Toronto, and the stolid security of office work.

My footsteps, scrunching on the gravel path, echo against the concrete wall of the clubhouse. It's a hollow sound.

Thirty-six hundred kilometres: that's what the odometer reads. Canada is a big country, and it's 3600 kilometres from the postage-stamp apartment in Toronto to the house in Edmonton. It's now three weeks since my visit to the Argyll Velodrome, and I have no direction, save one: go West and get a job. I had been in Toronto for only a few weeks, but realized that I needed a change of scene. For this disenchanted athlete there was to be no refuge in the normalcy of office routine. I hope that a new start will ease my disappointment. A friend is travelling to the University of Alberta in Edmonton. I'll go there, too, and find work.

My first interview is the day after I arrive.

"You have some gaps in your work history," says Lynne Turner, a human resources manager at Field Law in downtown Edmonton. I am being interviewed in her office.

"I used to be a bike racer." I guess that no one's ever used that one to explain a suspicious employment history gap. "But I have no intention of racing. If anything changes, I'll let you know."

The job is mine, and I'll spend the next five years there. I'm a floater, filling in wherever there's a shortage. Racing is out of my life, but the competitive instinct persists. I compete against the time clock to see how much I can do. The Field Law word-processing championship continues into the fall.

Still, it's not enough to quell my need for physical challenge. As soon as my interview with Turner was over, I race to the YMCA and buy a membership. I hope that joining the gym will also help me resolve my newest dilemma.

Riders love to eat, and because our training is so hard, we're food furnaces. When cyclists quit, they feel the foreboding of incipient fatness. The food frenzy has to end, or a fitness substitute has to be found. For me, the answer was to join the Y, and to follow the regime set out in *Body for Life* by Bill Phillips.

Phillips's regime, six days on and one day off, with a balance between strength and cardio, was perfect. It was the rigorous structure I needed. All this fitness, I thought, might come in handy. I'm working out, but not knocking myself out either. Not that is, until October 21, 1999.

Edmonton's Mill Creek ravine is a sinuous watercourse that runs from the Argyll Velodrome to the North Saskatchewan valley. My friends

Monica and David Nelson are mountain bike enthusiasts I met at Hardcore Mountain Bikes, a shop in South Edmonton.

"Let's ride Mill Creek," they say. "It's really good in October. The leaves are down, and the trails are easy to find."

"I have an old mountain bike," I say, "but I don't know how to ride off-road."

"We'll teach you," says David.

They are planning to meet several other mountain-bike riders, and take their pack along the narrow dirt paths woven through the heavily forested banks of the ravine.

My bike is an oversized twenty-one-inch yellow Schwinn. Bikes, like shoes, are sized and mine is the equivalent of a pair of size thirteen clodhoppers. Also, it has step-in pedals like ski bindings. A plate on the bottom of your shoe clips into a spring-loaded claw on the pedal. Nowadays, these pedals are standard equipment on good road and mountain bikes. Track riders feel the newer pedals are prone to accidental release. "They're wimpy," they say, "you can just walk out of them."

I am about to learn that this is not entirely accurate.

If track racing is the Formula One of the bike world, mountain bike riding is its motocross. Our group is sifting through the woods, and looping along the handlebar-wide trails. At least, the experienced riders are. I'm hitting trees where others are skimming through.

The Schwinn isn't a bike; it's a tank crashing through the woods, branches snapping and cracking. I'm used to a track bike, light, nimble and precise, like a scalpel. The Schwinn is a blundering mallet.

I can keep the others in sight only for a second, and then have to take evasive action to avoid a tree or a drop. The front wheel flicks left, then right, as I lurch around a kink in the trail. As soon as I'm back on course, I suck in my breath to negotiate a near vertical drop. The fit riders are at the front, and are goading each other to greater risks. I'm at the back, just trying to hang on.

Whack, goes a branch against the hard shell of my helmet. *Thunk*, says my front wheel as it drops into a dried-out pothole. My head is jiggling so much that I can't see where we're going. I feel like a passenger on a train that has lost its brakes going down a pass.

Finally, we break through the woods and onto a wider trail in the valley bottom. I can see more than three feet ahead and I relax. The path begins to rise along the creek's west bank. I get only a glimpse of this ramp because the approach winds around thick pine trees. I skim past their rough-barked trunks, and see the incline dead ahead. The trail leaps up the incline, and disappears.

For a moment, I see the exposed bank, twenty feet high, rising above the creek. The trail is on the top of a vertical retaining wall, built of river boulders. The thin track is cut into the side of the ravine: to the left is a steep slope, and to the right, a sheer drop to the creek. A small section of my mind—the cautious part—is saying, "Slow down," but the other part, the competitive part is, saying, "Don't get left behind."

As usual, the competitive side wins.

"Oof," I grunt as the front wheel hits the incline, and I pitch forward onto the handlebars. I nearly stop, but my legs are powerful, and the Schwinn leaps up the incline. I'm on the ribbon of a trail, teetering and wobbling as I thread the bike through water-filled potholes cratering the trail. The incline killed my speed, and the potholes are like tank traps. A bike stays upright because its wheels are turning and generating gyroscopic stability. My bike is creeping and not generating anything but inertia.

"Look where you want to go," I whisper, as the bike starts to topple. In the corner of my vision, to the right, is nothing but space. The Schwinn is tossed to the left as I try to fling myself up the bank and to safety.

It's too late.

Last chance. Get the feet out and jump.

The pedals won't release. I'm kicking my feet, doing a tap dance, but the sky and the horizon are spinning, and I have a feeling of tremendous freedom: I'm falling, and there's nothing to stop me. I remember Desmond's advice about falling: "If you fall, relax. You'll bounce." I hope there's water in the creek, enough to cushion the fall.

There's no water.

He's right. I did bounce.

When engineers want to find out how much strain a mechanical component can take, they put it onto a machine that shakes it to death. "There," they say, "We beat it 20,000 times, and finally, it failed."

Sometimes I wonder if I'm part of a giant engineering experiment— I have one gear, and when will I break? As usual, whenever I've been put under too much strain, I find out what my weakest part is. In the case of the Mill Creek plunge, I already knew what would suffer the most: my back. That year I had already experienced back difficulty. Massage, physiotherapy, and chiropractic therapy all helped, but my back had given out at the National Championships.

It was no surprise that the free fall onto the angular rocks of the creek bed would cripple my back. The emergency room doctors X-rayed me. "Amazing," they said, "nothing is broken."

However, a thermal imaging photo of my back muscles tells a grim story. A doctor holds up the colour-coded image. Happy muscles are green, and as the colour goes to red, the muscles go to sad. The muscles of my right side, are black, and are not sad; they're suicidal. They're so damaged and feeble that it's two months before I can walk a straight line.

In the past, and especially this last dark dismal season, I had needed back therapy to keep my back stable so it could withstand the total body commitment that is required for match sprinting. At the Nationals, in Calgary, I had pushed it too far, and it blew. Dropping myself onto jagged rocks did not improve the situation. Extensive therapy was needed so I could walk and work. Riding wasn't the issue; merely continuing activities of daily living was.

The fall into Mill Creek was, it seemed, the final stroke in the script that had written me off. A bike brought me deep into cycling, and a bike had taken me out. In fact, a bike had almost killed me. Each morning when I lay in bed, listening to the clock radio blare, I would steel myself to face the pain. Rising from bed, washing and eating, not to mention getting on the bus, felt like death-defying acts. The days wore on, and the pain chipped away at my good nature. I felt as if I'd been punished for riding and for thinking that the gigantic Schwinn could bring me deeply into life again.

Weeks pass, and the pain subsides to merely a constant ache. "Maybe," I think as I shuffle to the bus stop, trying not to slip on icy sidewalks, "I've been punished for another reason." Maybe I was punished for leaving the sport? I shake my head, and get on the bus.

Even though I had no plans to return to competition, I needed to be with my friends in the cycling community. In Edmonton, I had struck a bond with the Juventus Club. This organization ran the velodrome, and had been generous in giving me track time. A pleasant surprise was an invite to their Christmas banquet at the Chianti restaurant.

My old National teammate Steen Madsen, and his older brother Lars rode with Juventus. I was looking forward to seeing Lars again, and congratulating him on his Championship title. Steen did not ride the Nationals this year, but he asked me to help Lars. I gave whatever support I could, but Lars didn't need my help. He won the National Championship handily.

At the banquet, Lars was surrounded by well-wishers. But it wasn't Lars who stood out.

CHAPTER 7

RICH AND STRANGE

rich and strange / *phrase*. **1** a state of material abundance. Competitive cyclists are unused to this condition, and find it strange. **2** cycling is plagued with a rich supply of sincere, but often futile training schemes. That one should work is indeed, strange. **3** Steen Madsen's imagination.
—From the *Cyc.L.O.W.Ps*.

Who was this guy?

I knew it was Lars Madsen's brother Steen, but he was no longer the clownish figure I had seen the year before in Bordeaux. If his character in 1998 had been one of sunshine and gold, this new persona was overcast and grey. I remembered seeing him at the Calgary Nationals, waiting in the background, watching his older brother win the Championship. No doubt Steen was wishing he, too, was on the podium. He radiated a sense of yearning, something that I shared—feelings I had been pushing to the recesses of my mind.

His yearning was unsuppressed. Out on a pleasure ride, sixty kilometres out in the country, my chain had broken, and I hitched a ride to Steen's workplace, United Cycle. He was working part time while he pursued a bachelor's degree at the University of Alberta. While Steen puts a new chain on my bike, we talk. He's wistful, and I can tell he would love to race. Later, I drop off a National Team jersey for his father, Ole. Steen's face lights up, and I can tell that he misses the bike world. I don't.

I remember this as I stand in the banquet room at Chianti. Between sips of beer I realize the year has been a tough one, and not just for me. I recognize this as I watch Steen. Maybe it's the winter dark. Does it get to him too?

In Edmonton, at year's end, the night overtakes the day. When you rise and drive to the office, it's dark. Work all day under fluorescent lights, and drive home—it's dark again. Go to the gym in the morning, and it's dark. Go after work, and the sky is black. Life is a journey from one pool of light to another. Your work and play take place in brightly lit spaces, but the winter dark seeps into everything. For riders, it's an extra burden.

We need to ride, but have only two choices: take the mountain bike into the snow and ice, or ride inside. The only way to simulate riding a track bike at this time of the year is to ride indoors on rollers. Riding indoors is like eating chocolate without the flavour—no taste, just the chewing. You sit on your bike, drip with sweat, and count floor tiles.

Right now, though, I'm drifting towards the Christmas holidays. The beer tastes good, and I'm looking forward to a feast. Steen sees me, and I wave. We talk, but as we do, I'm asking the question again: who is this guy?

He's not the clown or the spectre, haunting the fringes of the infield pits. He seems harder, and although he's not saying much, what he's saying is something I need to hear. He's been transformed.

No one knows exactly what starts a transformation, what image, or word starts your brain on a course towards a goal. No one knows why an Olympic medal holds a siren-like power over your soul. Even today, I wonder if it was the medal I was seeking or some other result.

In any event, Steen's talking about taking on the big one. He was speaking about his audacious plan with the conviction of a street preacher converting a sceptic. If I was ever to make a comeback, I had thought Lars would be the ideal training partner. He is easy going, enthusiastic and generous. Steen is that, too, but there's something more: in spite of personal setbacks, he's refusing to quit. In fact, he wants two things: to ride the match sprint and win a gold medal at the 2000 Sydney Olympic Games.

"Me too," I say, amazed at the words that tumble out of my mouth.

Steen offers to help—he thinks I can do it. His faith is contagious. I drain the beer. It will be the last one for a long time.

"When," I ask, "do we start?"

The training schedule for 2000 is in my hands. My eyes are gawking at the codes: plyos, anatomical adaption, CompuTrainer, and spinups.

Steen's guiding me through it. Desmond was the apprentice's school teacher, but Steen is the university professor, trying to hammer elevated concepts into the freshman's reluctant intellect.

Every moment of every day is scripted. Each step—weight training, roller work, and bike work—is detailed to the second. Even the mental aspect, training the weakest link—the brain—is prescribed like some gigantic psychotherapy program. The detail is tremendous. For example, stretching involves over twenty-five separate tweaks and twists. This alone will take twenty-five minutes.

Steen is patient and earnest. How and what lies behind this recipe, I don't know and I don't question. It's a more detailed plan than I've ever seen or heard of. For Canadian women, there are two Olympic team berths open, both in the 500-metre. I know I can make one mine. Steen's own situation is desperate. The time standards, set by the Canadian Olympic Association (COA), are so high that it's well nigh impossible for him or the other guys to make it. Even though Steen and Lars are talented athletes, it will take everything to reach the time standards. And that's just to get to Sydney.

Steen's program is the cycling equivalent of a solo attempt on Everest. It will be long, hard, and dangerous. There's likely to be oxygen starvation and maybe a fatal plunge. But maybe, just maybe, if my body can hang in there, if my morale survives, I can reach the top—if I can hang onto the tail of this monstrous plan Steen has created.

After all, Steen believes I can, so why shouldn't I? But then again, why should I believe?

Year after year, and coach after coach, I had sought the perfect mentor. Except for Desmond, no one had been able to reach me and support me. My headlong plunge into Mill Creek mirrored what had happened to me without Desmond's guidance. Steen's appearance in my life was like finding a butterfly that has emerged from a cocoon.

Still, why should I trust him? This plan could ruin my health. This plan could set me up for another free fall. I reviewed the list of previous plunges: Cuba, Hyeres, Mill Creek. Would Sydney be the next? Over the last six years I had collected a number of medals, but also a number of disasters. Could I ever separate one from the other? Could I survive another success?

Was this one of fate's apples? Golden delicious or Red "deadlicious"?

I was thirty-four years old, and Steen was five years my junior. What did he know about coaching? I stare at the plan and see, like a card reader, potentialities of both kinds. There are two kinds of breaks.

Days later, we're at the Juventus velodrome clubhouse, reviewing the plan. "Lori-Ann," says Steen.

I stare at the page. I don't know if I can do this.

"Lori-Ann?" he says.

The workload is tremendous. It would bust an ox. And probably my back.

"Lori-Ann?"

Majority opinion says that, at thirty-four years of age, I'm too old.

"Lori-Ann," he says, "it will take a lot of work."

No kidding.

"But," he says, his eyes staring straight into mine, "it can be done."

Says who?

"I just have one question," he says, "how much time do you have? I need to know so I can work with you."

The buffoon has become the dark and fevered dreamer. Steen has just said, "work *with* you." He's trying to get to the Olympics, yet he's willing to take his own time to work with me. The magnitude of his generosity and his belief in me sink in. Who is this guy? Someone who believes in me. That's who.

"Time?" I say. "You tell me. How much time do I need to train?"

A gold medal. That's what he's talking about. Right now, my back is so weak that in the weight room I can only squat the forty-pound bar; no weights, just the bar. A world-level gold medal? Ha.

Nine months later, I'll come within one ride of proving him right.

Looking back over five years, it's hard to overstate the extent of Steen's help. It's easy to get used to being coached by someone who has a special gift. I was right that he would take me to the breaking point. Brinkmanship is, at the world level, the prevailing situation. If you don't go to the limit, some other clever rider will.

Go too far, and you're as doomed to fail as the slacker who skips training. Keeping the athlete on the knife's edge is where the art comes in. Make no mistake, Steen is an artist. The training volume was enormous, but the results came early. I look through my training diaries, and as I flip through the pages, the notations tell the same story:

"Jan. 13—On my last effort my heart rate got up to 174 beats per minute. I don't remember it being that high for quite a long time.

"Jan. 20—What an awesome training session: thought I was going to puke up my dinner on the last four spinups (maximal revolutions per minutes). Can't believe I finished it.

"Jan. 27—Rollers at Juventus Club—Pushed by riding with Steen. My form plus breathing was really good. What an awesome training session. Can't believe I pushed myself so much again!"

Page after page, the old diaries recount my renewal as a competitor.

Our hunger for international success pushed us to new lengths. Even Edmonton's fearsome January weather couldn't stop us from getting on our bikes. Of course, our velodrome was covered, but not with a roof. Once November hits, snow blankets the track until March. Therefore, we were condemned to ride the rollers. That's fine for practising the form you'll have once the bike is up to speed. But what about standing starts? The 500-metre event is timed from the standstill. Not being able to practise the start is like a 100-metre track sprinter not being able to practise in the blocks. But then again, this is Edmonton in January. We're not going to practise our starts in a metre of snow.

Not one to be deterred by minor difficulties, Steen phones me about an idea.

"We're going for a ride today," he says.

"We rode indoors yesterday," I say.

"Not indoors."

I stare out the window. There's an iron-like crust of ice on the road.

"Steen..."

"We have to practice our starts. Meet me at my condo. Bring your bike."

"Road bike?"

"Track bike. We're going to ride."

"In your condo?" I wonder how we'll fit into his living room.

"Underground," he says.

"Steen?"

"Tomorrow." *Click*.

We sneak to the underground parkade of his condo complex, and set up our rollers. It's dank, but after all, it's an underground parking garage. I spin my legs, and hear the hum of the rollers echo off the concrete walls. Bug-eyed drivers creep by, wondering whether they should call the security office. I ignore them. I have an Olympics to prepare for.

Steen and I spend thirty minutes puffing and grunting out our starts. It feels good to release the power that Steen's program is loading into my muscles. The entry for that day, the Tour de Parking Lot, says, "Great training session. Hungry to do more starts."

I'm so eager that after the garage workout, I hit the weights at 3 PM, and then more weights and plyometrics—jumping from boxes— at 5 PM. And, that day, a Sunday, there was also my morning workout program that started at 9:30 AM. Sunday a day of rest? For me, it's just a typical training day. At least I don't have to fit the training around my nine-to-five job.

Steen's also exercising my brain. His mental training consists of running an ideal race, from pre-race prep to post-event warm down, in your head.

On Monday I ride the bus downtown, and after getting a seat, close my eyes. Although I'm recuperating from a 6 AM workout, I'm not sleeping. While my bus mates are chatting about last night's *Friends* episode, or reading the latest paperback potboiler, I'm riding the World Championship—in my head. While the bus lurches and sways, diesel motor racing and brakes squealing, I'm on the home straight and rocketing for the finish line. The bus may be going thirty kilometres per hour, but I'm on my bike and hitting seventy kilometres per hour on the home straight. A steady drumming of feet on the aisle beside me snaps me out of the trance, and I rejoin the line of workers filing out the door.

The work-a-day world is like a holiday compared to Steen's program. Day by day I chart sleep, diet, and the actual training, so we can determine what works and what doesn't. I know that Steen has to keep me on the knife's edge of exhaustion. Not enough stress means not enough improvement. Too much leads to breakdown. There are blood tests used by wealthy sport organizations that can warn a coach that their athlete is about to go over the cliff. We don't have that kind of help. Instead, it's just Steen hoping he gets it right.

Weeks pass before I understand anything about the plan. The workouts vary in intensity and quality with no apparent pattern. Finally, in mid-January, he sends me a summary. The plan follows what he terms a *penta-structure* and has five parts: weights and plyometrics, aerobic, stationary-bike work, stretching, and mental training.

Steen's message, on this last component, says, "This training is to control your emotions both in training and racing. A race is won before you're anywhere near the race itself. You must believe you can win before you win."

Belief. It's essential to my relationship with Steen. Half the time, he doesn't speak. He nods, and off I go, jumping off a wooden box with weights in my hands, squat-lifting an immense chunk of metal, or spinning on the rollers until my eyes roll back in my head. His face betrays no emotion. During a workout, Steen reminds me of a grim-faced hustler in a high-stakes poker game.

His plan is so tortuous that it can cripple me. The only way I can keep up with the punishing workload is to have my own team of physiotherapists, masseuses, and chiropractors to pummel my overtaxed muscles back into position.

With Steen there's no simpering small talk, no insincere compliments. There are days when I come to the clubhouse for a roller workout, dying to share some event from my day. I'll be lacing on my shoes, nattering away, before realizing it's one of those days: a Thundercloud Steen kind of day. I'll look up and see the bleak look on his face that says, "Shut up and ride."

Steen will critique what I'm doing, and I know I have to accept it. He's got an incredible gift, and I'm fortunate he's sharing it with me. Believe in it? Instinctively, I do. Still, there's a cost.

After a month of this training, I'm irritable. One Sunday, before working out, I am quarrelling with friends. After my regular 7AM stretching program, I travel to the University of Alberta for an hour of weights. After, I head to the clubhouse for a roller workout. Questions rattle through my head. What is the point of all this suffering?

The Juventus riders set up, and the rollers start to spin. The metal cylinders, whirring beneath the high-pressure tires, whine as the riders hit training speeds. Layered over the metallic whining is a solid wall of industrial metal rock, pulsing out of a portable stereo. The music, an abrasive amalgam of angst and alienation, mirrors my frame of mind. Why am I fighting with my friends?

I am to blame: I'm strung out from all the work. I work at work, and I work on my bike. Work, work, work. My legs, my heart, are filled with cold sand. The workout stretches before me like a death sentence.

I close my eyes, and amidst the doubts, remember what Steen had taught me. It wasn't the plyometrics that helped my legs. It wasn't the aerobic training, the skate skiing, or stationary bike riding. It wasn't the previous roller workouts. And it wasn't the stretching.

It was the mental training on the bus. It was all the mornings of rehearsing the tiny details, the small steps in climbing onto the bike, and sailing out onto the velodrome. It was the vision of hurtling down the final 200 metres, my opponents' elbows lashing out, and my finishing burst of speed. It was the feeling of fulfilment when I crossed the line. First.

Today's prescribed efforts could have crushed me. But the mental training, the exercising of belief, let me succeed. When I imagined the finish line approaching I felt an intoxicating fluid, like a drug, pour through my veins and ignite my soul.

Steen had trained me to tap into the primal belief that I could win. Day after day, bus ride by bus ride, I had exercised my faith. And here, in the sweatbox of a concrete clubhouse, by a snow-bound velodrome, I realized that the hardest race was the one in my head.

If I could win that one, no one would stop me.

We warm down, the music is tuned to an ordinary rock station, and everyone's head is hanging between their shoulders. It's been the best session yet. Usually, I tell everyone how well the training's been going. Not today: it's a private triumph, and one that I'll keep close to my heart.

The day finishes at 9:30 PM with stretching.

The next roller workout is even better than the last. The diary says, "This was one hell of a workout. I can't believe Steen got me to do this. It was awesome having him and Lars doing the same session."

Belief. Is that all it took? There were two things more.

One was experience. In 2000, and at thirty-four years of age, I still felt like I was the apprentice. Still, there was nothing to do about it but keep studying. Not that I had a lot of time. Soon, I would summit either the top of the podium, or the peak of the scrap heap.

The last ingredient—the secret mystery element? It took me four more years and an Olympic gold to recognize it.

Stalking. Hunting. Nowadays, they're dirty words. Like any woman, I am disgusted with the violence that saturates our civilization. Yet here I am, stalking my prey, and my prey is Steen. His wheels swerve up the Argyll's velodrome banking to avoid a blob of dirty snow. I back off and position myself up the bank to better react to his jump. "Heh, heh, heh," I say to myself, "You're dead, man."

Steen's arms tense. Even through his winter riding jacket I can see his shoulders bulge, and he launches himself down the bank. I scramble to catch him. Dammit, he's fast, and I haul on the bars.

For an hour and a half, on March 25, 2000, we circle each other on the track. Like duellists rehearsing with wooden swords, we go through a ritual of jumps—accelerations to maximum speed. We're encased in constricting winter riding clothes, but I'm not complaining. In fact, I'm riddled with happiness and feel like a kid set loose for summer holidays.

The grim, grey days of indoor training are over. Even though blobs of dirty snow obstruct three out of four turns, we're weaving around these frosty speed bumps. Even though the low sun's slanting rays leave half the track in darkness, I feel the sun penetrate my bones.

While Steen and I warm down, I see a jack rabbit, leap from a snow bank. I wonder if he's the Easter bunny bringing me chocolate eggs.

On second thought, I hope he's bringing me luck. Today is my first day on the track. The season's first race, the San Jose Electronic Data System (EDS) cup in Northern California, is close at hand. "Better be quick, Mr. Easter Bunny," I think as I ride up to the railing and undo my toe straps.

"You've got four days before I leave."

Have you seen the Hollywood classic *Ben Hur*? The epic film's climactic action scene, with crazed charioteers and wild-eyed horses, is the epitome of merciless competition. Two thousand years later, the chariot race lives on in track racing. I've been on the track for only a few days, but I've qualified for the final of the Chariot race. Like its namesake, there are eight of us lined up closer than sardines. It's an all-out race, two laps only, and the money's good.

The gun goes off, but Steen gives me a wimpy push. I'm at the back, and there's only one way around the knot of riders, so it's up and over—the hard way and the long way around. I'm high on the bank of the first turn, and look down at my quarry. A power dive into the back straight, and I slingshot to the front. The throttle's stuck at the max, and it's first place, and a fistful of cash.

At this meet, I also advance to the finals of the Keirin—another free-for-all. The Keirin was devised in Japan, and is named after a beer company. The event is designed to create the maximum of risk for the entertainment of beer-sodden fans. A motorcycle paces the pack, usually eight riders. It tows the group up to speed, and the riders fight to get into the draft behind the motor. It peels off, and the riders who haven't spent themselves shoot it out for the finish. I make the final, and am beaten only by Tanya Dubnicoff.

The meet ends, only six days after my first ride on a track this season. Even so, I've collected two top-three results. It's unnerving how much Steen's focus on mental preparation has helped. I enter the races calm, but ready to ride aggressively. In the race, the mental rehearsal helps me convert the chaos of a mass start event into victory. Also, with Steen there I've got someone in my corner. My prize money helps pay our expenses, and I sense that this is going to be a great year.

For once, disaster doesn't accompany success, and the remaining races, in the run-up to the Sydney Olympics, put the lie to my usual pattern. I am closing on Dubinicoff and, in Texas, beat her for the first time. She's the 1993 World Champion, and was on the World Championship podium in 1998 and 1999. It's a sign that I'm closing on the world's best.

Finally, the National Championships, the critical qualifying event for the Olympics, take place in Bromont, Quebec. Steen the track sorcerer and his apprentice arrive early. The track is the old Wall of Death, previously ridden at Copps Coliseum in Hamilton. It's now longer because plywood extensions have been installed on the straights. However, the banking is still fifty-six degrees. The Wall of Death is now the Bathtub of Doom.

At first it seems to live up to its reputation.

Saturday morning, before the championship starts, Steen is warming up for his sprint. He's at full speed when a junior rider darts from the apron onto the banking. Steen throws his bike sideways, and tries to spare the errant junior. The two collide, but thanks to Steen's evasive action no one's hurt. No one, that is, but Steen's bike. His carbon-fibre front wheel and front fork are shattered.

My bike becomes Steen's bike. Throughout the championships we swap my bike back and forth. The saddle goes up half a centimetre for me, and down for him. It's not ideal, but it doesn't slow us down. The morning dew is another matter.

I advance to the sprint final against Dubinicoff. The second last race is hairy because it takes place at dusk. The evening dew is settling on the painted plywood, and it's becoming a skating rink. I lose, and I am itching for the next ride. Racing is called on account of the hazardous conditions, and postponed to the morning. Morning comes, and the racing starts before the night's dew is off the track. Dubnicoff and I have a drag race, but she wins the match.

Thirty minutes later, I'm on the rollers, warming up for the 500 metres. I'm preparing for the next event, and letting my legs float. My rear disk wheel, my only race wheel, hums on the rollers.

Kaboom! The rear tire blows, and the bike's back end fishtails on the rollers. I weave on the spinning metal drums, but stay upright. *Thump, thump, thump* goes the shredded tire and my heart.

I have not been mentally rehearsing what to do if my tire explodes minutes before the most important race thus far in 2000. There are only ten minutes before the race where I am to qualify for the Sydney Olympics.

Steen comes to the rescue. He puts his race wheel on my bike while I do my final preparation. The bike is restored, and I'm waved to the start zone.

Now Steen's mental training takes over. The race plays out like one of my bus ride rehearsals. *Beep, beep, beep, beep, beeeep* go the five electronic tones that signal the start of my race, and I explode like a Sidewinder missile leaving a fighter's wing.

I cross the line faster than any woman has gone on the Bromont track. Dubinicoff does not beat me, and I have my first Canadian Championship.

I qualify for Sydney.

And I realize one critical fact: a transformation begins with belief—mine, yours, anyone's. I won because I believed I would. I was standing on the podium because Steen Madsen believed I could. I think about belief, and the strange riches it had brought. I do not think what would have happened if the tire had blown ten minutes later.

CHAPTER 8

MYSTERY

mystery /mis turi/ *n.* **1** the reason most riders, ride. **2** a hidden truth that
may sustain the rider. **3** the relationship between being accepted, loved,
and riding performance.

—From the *Cyc.L.O.W.Ps.*

At the Bromont track, friends and co-workers from my Toronto and
Quebec days surround me. Everything I had wanted when I was an aspiring Quebec team rider has taken place. I'm on the National Team, a
Canadian Champion, and I'm going to the Olympics. After the championship jersey is slipped over my head my friends engulf me. I'm transfixed
by their smiling faces. It's like looking into a field of sunflowers.

When I return to my home in south Edmonton, I replay the accumulated phone messages. As I bustle around the main floor, I lose
count—messages from strangers have deluged my answering machine.
It's the media. I have been discovered, and it all has to do with qualifying for the Olympics.

"What," I ask myself as I replay the messages, and jot down the
return numbers, "would they do if I actually won an Olympic
medal?"

Training resumes, and the media attention becomes a daily event. I'm
interviewed on the track, at home, and at the gym. It's important not to
get distracted, though. I have the Pan American Championships—in
Bucaramanga, Colombia—before the Olympics. The event is important
because I need a top-level event to help me prepare for the Olympics and
the 2000 World Championships in Manchester, England.

It takes four different flights, but on July 26, I arrive in Bucaramanga. The city is located in a beautiful clearing, surrounded by

mountains. Less attractive is the 250-metre track. It's bumpy and in previous years, this would have thrown me off my game.

However, thanks to Steen's mental training, I have a new ability to focus and exclude anxieties. In the flying 200-metre qualifying, and the standing 500-metre race, I am beaten only by Daniela Larreal of Venezuela. Still, I want a win. I need a win.

In previous World Cups, I had speed but no tactical sense, or tactical sense but no speed. In the match sprint final, I face Larreal, and let my legs ride the race I've dreamed about on the bus. My legs whirl like never before, and I win the gold-medal match. No matter what happens in Sydney, I've qualified for the World Championships.

On the return flight home, I have almost twenty-four hours to review this season. The dejection I suffered in 1999 seems to be a foreign world, a parallel and evil universe. With Steen and my friends in Edmonton, I have something like a . . . family?

Back home, Steen and I return to the track and I feel the mental and physical training knit. Motorpacing becomes critical: it supplies me with speed, speed, and more speed.

It's an Olympic year, and the competition is deep. Of the top three places at the last three World Championships, only three people have filled eight of those nine slots: Ballanger of France, Ferris of Australia, and my teammate Dubnicoff. Day after day I hurl myself around the Argyll Velodrome, feeling my bike hunker down under the g-forces of the turns and imagining I'm in Sydney. I'm hitting record speeds—speeds that make a medal possible.

At thirty-four, do I think I can beat these World Champs? This year has exceeded my most fevered expectations. Could the crevasse-ridden road of my life be leading to success? Maybe the sacrifices will soon pay off.

On August 26 I fly to our pre-Sydney training location in Adelaide, Australia. After the workout on August 30, I feel like doing a jig. Our manager is motorpacing us, and I think he's going too slow. Turns out that he isn't; I'm just going faster than ever. Steen's training plan has been perfect. At last, the seemingly inevitable and mysterious success-disaster link is broken. About time.

A toilet is a toilet. Canadian or Australian? Close up they look the same, unless you're on a plane, and then they look even worse. It's

September 9. I'm on the plane to Sydney and Houston, we have a problem. "Huuuggh," I groan, and hurl bile-laden stomach juices into the bowl. I gasp and feel cold sweat bead on my greasy brow. I'm panting, trying to focus on arcane trivia in order to distract myself. Northern hemisphere toilets, I recall, have a counter-clockwise flush. The ones here, in the Southern hemisphere, flush clockwise. Is it true? The plane lurches, and I clutch the toilet rim.

"Huuuggh," I groan and forget to check.

"It's the Aussie flu Miss Muenzer," says the doctor at the Olympic Medical Center. I am sitting in the examining room holding a prescription for Tamiflu. I stare at the scrap of paper. "Take it every twelve hours for five days." he says.

I try to focus my itchy eyes on the doctor. The lights send searing pain directly into my brain. "I'm supposed to be racing on the sixteenth." My voice sounds like that of an eighty-year-old chain-smoker.

The doctor smiles, but doesn't say anything.

"Thanks," I croak, and wobble back to the Athletes' Village.

Days pass, and the only training I can do is the mental training. The 500 metre race plays out in my head: a perfect race, ridden by a healthy rider. Considering my health, the rehearsal is sheer fantasy. Still, like the Black Knight in *Monty Python's Holy Grail*, I refuse to give up. I refuse to acknowledge that this pestilence has deprived me of the benefit of over ten years of training. I refuse to believe that the power locked up in my legs is being penned in by simple, blunt, disease.

Sleep, eat, sleep. That's what I do until I get the call.

"Lori-Ann."

"Yaaa," I mumble, and fumble with the cell phone. I rise from my bed, and try to remember what day it is: Thursday the fourteenth?

"I know you're sick," Steen says. He's calling from Edmonton. No Canadian man made the time standards.

"Uhum," I say.

"Go to the track."

"Go to the track?"

"You must go to the track."

"Must go. To the track."

"Do it, and then call."

I hang up and fall into bed, my head spinning like a top.

I go to the track.

At Sydney's Dunc Grey Velodrome, I check out the facility. The officials allow me to listen to the starting gate signals for the 500-metre event. The electronic tones remind me why I'm here. It's the best medicine I could have. The Black Knight may have no arms and is bleeding badly, but her legs are moving.

Next day, I'm on my bike, but my slow takeoffs remind me that I'm still recuperating. Steen calls to check up on me. He'd like to be here, but since he's not the official team coach, he wasn't sent by the COA. Even if I could afford to bring him over, I couldn't get him the necessary accreditation to assist me on the velodrome infield. I'm at the Olympics, surrounded by officials, none of whom are my own coach. Sounds impossible doesn't it?

It will happen again. Four years later, to be precise.

August 18, 2004, Athens Olympic Velodrome, 10:45 AM

I release the medal, and let it fall against my skin. I close my eyes, and let the warm breeze play over my face. After so many years of competition, nothing has changed. My competitors are well-supported. Their coaches are present with a smile, a gesture, a joke. Why is it that at the peak of my powers, fate hands me another bomb?

If Steen were here. If. But Steen is thousands of miles away. The explanation is always the same.

Once more, after all the meticulous preparation and the painstaking training, I'm blindsided. In Sydney it was the flu. In Manchester in 2002... I've kept the real story hidden. That time, my inner beast, a monster really, took me to the edge of brutal violence. Never told anyone about that, but I have a workout to do and a dragon to face. I'm confronting the old dragon, the ugliest one, and she's got a face I recognize.

I could call Steen. If the other teams knew of our arrangement—I'm coached by phone—they'd choke on their PowerBars. In an age of instant messaging, I can confirm one thing: there's nothing like the personal touch. Anyway, calling Steen won't help me beat this dragon—the one revived by the latest sign of official indifference.

This time it's personal. One of us will never return to the velodrome again.

I leave the cell phone in its holster and unpack my gear. I nearly rip the zipper off the gym bag.

The 2000 Sydney Olympics became the first of many times when Steen would coach me by cell phone. I'm like a radio-control vehicle, except the transmitter is thousands of miles away. Setting a pattern that will be repeated in the coming years, I call and tell him how the training went. He listens and gives me advice for tomorrow's workout.

Soon the week is over, and it's the day before the 500-metre race.

First, however, are the opening ceremonies. We start at 4:30 PM. Then we wait. Four hours of waiting for the Canadian team's entry to the Superdome wear me down. Riders dread standing for long periods because it saps their legs. Fortunately, a Juventus rider, Nick, gave me a folding stool as a going-away gift.

Finally, we're shuffling into the Superdome. The stadium is filled with over 110,000 fans, and they send vast waves of cheers over our team. The moment catches me by surprise. Pride at being a Canadian makes me fit to burst. My eyes water, and my throat starts to close up. Politicians and celebrities appear, but the most beautiful images were of the Olympic torch, passed from woman to woman, all of them past Olympians, and then to the Australian aboriginal runner, Cathy Freeman, who prepares to light the torch.

Before she does, a path is cleared up the ramp to the torch. Aqua, green, blue and white light shines on the steps, water flows down the ramp, and then the torch is ignited. The entire structure is elevated to the sky. The athletes and spectators are melded in one incredulous spellbound mass, staring at the beautiful symbol. Then the stadium explodes with cheers. The games have started. And in less than twenty hours, so will I.

The velodrome is filled. The start line, so modest-looking yesterday, is now the centre of official attention. My bike is fixed into the starting block. I get on the saddle, and have only fifty seconds to settle in and adjust my toe clips and straps. The straps are pulled tight enough to make my foot fall asleep. I am not going to walk out of these pedals.

Twenty seconds to go, and I look at my line, and then glance at the clock.

Ten seconds, and the timer begins to beep off each second.

Zero seconds, a last, long beep, and the gate cracks open.

The crowd disappears. The officials have vanished. There is no sound. Nothing exists, just the air exploding from my lungs and the long black line leading me to the first turn. The turn markers—rectangular brick foam barriers, set on the inside of the turn to prevent racers from cutting the corner—flash by in the bottom of my vision. The pedals are spinning as fast as they've ever gone, and I sit down, driving the bike down the straight.

Last turn, and I'm fighting against the searing pain in my legs telling me to quit. I throw the bike over the line, and, gasping for breath, I crane my head to see my result on the vast electronic scoreboard. My time is 35.846 seconds and good enough for thirteenth place. Dubnicoff is ahead of me, but out of the medals.

A minute later, I'm on the rollers, trying to work out the lactic acid, and I dial up Steen. He has to concentrate to understand my out-of-breath account of the event. I'm plucked off my bike by an athlete escort, and taken to the CBC's studio overlooking Sydney's old harbour and the stone sails of the Sydney Opera house. I give a more coherent account to news host Ron McLean.

Finally, I'm back in the village and tap away on my laptop, e-mailing an account of the race for my supporters. I sit back, wondering if I can make this moment last forever. No, I didn't win a medal. Yes, I went faster than ever. Both my first lap time and overall times are personal bests—all this while recuperating from the flu. I let everyone know that the difference this year has to do with my coach. It's Steen who's made the difference.

That, and the other element. An e-mail from my sister, Jennifer, is clipped to my training diary like a charm to ward off loneliness and other evil spirits. Her message is inspiring. "If I had to pick a sister," she writes, "it would be you." We've had our conflicts, but in recent years we have reconciled. The knowledge that she is thinking of me is like finding a shelter after fleeing a downpour.

I can hear music throbbing from a distant room. It's past midnight, but athletes are trooping down the hall, laughing and whooping. Someone tells another to be quiet. Not everyone's finished their event.

An Olympic Athletes' Village has a magical atmosphere. It is a gathering of the fittest and most optimistic people on the planet. We're all at peace with each other, and after our events are over, we're here to celebrate. It's like having a Christmas party, but one that only happens every four years. As a result, no one's in a hurry to see the Sydney Games end, and ordinarily, no one leaves a Christmas party early.

But I do.

The World Championships are in Manchester and just six weeks away. Six weeks is what Steen calls a *macrocycle*, a defined and complete training cycle of wind-up, peaking, and recuperation for the next event. I raced to a personal best with half a body. What could I do if I were healthy?

On September 21, I return to Edmonton.

At the velodrome, Steen warns me: "This week's training will be difficult."

"Why?" I ask. "Last week I rode a personal best."

Steen's got me returning to the basics, and at first I balk. I've been to the Olympics. Why do I need to practise the basics? Of course, he's right. After the first ride my legs feel as though someone's beaten them with a baseball bat, and I buckle down to the humbling training program.

A bright spot comes when I receive a call from one of the children at Grace Martin School. Earlier this year I had volunteered with the Edmonton Public School Board to partner with this school. I keep them informed of my progress, and from time to time speak to the students. If only one child is encouraged to take up sport, the time spent will be worthwhile. It's the end of September, and I've had a hard day on the bike, but my call with Louise Pick, a grade-six student from Toronto, brightens my day. She and I talk like old friends.

I can't help thinking how little it takes to make a child's day. Also, it's late fall in Alberta, and as the winds pick up and the temperatures drop, I need all the cheering I can get.

Steen and I are working hard, but no one's having fun. We're riding on roads, fighting traffic and gusty winds. Shrivelled brown leaves swirl in the wind, and the city has a bleak appearance. The cold weather forces me indoors and on the rollers. The rollers are sliding around the kitchen floor—yes, I'm riding rollers in the kitchen. Any place is better than the concrete block clubhouse.

October hits and it's cold. We trudge to the track and watch the bare trees shudder in the raw autumn wind. I'm trying to go fast, but it's hard when your legs are cold and constricted by heavy wool tights.

Children save the day again when I visit another school. Grades four, five, and six present me with a medal, a cup, a thank-you card, and a bookmark. The children mob me and ask hundreds of hilarious questions. Their natural lightness revives my spirit.

So does the mystery element.

I'm on the plane to Toronto, first stop in the trip to Paris, then Bordeaux for warm-up racing prior to the Worlds in Manchester. It's been years since my family has come to greet me. When I see Mom and Dad, I feel like there's never been any distance, but it feels like it's a new relationship too. My sister Jennifer and her son, Toby, are there also.

After a brief visit, I visit my grandmother at her nursing home. Her birthday was the day before I rode the 500-metre at Sydney. That night, before the race, thinking of her helped to reassure me. She had always believed in me, and I'm sure that wanting to please her was a reason I had willed myself to recover so quickly from the flu.

She's the one member of my family with whom I've never lost touch. Many days now she's too tired to talk, so I just keep her company. Today we have a good visit. She's always loved me unconditionally: she doesn't care if I'm an Olympian or not. Still, she doesn't hide her pride in my achievements. Too soon, I have to leave and return to the impersonal hallways of Lester B. Pearson Airport.

The final of the Bordeaux Grand Prix pits me against Felicia Ballanger, five-time World Champion. I'm leading but keeping watch. She's won the last five World Championships, and took the gold medal in Sydney in the 500 metre and the match sprints. What is she doing hanging back? I gamble, plunge down the banking, and charge for the line, elbows out, riding like I'm chased by demons.

Ballanger doesn't come around. I sit up and realize I have beaten the reigning Olympic and World Champion.

I return to the pits and it sinks in: the Grand Prix is mine.

What's more, I've recuperated, and the speed I knew I had—the speed to win a World Championship medal—was indeed in my legs.

That race is done, and I can enjoy myself. Children are coming into the pits, seeking autographs and chatting. During the event the organizer serves a meal and the celebration, awash in silky smooth Bordeaux red wine, continues for hours.

Later, I try to analyse why I had been so successful. The racing seemed familiar: it played out like my training sessions with Steen. Also, I felt secure knowing Steen was there. Unfortunately, he won't be coming to the Worlds. I'll be without his advice on equipment, tactics, and training.

"What am I going to do?" I ask him as we pack our gear.

"Call me," he says.

"Phone you every time I have a question? I always have questions."

He nods.

"I'll be calling after every race!" I say.

"Yup. Call anytime, even if it's the middle of the night in Edmonton."

"Anytime?"

"Anytime."

I pretend it will be as good as having him beside me.

The TV crews are walking behind me, dragging heavy black cables. The cables hiss as their rubber casings slide on the Manchester velodrome lobby floor. I'm at the payphone, plugging one ear so I can hear Steen's voice. I'm wearing my Canadian National Team garb and arm and leg warmers. Although the velodrome is indoors, it's October 27 and Manchester is in northern England. Every time the lobby doors are flung open, a blast of frosty air swirls in. I'm trying to tell Steen about the World Championship's 500-metre event.

"Markovnichenko won," I yell into the clunky handset.

"What?"

"I got fifth," I yell.

"Fifth?"

"Awesome, eh?"

Steen is trying to make sense of my babbling. At least it's 1 PM in Edmonton and I haven't woken him up.

"And I beat my Sydney time," I say, shivering as the doors open again, and a gust of nighttime Manchester air swirls around my throbbing legs.

"Get on your rollers," says Steen.

I laugh. For someone so young, he's like an overprotective parent. The next day I'm on the phone again. CanadaDirect, the phone plan I've signed up for, is making a bundle off of me. I'm back in the lobby, but it's 9 AM in Manchester.

"Steen?"

"Huuh." This time he's waking up. I cringe, and imagine him putting the phone to his forehead, wondering what kind of nut is phoning him at this hour.

"Steen, I've qualified third."

"Third?"

"In the flying 200-metre. Markovnichenko is first. She hit sixty-four kilomtres an hour. Jennie Reed is second."

"Huh?"

"Second. Jennie is second. I did another personal best. I know I can beat Jennie."

"Don't beat Jennie," he says.

I hold the phone away from my head, and stare at the receiver.

"Don't beat her?" I say.

"Beat Markovnichenko."

"Right," I say, and hang up. Beat Markovnichenko.

Any European, seeing that I'm being coached over the phone, would stare in goggled-eyed amazement and then burst into laughter. After the snickering they would say, "You ask your coach for directions by phone?"

"Yes," I would answer, "and I have to wake him up too. He and his wife have day jobs. Otherwise, I'd call more often."

Another call is equally valuable to me. I call the Manchester Comfort Inn to retrieve my messages. My heart stops when I'm told there's an e-mail for me—from my mom and dad. I ask that it be read over the phone. The concierge, in her flat Manchester accent, reads the following words: "I'm ready, world. Are you ready for me? Go for it. Love, Mom and Dad"

With Steen behind me and my parents' support, I feel invincible.

I win the eighth final later that afternoon against Tanya Lindenmuth of the USA. The racing is done for the day, and I contemplate my upcoming ride against Galina Enukhina of Russia. Enukhina is the 1994 World Champion, and has massive calves that are the size of my quads. She's been on the circuit for years, and has a wealth of experience.

That night I'm on the phone to Steen, recounting the day's events and receiving instructions for tomorrow. Steen prescribes some mental preparation for tonight, tomorrow morning, and then a good warm-up. Also, he wants me to try, when I'm off the track, to distract myself. On the track, your focus has to be total. After the ride, it's the opposite: find something mindless to do, and avoid burning up energy that you'll need for the next race.

The last piece of advice will prove to be dead on, unfortunately.

The morning starts well, and I beat Enukhina two straight. I'm into the semi-finals, and so is my old competitor, Reed. For years she and I have been evenly matched. This will be anyone's race, and the winner will go to the gold-silver round.

First ride, I'm following, pushing her, hoping she'll keep the pace high and I'll draft her. Reed leads into home straight, and I catapult out of the saddle and edge her at the line. It's close, but it worked.

Next ride, I'm in the lead. She is vigilant; I'm not, and she dives underneath me when I glance forward. Reed picks up the pace, and tows me into the finishing straight. I churn the pedals like never before, and I win. It's a sweet feeling, and one of vindication—not only for me, but for Steen. His long-distance coaching has put me into the gold-medal final.

"Steen, Steen, it's Lori-Ann." I'm on the velodrome lobby phone again. "I'm in the final for the World Championship,"

"Of course you are," he says.

"How..."

"In Bordeaux I could tell that you were on a roll."

"But you didn't..."

"I didn't tell you," he says, "because you had enough to worry about."

"Thanks," I say and laugh. "What do I do now?"

"Nothing,"

"Nothing?"

"Just chill out and forget about the race. Twenty minutes before your ride, get on the rollers. When they come to get you, go through everything in your head. Until then, do nothing."

"Nothing," I repeat.

"Call me after the first ride," he says and hangs up. My lifeline with my coach and friend is now just another phone hanging on the wall. I turn and look at the fans milling in the lobby. No one takes notice. On the track, I'm a somebody. Off it, I'm just another rider using the payphone.

My opponent, Markovnichenko, has hard, dark eyes, and later will have a scary-looking tattoo applied to her forearm. Plus, she smokes cigars. More importantly, she won the 500-metre and qualified first in the 200-metre. I know that for her the title could be the way out of poverty. For me, it's worth more than all the money I could ever earn. There will be no easy ride for either of us, but I know that I could be World Champion.

The potential for this inspires me and, at the same time, scares me to death. Steen was right. Think of nothing.

I'm thinking, my mind whirring like a top, in the first ride of the final. Markovnichenko is barely moving, creeping around the bottom of the track. What is she doing? I'm following, but somehow I can't shake the feeling that she's stalking me.

By the bell lap, the speed's picked up, and I jump. She moves up the bank, and I flare upwards. She holds me there, still accelerating but controlling me, and dives for the pole.

It's 1–0 for Markovnichenko. I have thirty minutes before the next ride.

"Steen? Steen? Are you there?" I'm on the phone again, praying that he's going to answer.

He answers. I can't keep the anxiety out of my voice. "Steen, I lost. I don't know what to do."

"What happened?"

I tell him. The TV crews are still dragging cables over the floors, but my eyes glaze over as I describe the ride to my coach. "I don't know what to do," I say. Why can't he be here?

"Relax," he says. "Control the race. Keep her against the bank. Make her come around you."

"How? She's cagey."

"You're both fast, and the last turn is critical. You lead into it and you've won."

"She'll never let me."

"Yes, she will."

"Steen? I say.

"She will," he says, "if you make her."

I clench the phone as I steel myself for a confrontation with a World Championship veteran.

"Lori-Ann?"

"Yes?"

"You can do it. It's just another ride."

I hang up, and in the lobby of the Manchester velodrome, surrounded by TV cable, and fans, I tell myself it's just another ride. I feel as though I'm watching myself from a great distance—as though I am a photographer with a wide-angle lens, reducing the detail, and looking only at the big picture.

What did I do to spend the thirty minutes? I don't know.

I next remember forcing Markovnichenko to the railing, keeping my hip at mid-bank, and climbing with each pedal stroke. She's feinting, making head moves like she's going to dive, but I keep her there, denying her a straight run down the bank. We're accelerating as the bell (last) lap approaches. The bell clangs, the ringing changing in pitch as we leave it behind and I dive for the pole. The crowd noise is like a wave breaking over my head, and I accelerate. The last turns appear, and I'm smashing the pedals.

I'm first and have no idea how the whole thing happened.

Later in Edmonton, I see footage of this ride and notice that for a brief moment, coasting around the track, I raised one hand and held an index finger up, signalling "Just one more."

As I warm down, I realize that thirty minutes from now I could have the Rainbow Jersey. The World Champion's jersey is white, with horizontal bands of red, blue, black, yellow, and green—the rainbow. Like the Tour de France's Maillot Jaune (the Yellow Jersey) the Rainbow Jersey holds a huge power over its seekers.

Thirty minutes pass. I'm thinking, my mind whirring like a roulette wheel, the same thought—the thought of winning—rattling like the ball over the spinning numbers: *click, click, click.*

After the race, I coast, my feet moving with the dying inertia of my bike. The spectators are moving towards the exits. I roll to the finish line and see Markovnichenko, the victor, get mobbed in the pits. I had allowed her to take control. She'll go on to win another World title in 2002 and a silver in 2003. For me there will be no Rainbow Jersey.

Still, I've got a World Championship silver medal. When I come home, a photo is taken of me on my return. The smile on my face stretches from ear to ear.

I had always been a dark horse, missing more often than hitting, yet in Manchester, I had come within one ride of proving Steen's prediction that I was capable of a world title. There were a number of factors to my success. Steen's coaching was critical, but there were other aspects buried deep and disguised. It would take four more years to see the whole picture.

At the moment, I had a silver medal to celebrate.

With Mandy Poitras, the Canadian points racer, and other friends, our last stop is the Nag's Head pub. Good thing it's at the end of our street. Years of clean living, infrequent drinking, and a few pints of Guinness are a potent combination.

"Can you feel your nose?" I ask my friends.

"Why?"

"If you can still feel it, keep drinking," I say, and take another draught of the chestnut-brown ale

Truth be told, the beer had little to do with my intoxication. I'm delirious with joy and relief: at last my plans have panned out. Sharing my adventure with friends makes the whole night even more rewarding. We're singing and celebrating with other competitors who have drifted in. For a few hours, names, faces, languages blur, and we're all each other's best friends.

Forty-five minutes after I lie down, I'm up at 5 AM to pack my bike and begin three weeks' holiday in Greece. It's snowing in Manchester, but the sun will be shining in Greece. Two days later I'm in Athens, gawking at the Acropolis. For a moment, I wonder if I'll return for the 2004 Athens Olympics. The prospect seems remote, and I return to sightseeing.

I sleep the days away. At season's end it's exactly what I need. I drink beer, eat Greek salads, and play cards. The little things of life work their magic. One day is like the other: only the names of the hotels or the sidewalk cafés change.

Two weeks later I'm bored.

On November 30, 2000 I'm in an Edmonton weight room, sweating, straining and training.

Snow falls, and Steen has me take up skate skiing. Steen's a biathlon coach, and on top of his studies, coaching me, and part-time work, he is one of the Edmonton Nordic Ski Club coaches.

I flounder in the snow, trying to master the intricacies of gliding on one ski. Eventually, I can keep my balance on the skinny skis, and chase Steen around the club's Goldbar Park loop. Skiing for a cyclist? Makes sense—both activities require a powerful leg extension.

Also, I learn Steen is finding new ways to make me see black spots and feel like puking. Skiing, I understand, but holding your breath and diving for rubber weights in the deep end?

It's now December 31. Steen and I are at the Grant MacEwan College fitness centre for a year-end fitness feast. The main course is in the weight room and on the indoor bikes. Dessert is in the swimming pool. Steen has me dive to recover a weighted ring. He's forcing me to hold my breath and work hard, legs thrashing, and eyes bulging, swimming half a length underwater.

Why? I don't know. Steen's the scientist—a mad scientist. He can tell you himself.

Anyway, he's like family. If he told me to jump in the lake...

CHAPTER 9

COACH

coach /koche/ *n. & v.* **1** an artist who teaches the specifics of a discipline. **2** an individual so scarce as to be (in track cycling) almost non-existent. **3** in ancient times, a mystic, often tortured for their insistence that they know the truth. Nowadays, merely ignored. **4** Steen Madsen (see **1, 2 & 3**).

—From the *Cyc.L.O.W.Ps.*

On Being the Coach, Rabbits, and Picasso: A Post-Athens Discourse by Steen Madsen

Beginnings
As much as our results in Athens relied on science, our ultimate success relied on art. And, on one artist in particular, Picasso. I love Picasso's work. The taking of an object, and the transformation of its soul into an artistic maximum, is what intrigues me. His distortion of perspective—people with two eyes on one side of their face—shocked the world.

Picasso was an innovator and an illuminator. His work attracted scorn and insults. For better or worse, he was thrusting his hand into the chest of the world, tearing out its heart and exposing it to view. His famous mural, *Guernica*, a shrieking and frightening collage of images depicting the terror bombing of a helpless Spanish village, is the best example of his power—the power to illuminate the truth.

The artist and the scientist are interested in truth. The inner workings—the truth—of an athlete's mind, had always interested me. Long before I coached Lori-Ann at the 2000 and 2004 Olympic Games, my interest led me to follow in my father's footsteps and become a cross-country skiing coach. Later, I took a degree in psychology at the University of Alberta. It was, I hoped, the beginning of a career in working with athletes.

Also, I had some athlete's business of my own to take care of. In 1998, I had just made the National Team, and was competing at the Canadian National Championships in Victoria when I met Lori-Ann on the track infield. She was sitting in a lawn chair, staring straight ahead and preparing, it seemed, for her last day on earth.

"Hi," I say, chancing a disruption to her total concentration. She looks up. I feel like I've disturbed someone in church. Eventually, a smile.

"Hi," she says.

The smile vanishes. She pronounced "Hi" like it was the sort of thing a fencer says when they run a practice dummy through. Lori-Ann returns to her staring. I wonder if everyone from Ontario is like this, and meander to my camp.

I tweak my bike for the next event and wonder, as I adjust the wheel, if she's as focussed as she looks. I have a feeling that her image of total concentration is a mask; that she doesn't have a plan.

This last observation is based on intuition, but no one needed a mystical inner sense to see the problem with her pedal stroke. As I watch her circle the Victoria 333-metre track, the problem is obvious. The pedal stroke is supposed to be circular. Instead, Lori-Ann's pedal stroke is not a circle; it's pear-shaped, with the pointy end at the top of the stroke. Her weak foot comes up and jerks the rest of her body to the side.

"Smoothness is control," I remember my father saying to me and my brother Lars when he coached his budding BMX-racing sons. His pronouncement still holds true. So does Dad's follow-up statement: "Control is speed, and speed is power." He didn't need to add that power equals winning.

Maybe Lori-Ann Muenzer had a plan, but she didn't have a smooth pedal stroke.

I saw her later in the afternoon, and she was still all focus and concentration, even though racing was finished for the day. I know, from my coaching background, that when the competitive switch is on, your body is in a state of heightened awareness. Her overworked psyche was pouring energy down the drain.

After Victoria, we travelled to the 1998 World Championships in Bordeaux, France. Lori-Ann seemed disillusioned, and it became apparent that my guess was right: she didn't have a plan. The appearance of total focus *was* masking her frustration. At this event, I'm videoing everything in sight. When I stick the lens into her vicinity, she's shooing me out of her way.

"Lighten up," I tell her.

She's too polite to be rude to me, but I can tell she thinks I'm a clown.

She's right—to a point. Off the track I'm having fun, but it's proof I can turn my switch off. On the track is another story. *Click*, the switch is on, and I am as stone-faced as anyone. I had been a boxer and know better than most what it takes to step into the arena. Step into the boxing ring without your competitive switch on? *Blammo*—watch your adrenaline-crazed opponent send your noggin into the stands.

But this led me to a realization about Lori-Ann. Clearly, she was someone who could use a coach. Too bad our team resources are so tiny that she and I, starting at bottom, were on our own. For North American track riders, making it in Europe is equivalent to an uncoached kid from Provence playing hockey in the NHL. In other words, it's not likely. In fact, it would be a miracle.

If someone said that two years later I would be her coach, I would have asked, "Are you feeling well?"

If someone had predicted that I would coach her to an Olympic gold medal, I would have said, "Now that *is* a miracle."

Miracles do happen. You can pull a rabbit out of a hat. But first you have to put the rabbit in.

Picasso and the Rabbit: 1999 to 2001

By the end of 1999 it was clear that making it to the 2000 Sydney Olympics would require something drastic. Of course, I had no idea that part of the solution would involve Lori-Ann falling off a cliff.

By the summer of 1999 we had developed an acquaintanceship. In July I had met Lori-Ann at the Canadian National Championships in Calgary. My brother Lars was having a good year. He won the championship, and Lori-Ann came to our camp on the infield to congratulate him.

"Hey," she says, "I might be moving to Edmonton."

"No kidding," I say, and can tell that what she's really saying is that she *is* moving, and is looking for training partners. I hope my suspicions are correct: she's lightened up, and I enjoy spending time with her.

I ask, "You want a training partner?"

"Awesome," she says.

Lori-Ann knew I was determined to reach the top. I knew she wanted to get there too, but didn't have a coach, a training partner, or a velodrome. Moving to Edmonton would give her two out of the three. At this time, there were no experienced professional track coaches in Edmonton, or anywhere west of Ottawa for that matter.

By the autumn, I'm riding with her and talking about my hopes for the Sydney Olympics. Lori-Ann's dropping hints that she had given up. I didn't feel close enough to say, "Don't quit." When an athlete says they've finished, it's a decision that's involved a lot of agonizing. I thought she just needed a sabbatical.

There are a lot of ways to take a sabbatical. Normally, you don't have to fall off a cliff, but Lori-Ann did, and two things happened. First, she survived. Second, she learned how much she loved to ride.

As bad as it sounds, sometimes the best thing for a burned-out athlete is to get hurt. The injury forces them to contemplate life without their sport. Usually they don't need retirement; they need a rest. In Lori-Ann's case she sustained a massive injury to her back. She narrowly escaped becoming a paraplegic. Ironically, the muscles that had been crushed were the tissues that protected her spine when she landed on the stones of Mill Creek.

For Lori-Ann, the damage to her back was critical because it affected her core strength. No back strength? Then there's no anchor for the arms and legs to work against.

At the 1999 Juventus Christmas banquet, I watched as my club mates gathered around Lars and clapped him on the back. I wasn't surprised at the acclaim he was receiving. However, I was surprised by what Lori-Ann said.

She and I were standing off to one side, holding our beers and talking. I told her of my vow to make the 2000 Olympics, and laid out my desperate training plan: I'd keep the accelerator down, and hope I didn't break. If the plan failed, I would be an empty husk. If it succeeded, Sydney would be the reward.

Lori-Ann wanted to be my training partner. That wasn't too surprising. The more people you can attract in a training group, the more fun the training is. Also, she wanted a coach.

Now, here was the astonishing part: she wanted *me* as her coach. At this stage I don't know anything about coaching a track rider. I was a university student, a part-time ski coach, and a National Team athlete. I was also working part time, and didn't even have a CCA level one cycling coach accreditation.

But I do like Picasso. And I had seen how events had turned Lori-Ann inside out. Have you ever seen a Picasso painting, one where he takes the inside of an object—its guts or brains—and turns it inside out? He took the essence of his subject and exposed it to the world. I took his approach and applied it to sport science. To me a good coach is like a good artist. And a great coach is like Picasso. The coach has to extract the maximum potential from the athlete.

The first step for a coach is to learn the range of techniques. Picasso could paint in a range of styles. Like him, I needed to know everything I could about my art: I needed to survey the physiology of sprinting and the basics of coaching.

I knew we would be facing the best athletes in the world and well-funded organizations. For every Steen Madsen there would be three coaches, an exercise physiologist, and a physiotherapist. For every Steen there would also be a mechanic, a team psychologist, and a team manager. For the athletes there would be training camps in tropical countries and living allowances. There would be the latest equipment and the finest of facilities.

Steen had Steen. Lori-Ann had Steen. Period.

Also, it was winter in northern Alberta, and the only things moving on our track would be the snowshoe rabbits. Clearly, general knowledge would not be enough. And I had only a few months to pull the rabbit out of the hat.

There was only one way to do it. Day and night, every spare minute I had, I spent at the Grant MacEwan and U of A libraries. I took out stacks of books and reams of academic journals. The small, black print of the abstracts merged until I was reading and re-reading the same articles. After months of study, recurring themes were evident.

Whether I was reading a study from Britain on the optimal cadence for a cyclist, or a boxing text about mental preparation prior to a bout,

I was reading the same message: to train the body you had to identify the energy systems that were critical to the event. But there was another system that had to be trained, one that was at least as critical. Like Picasso, you have to see the soul of the person you're dealing with. You have to turn their psyche inside out and understand it. Or not.

The first month, it's like two bulls in a china shop. The sock dispute was typical. We're at the velodrome, in March 2000, for our first out-door ride at the track. Up until now the riding's been in the clubhouse and on the rollers. Today, we've shovelled snow from the velodrome until our brows are bursting. At last we're suiting up for the ride. I see Lori-Ann's wearing socks. Socks!

Sprinters never wear socks. Lori-Ann is buckling up her helmet. The socks, pristine and white, glare like beacons.

"Are you road riding today?" I say

She stops at the door, wondering if I am talking to her.

"Socks," I say, pointing at her feet.

"Yes," she shrugs.

"Sprinters don't wear socks."

"Well, I am."

"Road riders wear socks. Sprinters don't."

She's staring at me, like a third eye on my head has just opened up.

"No sprinter," I say, trying to remember if I'm right, "has ever worn socks and won a World Championship."

"Yeah?"

"Absolutely. No one, in over a hundred years of sprinting, has ever won," I say, trying to recall the photos of old-time champions in my cycling texts. "Wearing socks, that is."

"How come we wear them when we're roller riding?"

"'Cause we're sweating."

"You don't sweat on the track?"

"I'm ready to ride, not argue," I say, sorry I raised the subject.

She's standing in the doorway, squinting at me.

"You're a sprinter," I say, trying to sound authoritative like a news-caster. "Don't forget it."

She closes her eyes. Her gesture says, "Whatever." Lori-Ann wore socks for a week, and then no more.

More than her sock habits had to be changed. She was recovering from a serious back injury, and I had to scale back the weight training.

Also, it was important for me to smooth out the bumps, bobs, and other extraneous motions of her pedalling technique.

Aside from the sock issue, she would accept everything I told her to do. It wasn't unquestioning, though: I learned that from the sock fight. Later I explained to her that there is a reason sprinters don't wear socks: it's to get a better feel for your feet. Pianists don't wear gloves, and sprinters don't wear socks. This was easy to explain, but what about the other drills I had her doing?

First, there was the parkade training. This was triggered by a grim reality for track riders in Edmonton. From November until March, the track is encased in snow. The World Cup season starts in December. Of course we could go for a few days to a warm-weather track camp, but a world-class rider has to have weekly track time. In January 2000, the distance between our reality and our Olympic goal wasn't just a gap, it was a chasm.

Then I remembered what my father had done for his BMX-crazy sons. In the midst of a northern winter he had built a start gate, a ramp complete with timing lights, in our basement. On it, Lars and I would practice the starts that are critical to winning a BMX race.

I convinced Lori-Ann to bring her bike to my parkade. There we practiced our standing starts, and later I built in an element of mental rehearsal when I played a tape of crowd noises to accompany our training.

Lori-Ann was excited about parkade racing, but not all of my innovations were met with enthusiasm. Combat breathing was one. I explained it to her on another snowbound January day as we began another parkade session.

"What kind of breathing?" she says.

"Combat breathing," I say, my voice echoing off the bare concrete walls. "It's what fighter pilots do." I explain: "At test-pilot school, they practice special breathing techniques in a giant centrifuge."

"A what?"

"They go into a pod, on the end of a giant arm. The poor pilot inside is like a ball on the end of a string. The arm whirls and the g-forces build until the g's suck the blood from their brains. Unless they're breathing the right way, they black out at three g's. And probably puke. Anyway, if they take a quick breath, hold, and then exhale," I say, "the pilot can hang in there to six g's."

"So?"

"So," I say, "this allows you to withstand external stresses on your breathing, and then..."

"Then?"

"Then you utilize the martial arts secret."

"Secret?"

"To cyclists. There's a way to get an extra 10 percent of power. When I studied kick boxing, we released our breath explosively when punching."

She's leaning against her bike, arms folded and silent. I suck in my breath, hold it, and then let it burst out. Lori-Ann flinches. She's seen this before: my enthusiasm for the unorthodox. I get an idea and unleash it on her. But on one condition—I try it first.

Earlier, I had snuck to the garage and tested my combat-breathing theory. I'm amazed at how it helped me overcome inertia in the most critical part of the standing start. My studies have shown that the first four pedal strokes are the most critical.

It's a simple event, so why all the study? Imagine that you're on the starting line of the Olympic 500-metre event. Your bike's rear wheel is locked in an electronically controlled vise. An electronic timer beeps away the seconds. If you start too soon, you're straining against the vise and burning up your precious energy. Start too late, and you're left behind. The most insignificant error, one that slows you down by a tenth of a second, can cost you three places. Once, Lori-Ann missed a World Championship title because her wheel strayed off line for a split second.

Another bizarre but effective technique was prompted by our lack of year-round facilities. In 2001 we had no money for a winter track camp. Sprinting and the 500-metre event tax the body's ability to generate anaerobic lactic capacity. In other words, the ability to keep your muscles moving when your body can't supply enough air to keep the muscles oxygenated. It's the power you generate in an all-out effort, one lasting up to forty-five seconds.

Of course, if it was June we could go to the Argyll Velodrome and perform sets of intervals, timed efforts followed by a specified recovery period. Interval training can be tailored to the energy system you need to train.

However, it's January, and the velodrome could also be called the Argyll Snow Bowl. What about the parkade? It's too small. I'd make it half way through a forty-five-second interval before cratering into a concrete wall. These undeniable realities mocked my ingenuity. "Ha!" they seemed to say. "What, Mr. Smartypants, are you going to do about it?" For the time being, I let my fevered brain gnaw on the problem.

At this time, I'm still on my kick about breathing or rather the lack of it. I studied obscure techniques where riders deliberately starved themselves of oxygen. American Ned Overend, a mountain biker, and Eddy Merckx, a Belgian pro, had dabbled in oxygen-deprivation training. They trained with special masks that reduced the oxygen available to their lungs. Were these two riders dedicated to the point of insanity? Probably. However, both men were World Champions, and Merckx won the Tour de France five times. I put the idea aside, and head to the ski hill. It's one of my nights to coach biathlon, a sport combining skate skiing and shooting.

I'm training one of my biathletes on the cross-country ski trails of Goldbar Park. We ski past the lodge, and I see my athlete's mom. She's a synchronized swimmer. I imagine her in the pool, hair done in a bun, nose plug fastened to her face, and legs twiddling, hands sculling. She's smiling for the camera. Must be tough, I think, to hold your breath, tread water and smile. She's probably submerged for forty-five seconds or so.

Forty-five seconds? I stop skiing and coast to a stop. Notwithstanding the image of a sparkling Lycra swimsuit and the waterproof eye shadow, I can see the answer. I buttonhole Synchro Mom and ask her advice.

Next day, New Year's Eve, I phone Lori-Ann and tell her to meet me at the Grant MacEwan fitness centre.

"We doing weights?" she says.

"Uh-huh."

"Anything else?" Lori-Ann knows that there's always something else. My plans always include at least two and usually three separate activities.

"Bring your suit," I say.

"Suit? Is the media going to be there?"

"Swimsuit."

"Steen?"

"We're going swimming."

"Great, I'm a good swimmer."

"You shouldn't be," I say. "You don't have any body fat. I don't want you to float."

"Steen?"

"I want you to sink. It'll be better that way."

"Steen?"

I don't explain. At the gym we push iron until our legs are ready to fall away. En route to the pool I feel like a marionette and the puppeteer is drunk. *You* might say we're exhausted. *I* say that we're "pre-fatigued."

We spend the last part of the last day of the year diving to the bottom until our ears ache, and clutching at rubber weights. We're swimming underwater until black spots dance in our eyes. Lori-Ann and I gasp for air, surfacing like exhausted submarines, gulping air before we return to the chlorine-laced depths. The training continues until the lifeguard blows her whistle.

We stagger to the empty change rooms. Everyone else is celebrating New Year's Eve. We're just happy to be out of the water. Our level of fatigue is amazing. My head feels like I've taken a left hook. I've put the magic rabbit into the hat, but one thought bothers me: I hope it hasn't drowned. I shouldn't have worried. Not then.

Nine months later, at the 2001 World Championships in Antwerp, Lori-Ann pulled a rabbit—a medal-winning rabbit—out of her hat. She would perform this magic trick not once, but twice. The medals were silver and bronze, and we swore that the next year, 2002, would bring a rabbit wearing a gold medal and a World Champion's Rainbow Jersey.

Two thousand and two started as per the plan, and a well-trained rabbit was put into the hat. Funny thing about magic hats. Sometimes you put the rabbit in, but a different animal comes out. In 2002, Lori-Ann pulled two wolves out of the hat. One would take her Commonwealth Games gold medal. The other would nearly take her life. But that was to be eighteen months from the promising beginning of 2001. Until then, the wolves would bide their time.

CHAPTER 10

ODYSSEY

odyssey /odisi/ *n*. **1** story written by an ancient, blind, and probably alcoholic storyteller. Plot involves a series of adventures encompassing successes and disasters: similar to a cyclist's career. **2** often confused with **oddity**. On cycling road trips, the two may become identical. **3** *Related to*: trips taken by popular musicians and politicians: miscues abound. A happy ending seldom results.

—From the *Cyc.L.O.W.Ps.*

Baaaw, baaaaw, bedaaaaw, boom, boom, boom, boom, boom, boom, boom, boom, boom, bedaaaw, doo-doo-doooo! Everyone's heard the beginning of Stanley Kubrick's *2001: A Space Odyssey*. Horns blare, and kettle drums thump away. Horns blare anew. The dramatic chords of the theme, *Also Sprach Zarathustra*, are engraved on the modern consciousness. In *2001* they herald the rise of the sun, and the dawning of a new era.

In my case, the start of 2001 was less dramatic.

On January 4, 2001, Steen and I are dining at McDonald's. It's 7 AM, and our last stop before the fifteen-hour drive to Burnaby on British Columbia's coast. We hurry from our warm van and into the fluorescent wonderland of plastic fixtures and greasy food. We're surrounded by worn-out workers, grabbing a last-minute coffee before facing the day.

I hop from foot to foot, waiting for the line to move. Two thousand and one is an exciting prospect, and I'm lucky to be on a new adventure. Also, the sweet memory of my World Championship silver medal nestles in my heart. It doesn't matter that few are aware of my achievement.

Sprint cycling is recognized in North America, but just barely. After Manchester, I returned to work at Field Law. My supporters there cheered my arrival, and then peppered me with questions: "How come sprinters go so slow, and then all of a sudden take off?" I explain that only the last 200 metres are timed, and the first part of the race is used to jockey for position. In our reception area I leave a photo album of photographs I've taken, and I go through it with any-one that's interested.

My McDonald's line mates are sullenly stumbling into the New Year, but Steen and I are full of expectation. Canada now has an indoor track, in Burnaby, and we're going to it. Now, there will be fewer of the mind-numbing indoor roller rides in the Juventus clubhouse. The next day our wheels are thrumming on the boards of the steep, forty-nine-degree banks of the 200-metre track. Under Steen's tutelage, I feel the speed pour out of my legs and onto the pedals.

We repeat the trip in February with a nine-day camp. It covers weight training, video analysis of our riding style, and, of course, a lot of track time. When the weather's good we head out onto the roads.

No one watches us, and we're like anonymous actors rehearsing for a play that's months away. It's tough to connect the training with the ultimate goal, the World Championships. However, Steen says that this period, January to April, is when the most important training occurs. Still, amidst the February's cold rain, June seems a lifetime away.

Any chance to simulate racing boosts our morale. Fortunately, one of my American opponents, Jennie Reed, is training here too. On the third day of the camp she and I are side by side, doing one-lap efforts Reed is doing well, but I have the advantage of Steen's training and she is straining to match me.

By day's end, my toes are numb, the result of the frigid and damp air in the velodrome. Still, as I coax my toes to life and change into my street gear, it's clear that Steen's plan is transforming me into a sprinter. An entry in my diary, on the last day of track training, reads: "Track: four hours...felt strong...starts with Jennie Reed. I killed her." Figuratively, of course.

Scrape, push, and heave. Scrape, push, and heave.

I wish that we had a snowplow. It's March 3, and the Argyll Velodrome is heavily laden with an encrustation of snow. I look across the track and see Nick, a young Juventus rider, working on his section.

Behind me, Steen is plowing through his own section. We've been shovelling for two hours. He rests his chin on his shovel handle and smiles.

"Is this another of your ideas?" I say, and smile back.

Steen holds his arms up to the sky. It's a bright, blue, Alberta spring day. The air itself is brilliant, and seems full of crystals. He laughs. "It's all part of the plan," he says.

After the track workout, we throw the shovels into our cars, hop on our road bikes, and spin into the countryside. The wind is warm and the snow on the fields is dazzling. The riding has never gone better and I feel a sense of complete optimism.

Other parts of my career are progressing. My Web site is up and running, and I use it to stay in touch with my small band of supporters. Also, my school speaking program is continuing. I speak to hundreds of children, and never fail to enjoy myself. At the schools, the children are as eager to tell me about their interests as they are to ask me about my career. The day after one appearance, a boy's mom e-mails me: "Danny was still just beaming this morning...I told him about the street hockey game invitation you wanted and he said, 'NO WAY, YOU'RE NOT SERIOUS!!' So I am sure he'll be asking me to ask you to come out and play street hockey very soon!"

Finally, I am about to be a homeowner. Part of my sense of isolation was my rootlessness. Living in rented condos and crashing for a few months with friends, would be behind me. I had made an offer on a fifty-year-old house in South Edmonton's Queen Alexandra community. On hearing of this, a friend e-mails me: "Now to be honest, Beautiful, I cannot see you in an old pair of mukluk boots shovelling snow in the middle of winter or for that matter in a pair of baggy shorts and T-shirt cutting grass behind a lawnmower in the summertime."

I don't have the heart to tell him that I *can* see myself shovelling the snow and cutting the grass. I welcome anything that gives me a refuge from the day-to-day frenzy of work, training, and travel. Even simple tasks, like grocery shopping, give me a chance to stop being the totally dedicated athlete. Music, too, is an escape for me. It accompanies me everywhere, and lets me open up my heart to the feelings that are so often put on hold. Feelings? Sure I have them. Time to experience them? Sorry, maybe some other day, I often tell myself.

So, too, do I find refuge in my Monday night photography diploma courses at Metro Community College. There, I am given assignments by instructors Peter Sauer and Bob Lamb. It's amazing that the class can be given the same task, but come up with vastly different ways of looking at a subject. I use my thirty-five millimetre Pentax K1000 that I carted around in high school, and have always taken to races. When I'm off the track, I like to record my surroundings. The photos go into an album, and I use this to show my co-workers what, for example, our state-supplied, machine gun–toting bodyguards in Cali, Colombia looked like.

From March to April Steen continues to work me hard. We're battling the usual gusty Alberta spring winds, but with Steen at the helm there are no bad surprises. This year, I think, will be the year. The first race, the Cuban Championships in Havana, takes place in mid-April, and the results support my optimism.

I miss winning the match sprints by one ride. I write in my diary: "I feel like I was leaving off from what I learned at last year's (2000) World Championships...I executed moves that I haven't ever thought about doing before."

I can't wait for the first 2001 World Cup in Cali, Colombia, and I imagine a World Cup gold medal around my neck. After over a year of mental rehearsal—of training to believe that I can win—and seeing the top of the podium from second and third, I know it's just a matter of time before my odyssey will pay off. This is the first time I've been prepared to the best of my ability. I feel like a cheetah ready to strike.

My eyes are burning, and I'm staring at my riding shoes. I've just finished my ride at the Cali velodrome, but it's not sweat that's making me scrunch my eyelids together.

"Lori-Ann," says Steen. "Don't let them see you cry."

My head is turned away from the other riders. Steen puts his arm around my shoulders, and steers me to the washrooms. We've just finished the 500-metre event, and I'm ninth. It was my best result, but it was so slow that my heart is dissolving.

I don't know what's wrong with my legs. They feel like they've been replaced with Silly Putty. I'm in knots with frustration, and can't put my finger on the reason for my weakness. It doesn't console me that there are nine riders within half a second of the winner, Markovnitchenko. I'm not here to make excuses; I want to win.

Steen's bundling me into the women's washroom. A knot of surprised women chatter in Spanish. Some mutter about Steen, but when they see my face, they give us room. Steen closes the door to the cubicle.

"Okay," he says. "Cry."

After my promising early season, the World Cup at the Velodromó Alcides Nieto Patiño in Cali has been heartbreaking. I stand and put my head in my hands. "Go ahead, tears," I think. My opponents will not see how distraught I am. No tears come.

"Aaaagh," I say. It's all I can muster. I take a long, shuddering breath. "I'll be okay," I say. Steen has his own races to ride, and I don't want to take any more of his time.

When I get to the hotel I take my team jacket off. There's a rustling sound, and I pull a scrap of paper from a pocket. It's my mantra: a list of words that I use before and during an event to trigger instinctive responses: "I am the fastest and the strongest. I am the best, tactic-wise. I want it more than anyone. I have the confidence. Don't be afraid to be aggressive."

They're all the right words, wishes and beliefs, except the gap between the belief and the reality is like finding out there is no Santa Claus. At the end of the list I see the problem:

"You have speed in your legs again—they're back." I only would have written that if I had doubt.

Ever notice that nothing goes right before a big trip? It happens to athletes, too. Prior to Cali, I had the flu, and was so dehydrated that I needed three intravenous bags of saline. Also, there was poor weather and Steen and I missed critical motorpacing sessions. Finally, there was the pressure of closing the house deal, and sixteen hours of travel before arriving here.

Finally, there was the pressure of living up to my goal—to ride the 200-metre faster than my previous best—11.68 seconds. To the outside world, it's just a handful of numbers. To me, if I can make that mark, then I'm a contender. On the other hand, if I fail, the goals become mocking, jeering phrases.

The worst critic is always the one closest to you: the person in the mirror. And, in the background, there's always the voice, the take-no-chances doubter, saying, "See? I told you. Look at what you gave up...for what?" Fear, poisonous fear, was corroding my confidence.

The next World Cup, in Szczecin, Poland, was less than two weeks away. I remember Steen's earlier warning: "If you're not fit by April, it's too late."

At this point it's now the end of May. The trip to Poland needs to go smoothly. If I'm rested and calm, I'll be able to make the cue words transform potential into reality. Please, I think, let this trip go easily. I don't need another odyssey.

There's a photo taken during the Polish odyssey that says it all. Steen is standing in front of our airliner. The Polish airline name, LOT, is on the fuselage. The caption reads, "Thanks a LOT." You might think the caption was sarcastic. After all, LOT did lose our bags, with our riding clothes and bike parts.

At the Warsaw airport our problems increase. The CCA did not issue us visas. Without the paperwork, we can't get into Poland. No problem, I say to Steen, and pretend the statement is true. We keep a brave face and leave the airport with the correct visas after breaking speed records for completing Polish visa applications.

"Okay," I say to Steen when we get to the track. "Where's our manager?" Steen finds him. His name is Fidelio. He is Spanish, but doesn't know anything about track racing. That night we find out what Fidelio does know. He is in fact a world-class performer in his own right: Fidelio is a top-ranked drinker.

He does his best work at night, and uses the World Cup's social events to improve his alcoholic form. We try to get Fidelio to go shopping for food. Although he knows the universal symbols for Happy Hour, Fidelio does not speak Polish. He complains that he is hungry. We find food, which he promptly scarfs down.

All of this I try to ignore. But how do you ignore a lack of clothing? Our bags are still somewhere in the LOT wilderness. We beg at the track. The Chilean team lends me cycling gear with a psychedelic tie-dyed pattern. Steen snickers. I point out that he is wearing a threadbare yellow skinsuit, also from the Chilean team. Clapped-out Lycra becomes a thin mesh, and Steen's suit is so scanty he's in danger of being arrested.

Also, it's cold. Eventually, by borrowing gear from three different teams, we have enough clothing to stay warm—indoors. There's only one part missing: Steen's handlebars. The French team's mechanic, Monsieur Jean, lends him a pair.

By day's end, I'm still trying to maintain a regal calm. I write in the training diary, "This is going to be very interesting." The evening meal, supplied by the race organizer, is hardly ideal: three hot dogs and slices of rye bread. Nothing to drink. My diary says merely, "BAD."

Steen races the next day against German Rene Wolff. During the match, Steen tries to decelerate, and back pedals. His rear cog comes loose, and leaves him speeding forward when he expected to brake. Wolff attacks and wins the race. The trip is becoming not just an odyssey, but an oddity.

Fidelio continues to drink and laze about.

I qualify sixth in the 200-metre, but end up twelfth in the match sprints. Enough is enough, I declare to myself.

That night, June 9, I sit at my desk in the Radisson SAS Hotel. I'm like a boxer who's taken an early-round shot to the jaw. I write a manifesto on the hotel stationery. I imagine myself on the start line of the 500-metre event, and write, "No mercy. No prisoners...Kill." I dream that the timer is beeping down:"...three, two, one...EXPLODE!! Go! Go! Go!" I picture myself riding the race and see the finish: "Fast, fast, pin it...You can go even faster." And, finally, "See it and DO it." And, that is what I do.

After the ride, on June 10, a World Cup bronze medal in the 500-metre is hung around my neck. What role did the overflow of frustration play in my ride? As I pack the medal away, I wonder if I should send LOT a thank-you note.

I don't have time to ponder this question. We're on our way to St. Denis, France. The Grand Prix is a huge event, and well-attended by fans from nearby Paris. I'm looking forward to it—this time I've got the missing clothes and something else I had left behind: self-belief.

The French countryside is living up to its reputation. Steen and I are spinning around the countryside prior to hitting the St. Denis track. The houses are surrounded by gardens, and the fields are high with green crops. The bronze medal in Poland and the June flowers have lifted my spirits.

This time, unlike in 1994, I am ready for the race. When I warm up on the apron, I note the track is as choppy as ever. I'm not afraid. Even though the races will be *three-up* sprints (three riders per match), and the tactical dimension is more complex, I feel confident, especially when, on the next morning's road work out, I see three rabbits. I've seen rabbits at the Argyll Velodrome and associate them with good luck.

Luck, chance, fate, call it what you want. It plays a part in track sprinting. The race starts out at a sedate pace, but the last lap involves a cascade of events that take place in seconds, determining the winner and loser. When you remove the mechanical and human factors, there is still the unexplained hand of fate.

Luck is also something I need, in between the scheduled events, to wheel our cube van through the Paris traffic to get Steen to the Adidas store. He is desperate to get to the Adidas outlet. Does he want something from Dior, Chanel, or Rive Gauche for his wife? No, he wants to look at Adidas jackets. I hope that we don't get eliminated by Parisian traffic before the French riders have their chance. The drive there is a frantic journey and the return is no better.

"I hope we don't die before getting to the track," I say, watching another speed-crazed Parisian blast past our wallowing van.

"This trip is absolutely essential to our racing success," says Steen.

I fail to understand the connection between risking our lives on a French secondary highway and winning a track race. In the oncoming lane a suicidal motorist pulls out in front of us, passes, and darts back into his lane. His wind draft rocks the van.

"These drivers are crazy," I say

"They're Parisians."

We pass a road sign proclaiming this year's highway death toll. "Look," I say, pointing to the sign. Steen has his head buried in an Adidas catalogue. "It's a tough job."

"Yeah?" says Steen still gazing at the catalogue like it's a long-lost love.

"The sign painter," I say. He looks up. "The highway death toll sign painter. He's busy. You know what the worst thing about dying on this road would be?"

"What?"

"I'm not sponsored by Adidas," I say.

We survive our bold adventure.

And, as the saying goes, fortune favours the bold. I advance to the match sprint finals. The racing is capped by Steen's victory in a mass-start event. He blasts off the line, swerves around the pack, and steams to the finish line. I win my final against two French National Team riders. It's a good day for Canada.

I wonder, on the plane back home, if Ulysses felt this way. One day a shipwreck and the next day golden apples. I begin to accept that reversals of fortune are part of life. It makes me appreciate that important parts of my life are constant.

In Toronto we switch planes. It's late, so I don't phone Mom and Dad, but I pop a card in the mail. We're becoming close again. I especially wish I could visit my grandma. She's in a nursing home in Toronto, and not doing well. During my last visits, she wasn't able to speak, but I sensed she was aware of my presence. I hope Grandma feels honoured that she has been part of my success. Her unfailing support helped me through the shipwrecks of my journey.

I long to see her again, but I won't get another chance. Two weeks after my triumph in St. Denis, I'm on the plane to Toronto, heading to her funeral.

CHAPTER 11

ROCKET

rocket /raw ket/ *n. & v.* **1** a term for successful riders, as well as for projectiles, both of which are propelled by explosive forces. **2** the volatile nature of their propulsion system ensures that these devices have an unfortunate safety record. Explosions are not unknown, especially when nearing the top of their arc. (See **rocket ride**: chapter 14).

—From the *Cyc.L.O.W.Ps.*

On the plane home to Edmonton, I join the post–Canada Day 2001 holidaymakers. They're snoozing after exceeding their limit of beer and hot dogs. I'm staring out the window, oblivious of the landscape below. The forests of Northern Ontario, and the vastness of the cultivated prairie, slide under the plane's wings. I remember my grandma and our last visits. Futile regrets torment me.

I could have spent more time with her if I had been riding less. Also, what of my sister, Jennifer? After the service her small son leapt into my arms and I held him close. She and I are closer now than when we were living on Morland Road. Has the distance helped? Or hurt? And what of my parents? What do they think of my plans? What did they ever think? My goals are a mystery to them and probably everyone else.

I look around at my seat mates. Tomorrow will be another day for them: another day of work, family, or summer holidays. Is that what I want? The little things, the family matters and domestic realities of a good workplace mean a lot to me. Why can I only take so much of it? Grandma, I ask, what was your life like? What would you tell me?

We all have hopes and dreams. Work, family or holidays, we all have dreams to fulfil. Some of us *need* to be taken to our limit. Some of us *will* be taken there, like it or not.

I need to ride my bike to the outer limit of what's possible. Maybe that's why I've felt so isolated. I'm riding this crazy carbon-fibre bike to the edge of life, and I've left a lot behind.

Left behind? Yes, but there's a lot before me too.

I see Steen and Lars laughing, and setting up for a track workout. I see my parents and Jennifer, eyes glistening from grief, but glad to see me arrive at the service. Both groups are in my heart.

Maybe I belong in both places: Workplaces and workouts. Tracks and buses. Planes to family, planes to races. A split personality? I want to kill my opponents, to crush them in a race, yet I love to hang with them after the meet. Or maybe they're just different sides of the same coin.

The flaps grind out of the wings, and the landing gear doors thump open. We're on the final approach to Edmonton International. Tomorrow I prepare for the 2001 Canadian National Championships in Edmonton. For once, the media is interested, and I sense that my sport and I are emerging from a shadow land.

I bounce in my seat, anxious to get onto my bike. A picture forms in my mind. I'm on the track, screaming around turns three and four. National Championship, World Cup, or daily workout, the feeling is the same, and I shudder with the remembrance of how much I love it.

I step off the plane, and the most important piece of baggage—my family—is not one that I'll get at the carousel. Was I wrong? Perhaps I'm not leaving them behind anymore.

But I am definitely wrong about one other matter. This journey's not on a bike; it's on a rocket. Steen lit the fuse in 2000, and no one's putting it out. This rocket is going all the way.

For me, hopping on a track bike is second nature; for others it's a death-defying experience. Prior to the racing, some of the media have plunged into the fray. The Championships are preceded with a media race, and I partner *Edmonton Journal* writer Nick Lees against the athlete-media team featuring CBC's Mark Connolly. Afterwards, the moist faced reporters are hauled off their bikes, and I am impressed by their bravery.

I win the Championship, and enjoy seeing Steen win his own Championship, too. The Argyll Velodrome is my back yard, and the racing is like a reunion with old friends. Wrong again. They're not friends; they're my other family.

After the Nationals I call my parents, and fill them in on the final races of the 2001 season. "My next race is in the US, then a World Cup in Mexico City," I say. "Then there's another World Cup, in Ipoh, Malaysia, followed by the Ted Turner's Goodwill Games in Brisbane, Australia. The final event is the Worlds in Antwerp, Belgium."

"That's nice, dear," says Mom. And she's right. It is nice—to hear their voices, that is.

The next day I feel the rocket sputtering. I work a full day at Field Law. But it's a Monday, and there's no training. This makes the day, July 23, officially a "rest" day. At the end of the work day, I push myself away from the computer, and wonder when I'll be able to stop scrambling for sponsorship. Tomorrow I travel to Portland, Oregon for an important regional event. My house closing is coming up in September, and I'm wondering how I'll pay for the upcoming races and make the mortgage payment.

In Portland I win the 500-metre, setting a track record, and my friend Jennie Reed wins the 200-metre. Rain wipes out the rest of the meet, so she and I never have a final showdown in the match sprints. Before the rain however, I do have a showdown with a wasp that flies down the front of my jersey and into my sports bra. The crazed insect whirrs viciously and is stinging me. I'm shouting, trying to get the thing out of my bra and not crash my bike.

Back to Edmonton for a week, I head to a nightclub to see the band Rough Trade. I'm there to indulge my passion for photography, but end up spending the night celebrating with band members Carole Pope and Kevan Staples. I leave their hotel at 9:30 AM—most un-athlete-like. Steen, if he knew, would not be happy.

At 2:30 PM I'm on the track for three hours. In spite of sleep deprivation, I'm riding like I'm on fire. Maybe, I think, as I walk to the clubhouse, I should break training more often.

One week later, I'm in Mexico City and qualify fourth in the 200-metre. It's good having Steen and his father, Ole, there. The afternoon ride, the quarter-finals against Hungarian Szilvia Szabolcsi, is tough. In the third and deciding sprint, I have a moment of panic. Coming out of turn two, I doubt my plan, the one Steen and I had discussed at length.

Steen and I had realized that 99 percent of the time, the rider who leads on this track's back straight, loses. So why did I become one of the 99 out of a 100 riders who lead on the back straight? My lapse leads to self-doubt.

My confidence continues to shrink in the fifth through eighth rounds. I ride against Kiwi, Elizabeth Williams, who hooks me and sends me sailing up to the rail. My rivals recede into the distance.

Hooked by my self-doubt.

That night I write my cue words for the 500-metre event tomorrow, August 12. I draw an oval, the track, and list the steps I will take during each segment of the race.

The next morning, after rain delays that try my concentration, I am wheeled out onto the track. The air is heavy with moisture, but the rain has cleaned some of the smog out of Mexico City's air. I feel the handlebars of my bike fit into my hands. It's as if one was made for the other. My cue words reverberate as the electronic countdown starts.

And, as the final bleep sounds, I explode and tear my way down the track. A kaleidoscope of images, of power and an intense flame, run like electricity through my body. The bike hurtles into the turns. The finish gun goes off, and I know I've done a good ride. It's three hours before I get the results, but I'm third.

The rocket's first stage is separating, and I'm waiting for the signal to light the second stage. I won't have long to wait. Ipoh, Malaysia is four days from my bronze medal in Mexico City.

The early signals were not encouraging.

We arrive in Kuala Lumpur, Malaysia, at 1:30 AM. The CCA told us they were sending Eric Van den Eynde as our coach. At the airport, there is no sign of him. Of course, it always helps to have a coach, but Eric also has our new Canadian National Team clothing. Later, we find out that he missed his plane.

After our 5:30 AM arrival in Ipoh, I go on a road ride. My rear derailleur cable breaks. The next day I try to ride the track, but constant drizzle forces me to use the rollers.

The words Cali and Szczecin are coming to mind. In response, I spend the next two days mentally rehearsing my sprint races. I write out the questions:

Q: What do I want to accomplish?
A: Medal in the sprints and in the 500-metre.
Q: How will I do this?

A: Be mentally prepared, ride one race at a time. Focus on my plan.

Q: What is my plan?

A: For the 500-metre, visualize my rides in Poland and Mexico.

Q: For the sprints?

A: If ahead, stay vigilant, and control the pole. If behind, stalk, be patient, and show no mercy. Take no prisoners.

On August 24, plan and performance merge.

I qualify second in the 200-metre. More plans are scripted. I advance through the quarters and semis to the finals. A new image, one of me chasing Steen on the motorcycle, is employed: I'm chasing it through turn four, trying to catch the ghost motor, straining to push my front wheel to its rear fender.

The ghost vanishes, and I'm the winner of the match sprints.

At first, I'm not sure if the result is a dream, a mere continuation of the mental imagery. I ride to the rail and unclip. The spectators are yelling at me, which never happens in a dream. The only thing better than this, I think as I walk my bike to the infield, would be to do it again.

On August 26, I'm in the 500-metre event. Once more, the imagery and my legs find a perfect match. I win and am on the top of the podium. It's only a little step up, from second or third spot, but it's a much better view.

In the morning, I see a small square of paper under the door. It's from my National Team roommate Erin Carter: "Lori-Ann, you're snoring again—just kidding. Good luck in the races to come! You have the strength and power to do whatever you believe you can do!"

The rocket ride continues. The next event is September 2, the Goodwill Games in Brisbane. Again, the plan and ride blend, and I set a new Australian outdoor record in the flying 200-metre qualifying round. My sprint tactics are coming, but this time I push too hard. I finish first, but the commissaires rule that I cut off Katrin Meinke of Germany. They relegate me to second place. Later, I talk to Meinke and apologize. She laughs, and I know that there are no hard feelings.

Back home, on September 8, I barely have time to unpack, and I'm moving into my house. My work mates, cousins, and friends storm into the house. With pre-marked boxes, and everyone whirling about, the entire move is done in less than ninety minutes.

My arrival from Brisbane, three days ago, already seems like ancient history. I remember being greeted by a TV crew and being interviewed by CBC sportscaster Mark Connolly at the airport. It's a sight I'm not used to, and I'm grateful for their newfound interest. Connolly's becoming a loyal supporter, and I want to give him something good.

"How do you feel about your results from Brisbane and Malaysia?" he asks.

I give him a calm, succinct answer, but I want to pour my heart out, to say: "I've been working on this for eight years. I've almost died, and I've sacrificed so much for it. For years, I've really been working two jobs. I've spent every cent I've had. I'm driven—don't know completely why—by my unrealistic ambitions. But you know what? It's worth it. To get a World Cup gold medal, it's all worthwhile."

At this point he'd be goggle-eyed, but I'd continue: "Wait, Mark, there's more. It's good, but it's not enough. I want a World Championship, and I know that I can do it."

Connelly deserves a usable sound bite, not a saga, so I keep the details to myself. Also, I didn't want to reveal my secret weapon—Steen's choice of pre-Worlds training venue.

He and I will travel to Bromont, Quebec, and train on a track identical to the Antwerp World Championship facility. Steen believes in training specificity. In other words, you train the same way you will compete. The bike set-up and even the track need to be identical to the big event. Steen's using the same pattern of mental and physical rehearsal used by NASA's astronauts, so that when I put my bike on the line, the race seems just like another rehearsal and I won't be distracted. It's so much like Steen: methodical and tinged with genius.

This year, I sense, the Rainbow Jersey could be mine.

Three days later, the 9/11 disaster takes place. Like everyone else, I'm shocked at the frightening conversion of peaceful aircraft into flying bombs. Like any professional traveller, I know that the future of travel will be less friendly.

Two days later Steen and I arrive in Bromont. The Quebec Cycling Federation has installed the 250-metre track from the 1996 Atlanta Summer Olympics in place of the Copps Coliseum Bathtub of Doom. This camp is no National Team exercise; we're here at our own expense. No Canadian had made the time standards for the Worlds. Steen will coach me, but will ride too, hoping to keep sharp and make the grade for next year's Worlds.

Our first day is a rest day, and I take Steen on a tour of Old Montreal. We visit the historic buildings, and take in Notre Dame Cathedral. It's such a contrast to western Canada. Old Montreal is more Old World than New, with its ancient stone buildings and gothic architecture. The predominant language is French, and we're transported, several days before we arrive in Belgium, to the Continent.

After lazing in the Old Port, we fall back into the athlete's life at the near-deserted Bromont facility. We push weights in the morning while the dew is burned off the track. By 11 AM we're on the track, sprinting behind the motorcycle. For once the isolation is welcome: there are no distractions.

We have one guest, though. National Team coach Eric Van Den Eynde travels from his residence in St. Bruno and helps with motorpacing and timing.

My diary records a complaint about Eric: he wasn't going fast enough. Eric is eager to help, and opens the throttle. Five days later, on September 21, Eric times me for the 200-metre. My time is faster than my qualifying time in Ipoh, Malaysia. The rocket is in good shape and getting better.

More good news arrives. Steen has received a wild-card berth into the Worlds. He's coming with me. Good thing he was helping me simulate race conditions, and brought most of his racing gear. Maybe, I think, race simulations and mental rehearsals are more than just learning to believe. Perhaps the process of visualizing something can make it happen.

It's like motorpacing. No coach can explain why motorpacing works. Your legs get used to going fast, but they can do that on stationary rollers. What difference does it make how fast the road is travelling beneath your wheels? Yet, it does. You feel the wind on your face, and somehow you're transformed. Maybe visualizing is like dreaming. We dream that something could be, and somehow the world is transmuted.

Steen and I pack up our gear. I feel fit and fully charged. The rocket's ready to blast off, and I can feel the Rainbow Jersey on my shoulders. Bring on the Championships. Somebody, light this rocket. *Sssssssssss.*

August 18, 2004, Athens Velodrome, the Track Apron, 10:55 AM

Zzzzip. Zzzzip. "There," I whisper as I cinch the double leather straps over my riding shoes, and prepare to push off onto the Olympic Velodrome. My toe straps are so tight I can't feel my toes. It's good to feel the bite of the straps; otherwise I feel numb. I have to feel something, do something. Otherwise? It's over.

I remember the last time I was shunned like this; in 2001 at the World Championships in Antwerp. That time, I felt *plenty*.

September 2001, World Championships, Antwerp Velodrome, 500-metre Event

Kapooow. A rocket shell has gone off in my head. A rage, a hot tornado of anger, is roaring in my soul.

I'm trying to get to the track infield, but someone won't let me—they're hanging onto my skinsuit. Stitches are popping. My weight-trained arm muscles are like steel ropes, and I'm grasping the air in front of me, and grinding my teeth.

Someone's talking—Steen, I think. I've just finished the last event of the 2001 World Championships, the 500-metre, but I'm not trying to warm down.

I'm second, but I don't want the medal. I want to punch our team director's lights out. No other Canadian has won a medal at this race. It's been years since a Canuck won a Worlds medal. I miss the gold, the World title, by a whisper. Does our director say, "Way to go," or "Tough break, but good job"? The director, Mal Cupric, does nothing. But talk. To a friend. It's what they've done all week: nothing.

A person can only tolerate disdain for so long. The more that has been invested, the higher your personal cost, the more overwhelming the rage. White-hot competitive ambition has morphed into a maelstrom of mad fury.

"Don't get in my way," I hiss and try to twist away.

"Lori-Ann, get on your bike."

It *is* Steen, and he's holding my skinsuit by the shoulders. I'm straining, the Lycra fabric taut, trying to lunge at Cupric.

Cupric turns, sees the look on my face, and shrugs.

ABOVE: My grandparents' anniversary at the cottage, Bay Lake, Ontario in 1978. Left to right is Grandpa, me, Grandma, Dad, and Jennifer. Years separate me from those carefree summer days, but the love of my grandma, Annie Rosena Abernethy, follows me still.

RIGHT: 1968, my first bike. Even at age two my bike has one gear, no brakes.

Christmas 1979. Dad, me, Jennifer, and Mom. At age thirteen, I dreamed Santa would bring me a Lloyds stereo. Days stretched like an eternity. Twenty years later, Steen Madsen, would inspire me to dream of an Olympic gold medal. The waiting then was just as hard, and a lot longer too!

LEFT: Sydney 2000. The racing is done, and I can, for a moment, play tourist.

BELOW: Athens, November 2000, the Acropolis. This time I left with good memories, and great photos. Four years later, I left with an Olympic gold medal, and a hint about the next chapter in my life's journey.

RIGHT: November 2000, my Juventus Club Fall Banquet. On the left is Lino "Mr. Rocco" Bovo. On the right is the late Jim "Mr. Guinness" Horner. My club mates became my cycling family, and Jim volunteered as my Edmonton mechanic. His meticulous preparation of my track equipment kept me in the game.

BELOW: Manchester, England 2000 World Championships. My victory here, over USA's Jennie Reed, set the stage for my first World Track Cycling Championships medal—a silver.

Kelowna, British Columbia 2003. My friends, David and Monica Nelson, and I congratulate friend David Ahrens on finishing his Ironman race. Forest fires nearly consumed the city of Kelowna, and led me to wonder if I had incinerated my career.

Steen Madsen and I at the 2002 Canadian National Track Cycling Championships in Bromont, Quebec. Steen and I both took three gold medals. It was, I hoped, the start of a rocket ride to Commonwealth Games, and World Championship golds. As events would prove, rockets have a poor safety record.

Argyll Velodrome, Edmonton 2001. Surrounded by trees, with a blue sky above the High Plains, my spirits soar and Steen's training takes me to within one ride of a World Championship. Photo by Matthew Sweet

January 2001 at the Burnaby Velodrome. Baby, it's cold outside, and inside here too, but I'm not complaining. Back home there's a metre of snow on the Argyll Velodrome, and outdoor training is a distant thought.

Argyll Velodrome 2003. It's another cold day. A long-sleeve jersey, leg warmers, and booties ward off the raw wind. Still, it wasn't enough to warm up my results that season. The pain from my listless results would, however, spark a fire in 2004. Photo by Matthew Sweet

Post Athens 2004. Another peak experience. World Champion, and all-time Tour de France winner Lance Armstrong invited me to his Tour of Courage fundraising ride in Alberta's Kananaskis Country. At the highest point on the mountainous road I caught up with the world's premiere cycling announcer, Phil Liggett.

Burnaby Velodrome, January 2004. I'm exercising my need for speed, and racing with the men. In this match sprint final, I lead out Kenny Williams, Ryan MacKenzie, and Matt Chatter. Photo by Greg Descantes

Burnaby 2004. After three laps against the men, it comes down to a photo finish where I took third place. At the World Championships, Australian Anna Meares would best me in another photo finish. In Athens, things would be just as close, but with a different result. Photo by Greg Descantes

ABOVE: If it's February 2004, and I'm indoors, it must be roller training in the Juventus Clubhouse. Not a dramatic setting, but in this sweatbox of a tiny room, surrounded by straining riders, the summer's medals are won or lost.

RIGHT: In Edmonton, a few days after the Olympic gold medal, hiding with my nephews in a hotel until things settled down. Two years later, life is still hectic, but new roles fill me with optimism. Photo by Jennifer Mikula

Hyeres, France, August 2004. Me, Steen, and his wife, Cyndi. The "last supper" before Athens. The meal capped seven days of meticulous preparation. Steen knew, like the artist he is, that I would win a medal. He didn't tell me though—he thought I had enough to worry about.

RIGHT: Athens, August 24, 2004, Olympic match sprint final. The smile says it all. After an eighteen year voyage, I've come home, and I've got an Olympic gold medal.
Photo by Greg Wood/AFP/Getty Images

ABOVE: Top of the Olympic podium, end of the journey, and buoyed up by my friends, family, and country. Proof that dreams really do come true.
Photo by Damien Meyer/AFP/Getty Images

RIGHT: Brenda Miller, at Jasper's Maligne Canyon, shortly before she was killed in 2002. The money she raised sent me to a World Cup race. Her faith in me took me to an Olympic gold medal, and inspires me to this day.
Photo by Heather Rask-Maynes, Francine Harvey, Bernie Kollman, and Karen Eastlake (all with her on her last cycling trip)

"Let...me...go," I say to Steen and lurch toward the director. I can hear a series of pops, the fabric rending. I'll be a wearing a shredded suit, barrelling down on this bumbling bureaucrat. What a sight! But I don't care.

"Lori-Ann," says Steen. He's controlling me like a NHL brawler, waltzing me away from big trouble. "Get on your bike, Lori-Ann," he says, his voice breaking through the blinding static in my brain. Now Steen's in front of me. He's scared. Steen never gets scared.

"Okay," I say and close my eyes. Steen relaxes his hold.

"Lori-Ann, it's not worth it."

"All I wanted..."

"I know," he says. "Get on."

Steen's right. A bike had plunged me deeply into life. A bike took me to the point of a blinding rage, and a bike would take me back to civilization. I coast around the infield. Athletes are waving, congratulating me. Spectators too are waving, and I grin.

Almost—I almost had it. I roll past the part of the track where I lost the gold medal.

The night before the race, I had scripted the event, and inscribed a list of cue words:
"five-four-three—back pedal—two-one—EXPLODE!!" And so I had.

Like a booster rocket flaring, I had burst out of the gate. I hit the turns, the speed-induced g-force pressing me into the saddle, and launched onto the straightaway. On the last turn I had, for an instant, flicked up the bank by one metre. For a split second my arms had tensed and let the speed carry me off line. Go up, and you go longer. The shortest way is on the black line, the pole line.

A gold medal is unforgiving. In the moment my wheel slipped up the bank, a Rainbow Jersey slipped away.

I remember rolling into the infield. Everyone knew I had nearly won the Championship, and the Canadian Team knew I had ridden to my second medal of the Championships. I had tried so hard that my vision had faded—a red film covered my eyes as I whistled down the home straight.

I coasted to a stop, and saw the riders moving to help me off. Bright faces and full, blossoming smiles greeted me. Teammates Mandy Poitras and Jeremy Storie came forward. Steen was there too, grinning. I had earned their respect and their congratulations.

Cupric, where was Cupric? Loitering in the infield. Our regular Canadian team coach Van den Eynde couldn't make it to the Worlds, and sometime Canadian team coach Kurt Innes had his hands full, so Cupric was assigned to some of us. I was the only Canadian rider in the event, but it was, apparently, too much. Need a water bottle? Get it yourself. Need a wrench? Use your own. When's the next time the track is clear for a warm-up? Find out yourself. I've been training for years to get to this point, and all I'd asked for was a little help; the last thing I needed was indifference.

This frustration was boosted by my disappointment at missing the Rainbow Jersey. The blow-up hinted at the existence of a beast I would face again and try to tap into. For now, it was just a mystifying melt-down. My flashing into a rage left me with a sick feeling.

Steen helps me prepare for the medal presentation. His quiet and steadying presence has been important, and not just for forestalling my attempt to savage Cupric. The night before the finals Steen put a note under the door:

Hey champ:
Very nice rides against the last two riders. You controlled it and were very smooth! Awesome! Now let's keep doing the smart strong rider and go for a new jersey! (the Rainbow Jersey)
Steen

His encouragement helped me ride the eventual 2001 World Champion, Russia's Svetlana Grankovskaia, to her limit. In our semi-final confrontation, she edges me by three hundredths of a second. I'm shunted into the bronze round, and take it two straight. Notwithstanding the loss, I entered the 500-metre prepared to win.

At Antwerp I saw how close I was to the Rainbow Jersey, yet it's not enough to be the fastest in terms of raw speed. In the match sprints, you have to rely on instinctive response as well as sheer speed. In the 500-metre you must let your upper body steer the bike on the optimal path.

After the ceremony, we pack our gear. I'm looking forward to 2002. The rocket was ready, but its guidance system needed work. There were the inexplicable cases where I *let* other riders draft me to the line, or obstruct my path to the finish. I figure that after making a couple of quick adjustments, I'll be wearing a gold medal and a Rainbow Jersey.

I should have known that there would be no easy bargain made with fate. In the next year I will learn three things:

1. The hardest repairs to make are the mental ones.
2. When a rocket explodes, it takes a long time to find the pieces.
3. It's good to be alive.

CHAPTER 12

LIGHTING THE FUSE

fuse /fuz/ *n*. **1** a pyrotechnic material used to detonate an explosive device. For cyclists, self-belief or faith, triggers the cataclysmic effort. If coupled with material support, so much the better.
—From the *Cyc.L.O.W.Ps.*

One October night, prior to the start of a roller training session, I meet Steen at the clubhouse for a planning meeting. We're alone, and sitting on a battered couch. Photos of previous track champions and Formula One race cars line the walls. Steen asks me what my goals are.

"I want to win two golds at the 2002 Commonwealth Games in Manchester," I say

"Anything else?" Steen isn't being sarcastic.

"The new jersey," I say. "A World title."

Steen makes a note in his workbook. He sits back, and stares out the window. He's like a psychiatrist who's been told of a patient's bizarre dream.

"It's so close that I can taste it," I say.

He's still gazing out the window.

"You did it before," I say, wondering what the problem is. Part of my anxiety comes from needing to justify his faith in me. Steen's investment in me is huge. He's got his own career to look after too. After all of his pondering, his question is the same as ever:

"How much time do you have to commit?"

"What do I need to do to become champion?" I ask. "What do I need to become the fastest woman on the planet?"

Steen faces me. His dark eyes, a legacy of his Spanish heritage, stare through me.

"You know I can do it," I say

He closes his eyes and nods. A decision has been made. What, I don't know.

"Here," he says, and hands me the program. "It's the outline for the whole year. I'll give you a more detailed one in January."

Steen got me to the podium last year, and there is no question where I'm headed—a gold medal. Maybe two. We've got this thing wired. I don't have any doubt about it.

Still, there was a mountain of toil, training, and searching for sponsors on the horizon. You don't tackle a mountain unless your body *and* soul are in peak condition. Accordingly, Steen's planning includes a section about life outside of cycling. It's not just a sop to the self-help industry that he wants me to develop my whole being. Life is good, so enjoy it. And if you do, your game will improve.

The development of a life outside of sport is neglected by many athletes. The failure to develop your full potential leaves you high and dry when the games are over. Steen, more like a psychologist than a coach, steers me to do something—anything—not related to riding. At age thirty-five, I crave a break from the relentless demands of working and training. And every Monday night I continue my photography diploma course where the instructor helps me break out of the cycling box. Each week, for three hours, I'm just another aspiring photographer struggling to communicate a meaningful image to the world.

I am especially impressed by the work of Herb Ritz and his photographs of ballerinas. I'm stunned by the blending of grace and athleticism. The mixing of strength and technique is something that I strive for on the velodrome.

Taking this course lets me meet people who are not work mates or cyclists. I don't know their world, and they don't know mine. It's one of the only chances I get to socialize outside my small universe of work and riding. I can't do the things I used to do—play recreational sports, or go out drinking and dancing—so these routine social encounters are valuable for me.

There are also new efforts to gain sponsors. In spite of my World Championships medals, IMG, the worldwide conglomerate of sports agents say my results aren't good enough. However, my increased profile helps me find a solo agent. Maybe, after ten years of do-it-yourself fundraising, I'll have some luck.

Also, I'm continuing to rebuild my relationship with my family. I return from a visit to their Toronto home with a family treasure, my great-grandfather's rocking chair. I suspect it is the only rocking chair actively used by a World Championship silver medallist. The chair brings a sense of permanence into my new old house. There's little more steadfast than a rocking chair.

The training is carrying over from the last season. Steen has me swimming and skate skiing, and, of course, riding, indoors and outdoors. By December, the snows are here, and my road bike is parked for the winter. By the end of the year I can tell Steen is ramping up the training: I'm dragging myself home, my jaw numb and my mind a blank. Some days I'm in bed by 6:30 PM.

December gives way to the New Year 2002 and I'm wondering: is Steen Chinese?

He had told me his father was Danish, and his mother's side Spanish. We're in the clubhouse, and I'm reading his preamble for the January 2002 training schedule:

"We will train like horses this month. Horses are trained very hard. They accept whatever is given to them in the form of training and never complain. They just grind it out and complete their routines and exercises.... We will train like the Horse, naturally smooth and fluid in exercises we complete. This month we will be horses."

I look at Steen and gaze at his features. No, he definitely does not look Chinese. He's dark-haired, the result of the Spanish connection, and has strong Scandinavian features—tall forehead, strong jaw, and wide cheekbones. Definitely a Viking. There are no Chinese Vikings. So why is he following the Chinese Zodiac Animal Calendar? I know that 2002 is the year of the Horse, but does he?

I don't ask. I am no longer a rocket. I am a horse. It's more accurate. After all, "horses accept whatever is given to them." I read the list of activities, and struggle not to exclaim, and be un-horse-like. Steen's prescription includes:

1. Rollers twice a week.
2. Spin classes (another form of indoor cycling).
3. Upper body exercises with weights.
4. Leg training with both light weight and high repetitions, and high weight and low repetitions.

5. Massage. Steen says, "Do it yourself if needed." (!)
6. Cross-country skiing.
7. Cyclocross or mountain-bike riding on Sundays. ("Like church— every Sunday no matter what," says Steen)
8. Psychological and positivity training on Sundays.
9. Diet: cut the sweets and fat. Time to get fit and trim.

It's a program that would break most horses, especially those with full-time jobs. On the other hand, horses just grind it out.

"What do you think, Lori-Ann?" asks Steen.

"Awesome," I say, and smile with a naive enthusiasm.

It is awesome, in both the frightening and encouraging sense of the word. I recall Steen's prediction in 2000—the programs would pay off or break us. They paid off, but a thought lingers, like an unexplainable noise made by your car. I cease any deeper analysis. This horse, I vowed, is running for the finish line and wants to get there first. Bring on the Commonwealth Games and serve up the World Championships for seconds.

Weeks later, I have more paper in my hand. It's the printout of my U of A sports performance unit Wingate tests. The Wingate tests are a standard test protocol, done on a special exercise bike (an ergometer) that measures power. Nowadays, everyone in the cycling community recognizes that power output is the best indicator of performance. Bird, beast or person, it's the amount of power per pound that determines how fast you'll go.

Most nations' cycling organizations have power meters. The best one, the Schoberer Rad Messtechnik Laboratory's device (SRM), is common equipment for my competitors' teams. Not for Canada's, however, and the $5000-plus price tag has put it out of my reach. I have other urgent demands on my wallet—a failing battery in my ancient Honda, for example.

As a second best, Steen has lined me up (at $33 per session) with the U of A's test facility. Like the horse, I have taken on the workload and the tests prove Steen's regime is on the money yet again. In less than one month my power output has risen 3 percent, and my ability to sustain a maximal effort has increased by 6 percent. In fact, the tests showed my power output was nearing that of male cyclists from top national teams.

There was no time for pondering the toll of my unyielding commitment to ambition.

By the end of January, the horse's eyes are bulging from the strain. I record, in my diary entry for January 29: "Almost 'exhausted' feeling. It would be great if I didn't have to work five days a week so I could have a chance to recover and 'be normal'."

The reference to "almost exhausted" I made without any humorous intent. Naturally, a horse may observe a state of exhaustion, but will never complain. A few days later, Steen's handing me another piece of paper. It's the February schedule, and there's a new animal of the month. Steen's turned us from horses into grizzly bears.

Okay, he's not a Chinese Viking, but he doesn't look like a shaman either. I look at Steen and try to visualize him as a fur-clad medicine man. No, he's too well groomed. How about a medieval wizard—gown and conical hat painted with stars and planets? No, Steen's too muscular. What about a Danish Calvinist minister, preaching hellfire and brimstone from a pulpit, hurling heavenly lightning bolts into rows of blond-haired parishioners? They'd be scared stiff, waiting on the word from Steen. Yes, that's it.

And, like the astonished parishioners, I am receiving the sermon from Steen. "We are about to awaken from our deep winter slumber," his notes say, and I wonder how it's been possible to sleep with all the training going on around here. Not that I'm complaining, of course, because horse or grizzly bear, I have a huge appetite for work. I read on:

"The Bear is lean and mean upon first exiting the burrows of the earth. He (or she, I add) looks upon the spring natural habitat as an opportunity. We will treat this month with the same vigor and vitality, comparing directly to the Grizzly Bear."

I shake my head, and continue reading: "We will train like the mighty Bear and claw down anything in our way, attaining our rightful place at the top of the food chain." Now that's what I need to hear.

"Now," his notes add, "is the time to start imaging specific events of the year: World Cups, Nationals, Commonwealth Games, and Worlds. Focus on the year ahead, but still remember the positive successes of the past."

It's exactly what I need to steady my mind. I close my eyes, and try to relight the fierce spirit that led me to World Championship medals in

Antwerp. Further down the page, Steen, like a good preacher, ends with a warning, and a promise for the future:

"You should be acting like a champion both on and off the bike, acting professional, relaxed, and focussed when you need to be....This year will be the proving ground of the champion...only those select few that have the last 5 percent of discipline, will, and determination will achieve this end....Let's make it happen."

The preacher's words electrify me.

Although I'm staring out the windows towards the barren trees, my eyes are seeing a different scene. Memories of the towering clouds and turquoise skies of Cuba, and of Havana's white sand flood my mind. The first race is the Copa Cuba de Pista 2002, and it's only two months away. This grizzly had better get out of the den.

Hold it, that's not correct. This *champion* grizzly had better get a move on.

The tactical weakness of this grizzly's mind is being trained too. Steen has me reviewing videotapes of previous World Championship races and adds this to my regular mental training.

The school visits continue and I am amazed, by the end of February at St. Lucy's Elementary School, that some of the children recognize me. They are excited about my prospects for the Commonwealth Games, and want to be kept up to date on my results.

In the lead-up to the Commonwealth Games I'm recognized by my media loyalist, the CBC. They do a feature about a day in the life of Lori-Ann Muenzer. For laughs, a number of scenes are played at double speed. For me, it just looks like real life. A local TV station puts me on their morning show, and I'm billed as "the second fastest woman in the world." It's a billing I plan to change.

Also, my agent and I meet prospective sponsors, but, alas, with the usual results. The World Cup schedule this year involves far-flung venues: Monterrey, Mexico; Sydney, Australia; and Cali, Colombia. Without a sponsor, I'm going to have trouble attending the meets. Without the meets, I won't get the pre-games training. Without the training? I don't take the line of thought any further.

I'm also coming up blank in another area. A sensation of fullness, in the lower abdomen, has me wondering. Are my pants too tight? I know that I haven't put on weight. The persistent bloating sends me off to see a dietician at the university. The dietician sees nothing wrong with my eating habits, and I shrug it off. In the run-up to Cuba, the tight waistband was easy to ignore.

March comes and I'm in the clubhouse receiving the new schedule. Steen's notes say, "It's a hard month. We will be converting the indoor work to the demands of outdoor riding. Our bodies are going to adjust, but it will take extra energy."

I write this explanation on a piece of scrap paper, and attach it to my diary. I add the phrase, "burn-out month." Was it a statement, a question, or a prediction?

I don't have time to ponder the observation. The champion grizzly is up against a world-class wolf: the one at my front door. In one day alone, March 25, I call Labatt brewery about their adopt-an-athlete program. I contact two other prospects, and follow up by calling a battery shop, an office furniture store, and an engineering firm about a sponsorship proposal. No one is safe from my questing phone. I even hit up my gym and convince them to give me a break on my fees. By 5 PM, I've had enough, but still have an empty sponsorship plate. Unfortunately, the wolf's growling can be heard loud and clear. At 6 PM I'm dropping off a mortgage and car loan payment to the Bank of Montreal. Six days later, my car won't start.

The next day I'm road riding, and have to grind my way home through a spring snowstorm. My face is so cold that I can't speak. The wind has driven the snowflakes into my skin and I feel like I've kissed a porcupine.

The Copa de Cuba is just days away. I've won this race before, and last year placed second. The grizzly's hibernation, I vow, is about to end.

The Keirin race is over, and I'm third. It's April 13, late in the hot Havana afternoon. The Keirin is the last event of the Copa de Cuba, and I've learned which one of Steen's animals I truly am.

Last year I was a rocket, this January a horse, and now I'm a grizzly, a tired, sleepy grizzly, who's rubbing her eyes. Against the Latinos, I'm second in the match sprints and third in the Keirin. The Latin American riders are aggressive, but they're not as good as the Europeans. What will happen when I get to the Continent? After these results, I'm like a grizzly who's put her snout into a bee's nest, and I hope the stinging stops soon. It doesn't.

On April 17 I arrive in Monterrey, Mexico for the first World Cup. The Keirin follows the same pattern as the one in Havana. I squeak through to the semis, and then I'm boxed in, boxed up, and delivered as fifth place in the final.

On the other hand, the match sprint starts well, and I qualify third. Forget about the grizzly, I think. The World Championship medallist rocket is back. Following the routine I used in Antwerp, I script out my next ride. The race follows as surely as my handwritten scenario. I beat Mexico's Nancy Contreras in the eighth final. The long-dormant fuse lights and the win is an expression of power, and confidence.

So, in the quarters, what happened to my rocket? Who, or what, put the fuse out?

The USA's Tammy Thomas beats me two straight. Afterwards, I am churning with bitterness, and take it out on my notebook. I'm so agitated I can't write sentences; only points are dashed off. I write:

- It really burns and bites.
- I lead her out in both races—BAD—she likes to be lead out.
- My focus wasn't there—need to flick that switch.
- Before going into your heat, never second-guess your gearing, your ability.

The next words I write are too profane to repeat. I usually avoid swearing, but I've lost control of my feelings. The notes continue: "MUST GET RID OF THIS DOUBT—HOW TO DO THIS?"

Racehorses don't have second thoughts. Grizzlies don't hesitate. Rockets don't have doubt. Humans do. I don't feel like a champion. I feel like a thirty-six-year-old woman who has put everything on hold for a dream, an expensive and extravagant vision that is no longer a cherished dream leading me to a lifetime accomplishment but an odyssey that's turning into a nightmare. My march to self-fulfilment is turning into a parade of folly.

The next World Cup takes place in Sydney, Australia. My main opposition for the Commonwealth Games gold medals, the Aussies, will have home-turf advantage. I'll be up against a powerful sister act, Kerrie and Anna Meares. Over the last season these two have been advancing through the international rankings. Last season, Kerrie's results were approaching mine. The Meares sisters are products of a well-funded Australian National Team track-cyclist factory. The women train with the men, and the men are renowned for their reckless riding style.

There will be no easy bargain at Sydney's Dunc Grey Velodrome.

I need money. I need speed. Anything else? Faith. I need faith—faith in myself. Something or somebody has to extinguish these doubts.

Faith is a gift. Sometimes it comes in the shape of a person, and sometimes as an angel. In my case, Brenda Miller was both. Her arrival was the best gift I had received in years.

She and I worked out at the World Health Centre Club. Everyone there knew who I was. Monster Gym, or WHCC, each gym has its own culture and hierarchy. I was the stubborn cyclist, and sometimes spin-class leader. Brenda was an ardent squash player and fitness enthusiast. She was a sparkling, vivacious woman with the six-pack abs I have dreamed of but never developed.

Brenda would enter the gym, work out, and socialize more effectively than anyone I have ever met. I'd be all business, grunting and sweating through a weight workout. Brenda would work out too, but through it all she would talk people up, and still be changed and out of the locker room in less time than anyone I'd ever know.

If I was the grizzly, Brenda was the butterfly.

She knew that I was short of money for the Sydney race—$8000 short to be precise. I had called so many people in town that I'd be surprised if anyone didn't know. It's now the end of April, only two weeks from Sydney. The endless meetings with potential sponsors had netted me nothing. Less than nothing, in fact, if you took into account all the energy I had spent.

In the end, it was my boots and Brenda that brought me the money.

At the time I wore a pair of Fluevog Brogue boots. Of course the businesswomen who attend WHCC opt for less stolid footgear. The clients at WHCC always knew when I was working out: the Fluevogs, parked amidst a sea of sensible black pumps and dainty heels, let everyone know I was there. Near the end of April, I'm picking my way around the shoes at WHCC, and reaching for the Fluevogs. I see a slip of paper poking from a boot top. It's a cheque for $500. Another $2500 would come in that week from Acron Roofing. More would follow a few days later. It was more than I'd raised in years. Brenda had twisted arms, buttonholed friends, and beat the bushes, raising money for a woman she knew only as an acquaintance. It wasn't just a fundraising exercise. It was a demonstration of belief.

How could I fail?

I wish today that I could show her the pay-off. Events later in the season showed me how ultimately fragile life is.

In the meantime, I arrange for a private manager, a physiotherapist named Rochelle Shapera, to accompany me to Sydney. She had been my physiotherapist when I lived in Toronto. I've been at this game long enough to know that one of my biggest enemies is isolation. Steen won't be at the race, and I'll need someone else that I can trust to do the manager's job for me.

Managing a rider is not complicated. You make sure they're aware of the schedule, fed, watered, and brought to the line for their event. Ideally, a manager would maintain the bike too, but I can't expect a track rookie like Rochelle to do that.

"You've set a record," says the female commissaire. I recognize her as one of the chief officials here, on May 10 at Sydney's Dunc Grey Velodrome. I'm riding my rollers, and warming down from my fifth place in the World Cup Keirin-qualifying ride. How could I have set a record with an inferior ride? The woman is smiling, like she's sharing something of vital importance.

"Uh-huh," I say, and keep churning the pedals. "A record, eh?"

"I've checked," she says in her twangy Aussie accent, "and according to the UCI (Union Cycliste Internationale—the international cycling governing body) records, this is the first time a female coach has taken her rider to the line for every race."

She's grinning like a kid who's won a prize at the midway. I don't have the heart to tell her that before today Rochelle has never been to a track race.

Inexperience doesn't hamper Rochelle. She makes sheaves of notes on everything from what to feed me to how to hold onto my bike at the start line. Her presence and her attention to detail buoy me.

Except for the Keirin, I ride well and aggressively. The horse and the grizzly have been left behind, and the rocket's flying again. It doesn't matter that the field here is the strongest all year. I take third in the sprints, and follow up with another third place in the 500-metre.

The medals are good, but the sensation of relief is better. Groove, mojo, morale or self-belief, whatever you want to call it, it's good to have it back. And not a moment too soon: the Canadian National Championships in Bromont, Quebec, and World Cup III in Cali, Colombia, are the last events before the Commonwealth Games in Manchester, England.

On my return, I field a flurry of media interviews.

"So," the interviewers would ask, "Tanya Dubnicoff won gold at the last Commonwealth Games."

"The last two games," I would say. "Duba is a tough act to follow, but I plan to."

"And you were silver and bronze at last year's World Championships, so it looks like gold for you this year in Manchester?"

I'd *like* to say: "My friends, especially Brenda Miller, have renewed my shaken confidence. I'm now on form—finally. I want those gold medals so badly I can smell them." Instead, I restrain myself. "I'm going to Manchester, and giving it my best shot," is what I say.

The public attention comes with a price. Everyone expects me to win two gold medals. It's hard enough having high expectations for yourself. Fortunately, my form continues to improve, and in Bromont I set a new track record in the 500-metre. Mediocre results at the World Cup in Cali don't faze me, and I return to Canada for a final bout of training. My faith has been tested and it's held. The games are in Manchester, the site of my first World Championship medal. Steen will be there, and I'll have a large Canadian contingent to cheer me on.

With the early season crisis of belief behind me, I know that there's little that can stop me. Over the years I've eliminated every possible obstacle, as well as some seemingly improbable ones. I visualize, in my mental training, a smooth path to the gold medal.

But that, of course, is not to be.

You can't possibly imagine everything that will happen. Some things are too perverse to dream of. Giving up a gold medal, for instance—just letting it slip away. It's unthinkable. Bizarre. It happens.

CHAPTER 13

BURIED TREASURE

buried treasure /ber ryduh tre sur/ *n*. **1** moral values (forgotten by riders in their obsessive quest for success) that surface at a later time. Viewed by some as a burden; by others as a blessing. (*See also*, entry for **character = fate** theorem) **2** valuables buried out of reach, the memory of which continues to inspire.

—From the *Cyc.L.O.W.Ps*.

There was a fight going on, a battle between two deeply entrenched forces. Buried, deep in my head, was the key to success. Also buried deep in my noggin was the cause of my early season sluggishness.

I pondered this from my empty room in Manchester, England. Today, July 28, 2002, was the 500-metre event, my first race of the XVII Commonwealth Games.

I was on my own. Steen was spending time with his wife Cyndi, who was staying off site. Eric Van Den Eynde was not in Manchester, and Kurt Innes was the coach assigned to the Canadian track cycling team.

Also, my stomach was acting up, but this I chalked this up to a traveller's stomach bug. Further, there was the pressure of having to live up to my media ranking as the number one contender at the Commonwealth Games.

"Is this what it feels like to be number one?" I ask my silent room.

Steen has trained me to believe. I've willed myself through a lean early season and onto a precarious perch near the top. In my head there is a battle between faith and doubt, between hope and haplessness.

Aside from my unruly stomach, my body feels good. Wilbour Kelsik, the Canadian team chiropractor, has given me a great adjustment. Every time I've set a record, a "Wilbour adjustment" has paved the way. I pack my gear and head to the velodrome. Outside, it's a blue-sky day, and I talk myself into ignoring the bleak forebodings of my psyche.

Kurt holds me for a practice start. I jump the gun and go too early. I head to the pits, alone, and prepare for the 6 PM start of the 500-metre. My head is buzzing. Nervousness, I guess. More than I've ever known.

"Breathe, Lori-Ann," I whisper, and start my relaxation exercises. I concentrate on breathing my way to inner peace. I rehearse my start, and repeat my cue words. The familiar words of strength and power toll in my mind. The velodrome dissolves around me, and I leave the venue behind.

The other riders take to the track, but I'm oblivious.

"Lori-Ann," says Kurt, "it's time to go on deck."

I snap my eyes open, and nod. He rolls my bike to the apron. I strap on my aerodynamic teardrop helmet, and take my place on deck.

The *now* of the games overwhelms me. The cue words are left behind, like the packs dropped by retreating soldiers. I feel like an amateur actor, intimidated by the crowd and not using their excitement to boost my performance.

My bike is locked into the start gate and I mount up, my hands passing lightly over my toe straps, hastening to tighten them. The rules say I have only thirty seconds from this point to strap in. My hands fly to the bars, and I look up, expecting to see the digital timer counting down the remaining seconds, usually ten seconds at this point.

The timer is not moving. What?

The clock finally starts ticking.

The timing process has been changed! No one warned me!

"So what," says the warrior inside. "We're here to race."

The white digital numbers flick their way to zero. I lurch forward, my breath a hoarse shout.

The bike does not move.

I rock back, my muscles now stuttering against the iron grip of the start gate.

Click. Now it's open. Go! Go! Dammit, go!

My muscles, drained from the longer than usual countdown, taxed by the too-early start or the malfunctioning gate—I'll never know which—are flaccid and reluctant. In spite of the botched start, I claw my way down the track and ride the pole line. The finish comes up, and I'm third. Considering the start, I'm glad my time is not dead last.

Kerrie Meares from Australia wins by half a second, a big lead in a thirty-five-second event. I smile during the medal ceremony and throughout the media interviews. Outside, I'm radiating positive messages.

Inside? The battle's raging, and I'm dreading the coming postmortem with Steen. I feel like a small child who has broken her mother's favourite vase. Steen and I step out of the Canadian Team pit.

"Sorry," I say. "I let two people down. You and me."

"I'm not surprised," he says.

"Huh?"

"Your times in training weren't good. I didn't think you'd have a stellar performance."

He may not be surprised, but I am.

"Go back to your routine," he says. "You're going to be fine."

I am desperate to believe him. His wisdom is clear: it's Sunday, and the 200-metre qualifying is on Wednesday. Steen doesn't want me wasting precious mental energy fretting about the 500-metre event. He's right, and I try to leave it behind.

The feeling of loneliness is not so easy to avoid. Even though Steen's here, he's less accessible than when I was in the lobby during the 2000 World Championships, waking him up with my intercontinental phone calls.

By the end of Tuesday, my stomach is settling down. I end the day by rehearsing the 200-metre, and script my notes about the upcoming sprints. My battle for belief comes to the front. I will the pen to extinguish any doubt: "I need to regain my confidence. I need to believe. I need to see it. *I have only one more day to do it.*"

I look up from my desk. Sydney's World Cup was the turning point. Why? I had someone in my corner—Rochelle. She was reliable, but, more to the point, she believed in me. Rochelle and her husband have long been believers in me. What did they see? I gaze at an album of photos from the Sydney meet and wonder what it was that Rochelle told me. She didn't tell me anything. She wrote me. I remember her, at the velodrome in Sydney, writing me a note. The note says, "Lori-Ann, you have strength you have not yet found."

The remembrance washes over me like a wave. Smarting from the debacle in the 500-metre and ashamed at myself, I find the strength, which is like buried treasure, and I unearth my belief. My pen flies to the page and writes as though guided by a new hand:

"I know that I can put it together for Wednesday and Thursday. I'll be there. I know it. I feel strong."

It's July 3 and I'm waving to the crowd, their faces lit with smiles. The cheering is boisterous, like at a twenty-first-birthday celebration. The scoreboard flashes: "New Commonwealth Games Record in the 200 M." I realize that I've got all the speed I need.

This is not a drill.

All of this is taking place, not in my mind in the quiet of my room, but in the midst of the Manchester velodrome. Belief has become reality. After a victory lap, I glide to the apron.

"You set a games record," says the commissaire. The British officials are usually spare in their commentary, but they're full of congratulations for me.

"Yessss," I say, and roll onto the infield.

The commissaire is holding my bike and says, "You've got the fastest qualifying time, and have a *bye* straight into tomorrow's semis."

"Thanks," I gasp, and slip off the aerodynamic helmet.

My faith had come through in the eleven seconds that I took to cover the 200 metres. It supported the blaze of effort that propelled me around the track faster than anyone else in the history of the games. The challenges of this uncertain season had tested my confidence and today was the pay-off. After all, everything that comes through the fires of adversity is refined and resilient. Steen had taught me and countless friends had supported me on my difficult journey. Finally, I thought, as I walked to our pits and put on my National Team track suit, the rocket's back and going for the top—for the gold medal

Rochelle was right: I do have strength I never knew. The next day, I'll need it. And not to win the gold medal; quite the opposite, in fact.

Wham! Whoa girl, I say to myself, and cut hard left. Meares has swerved in front of me like a drunk weaving in traffic. The first heat of the Commonwealth Games match sprint final just started, and our wheels are barely turning.

Her bike is leaning crazily, and she's pushed me to the apron—off the apron, in fact. Has she blown a tire?

No, she's veering towards me again. I see a glimpse of her face, the smirk and the sneer. I had seen this expression on the start line and ignored it. I realize too late that Meares, like the cocky nineteen-year-old she is, had been sizing me up.

The hook was no accident; her swerve, more like a kamikaze's dive, was deliberate.

Now, she and I are moving up the bank, but she lunges again, hooking me, and driving me down.

We haven't got to turn one.

"This hook's for you," her face says. Meares knows I'm slightly faster, and she's put her cards on the table. Like a sweet-faced gargoyle, she's trying to intimidate me. I know that she'd ridden England's Victoria Pendleton into the boards in the semi-finals. Meares had been warned, but not disqualified, and advanced to the final. Undeterred, she's running me into the apron, trying to keep me from the front.

Fine. I back off and ride up to the rail. Meares, staring over her shoulder, careens towards me, throwing another hook, stopping me from taking the lead. I don't want to collide and hurt her or myself. I decelerate, create some breathing space, and climb to the rail again. Meares throws another hook. Four hooks in less than half a lap. I've never seen anything like it. Neither has the crowd. The gasps of surprise are being replaced by boos and shouts.

It's okay in match sprinting to use the whole track, but the rules say you have to give your opponent room to pass. She's not just trying to come close—she's trying to collide and play the percentages. In most collisions, the lead rider stays up, and the second rider tumbles.

I know the percentages too, but I'm not about to let her steal this medal.

Second lap, and Meares is sweeping, cutting across the track, knowing I have to make my move or it's over.

I surge forward, my right elbow on the rail, and try again to pass above her. Meares hooks me once, twice, and I'm close enough to see the weave of her Lycra skinsuit. My tire is jammed into the seam between the banking and the boards. She's doing the same with me as with Pendleton, but no commissaire is blowing the whistle.

It's the same in playoff hockey. The refs are frightened of making a call that will change the outcome. They put the whistle in their pocket, and turn their backs.

Meares dives for the line, and we head into the final—the bell—lap. The crowd noise obliterates the bell, and I have to go the long way around her. She flicks to her right, as quick as a cobra, moving over the sprinter's line, the red line that the rules say she can't cross once committed to the sprint. My bike is moving over seventy kilometres per hour and I'm balancing on the tiny contact patches of my rock-hard tires. One touch of her body, and I'm going for a skin-shredding slide on a splinter-infested surface. Meares's trick forces me farther off line.

There are two results. One, she wins. Two? I see the sneer on her face, a tiny, teenaged half smile. I know what it means: "Rules? What rules?"

The commissaires huddle by the start line. I can see one of them making notes on a clipboard. The announcement is made: Meares is *relegated*—cycling terminology for disqualified—and assigned last place. It's small comfort. She's been warned, booed, and now relegated. It won't stop her. She can't out-speed me. There's only one way for her to stop me, and, I think, only one way for me to stop her.

I head to the pits. Someone hands me a cell phone. Who could be calling at this time?

"Lori-Ann?" It's Steen.

"Where are you?"

"I'm watching, back at Athletes' Village. I saw what happened. She's trying to intimidate you—maybe crash you."

"Wild, huh?" I say, not knowing what other description to give it.

"Go up."

"Steen?"

"You must go up a gear—to 93.5."

The approximate measurement, 93.5 inches, is the mechanical equivalent of the wheel size your gearing gives you. The bigger the gear, the farther you go per revolution of your pedals. How can Steen tell I need a bigger gear? He's watching a tiny, low-definition TV in the athletes' lounge. Still, he always knows.

"Anything else?"

"You're faster, Lori-Ann."

I pause, hoping for a feel-good answer. How about, "She's going to play fair now, and you won't have to make this awful choice?" Or, "It's just a mental rehearsal. Kidding."

There is no other answer. There will be is no easy way out.

Go up a gear, sure. But what about the only way to stop Meares? I don't want to think about what I'll have to do. My mind churns on the issue as I wrestle with my wheel, and blacken my hands with the oily cogs. The gear change seems to take forever. Kurt appears.

"Time to go," he says.

I look at my hands—they're black as death. I can't wipe them on my suit. I'll have to live with them. One way or the other, I'll have to live with my dirty hands and their handiwork. If I lose, I'll have to face millions of disappointed Canadians, thousands of fans, scores of friends, parents, Steen. If I win by doing what I know I must, I have to live with that most problematic person—myself.

My feet clip-clop, the cleats clacking on the infield. A corridor between the other countries' encampments leads me to the deck. No one talks. Everyone but me is still.

I can see hordes of curious riders, silent spectators, the officials, all awaiting my arrival. The whole scene is frozen, as if made of glass. The entire velodrome knows that this is the showdown. The cards are out, and the betting will start. How much is each rider willing to pay? Meares has made her bet. Now it's my turn.

I stand on the deck, black hands, black heart. Meares is on the line. She's leading this time.

I know the percentages. And I know how it can be done. It's seldom attempted, but we all know how to take someone out, and put them down. You see it a couple of times a year. We all know the percentages. Plus, in my case I'm bigger, stronger, heavier—a grown woman against a young woman not out of her teens. She's on the line, the half smile still there, confident whispers with her coach. She thinks I'm too old, too afraid, beaten, and bullied. Finished.

She's right. I am finished; finished with her juvenile contempt and disdain. I reef on the toe straps and feel a hot surge of anger flood my body. I'm trying hard not to quiver. The adrenaline is roaring through my body. I don't have blood anymore, I've got napalm, and I'm frightened of what will happen when it blows. The rage in Antwerp is nothing compared to this.

The whistle blows, and she leads off, looking over her shoulder, watching.

She thinks I'm the target, I'm the victim.

We ride to the turn, and she glides up the bank.

Predictable. Meares wants me to follow on her right side, and then she'll ride me to the rail, squeezing my front wheel in a vise made by her back wheel and the boards.

Not this time. Not this ride.

Meares assumed I didn't want this as much as her. Thought I was afraid. Wrong on both counts, mate.

We're high on the bank, and—thanks to Steen's gearing advice—I'm moving faster than last time. I'm on her right, and have drawn even. My shoulder is coming down, my bike is veering towards her, and I'm preparing for a bone-crunching side-swipe. In a split second it will be two minutes in the penalty box for charging, boarding, and roughing. She'll be crumpled on the track. I'll be relegated. So sorry. Of course I didn't mean to, I'll say. After all, I thought that was the way we were playing this game: anything to win, old sport.

He has a name. I never found out, but today I would write him a thank-you card. The mystery man leaned over the rail, spellbound, to see the cycling equivalent of a lumberjack chain match—two go in, and only one goes out. Mystery boy leaned over the railing, and his expensive watch, a glittering lump of chrome, slipped off his wrist. It could have slipped off a thousand different times and in a thousand other places, but it decided, on the track ahead of Kerrie Meares and Lori-Ann Muenzer, to make its dash for freedom.

Sprang, kachunk, bonk, bonk, bonk. The watch toboggans down the forty-five-degree bank and halts on the apron.

Bang, bang. The shots come from the commissaires' starting pistols—the firing signals an instant halt to the race. The watch is a hazard. It's the cycling equivalent of a squirrel stealing a golf ball on the green of the eighteenth hole of the Masters.

That's when it happened: I saw the only true way to win this thing.

Self-belief is more than a way to win a bauble, a trinket. Self-belief and faith is a means to a result you are proud of. Standing on a track, watching your opponent writhe in pain? Living with the knowledge that you deliberately hurt someone?

I saw my journey and my path. There was no doubt. I knew I was the fastest, and would ride my way clear and clean. There would be no harm passed off as miscalculations or other legitimate encounters with unintentional injury. I would not say, as Meares did later in explaining her dangerous riding, "I'm inexperienced."

Grace had given me the chance to avoid both a disaster and a gold medal covered in blood. It was the best gold medal I never won.

In the next two rides Meares used every hook in the book, and then some, to confront me, crash me, or provoke me to break the rules. In our second try at ride number two, I'm leading in the final straight, surging for the line. Meares is behind, knows she's in trouble, and has to come around the long way. She leans on me, levers her left elbow under my right elbow, and flips it up, hoping to dump me to the left and out of her path.

It doesn't work. She does it again. And again. And again.

Finally, I know it's only a matter of time until there's a crash. I put my head down, grinding my teeth, and let her pass.

The commissaires keep their whistles in their pockets.

The final ride is, of course, much the same. Even so, I'm beaten by only a hand's width. After her win, she circles the track, riding hands off, blowing kisses. The velodrome is silent and unsettled.

Go ahead, Kerrie. Enjoy the medal. Accept my congratulations. By the way, thanks for the lesson. It's like finding buried treasure.

The greater the price paid, the more valuable the lesson, but what a price. And how to explain what had happened? There was no way, then, to say, "I gave the medal away, and you know what? I'm glad. I almost descended into violence. A stroke of luck saved me from it, and probably a gold medal."

How do you say all of that, and tell them that you've had to give up part of the pay-off, part of the bargain for sweating and struggling your way to the top?

The Canadian press was outraged at my treatment. Even hardened tabloids like the *Edmonton Sun*, a paper that's pro-sports mad, featured me on the front page, with a huge black headline, denouncing what Meares had subjected me to. However, I didn't have the time to elaborate. To explain it all would have taken a book.

Instead, I did the only decent thing a top athlete can do—two things, actually: First, move on and look forward to the World Championships in Ballerup, Denmark. Second, party.

I drink with the games-mad crowds populating the city, and party with the other athletes whose events are over. Like an army on leave, we're out early, drinking, dancing, and returning late. After the sprint final, I'm home at 3 AM. The next day, it's 4 AM, and the one after that it's 5:30 AM.

I leave the seventeenth Commonwealth Games with two things: First, I know I'm the fastest, and the only person who can stop me is myself. Second is the honour of being selected by the other athletes and staff of Team Canada to be the bearer of the Canadian flag during the closing ceremonies. I earned the right to be an example, and it's one medal I'll never give away.

On August 5 I'm riding through Manchester with Steen, and we spin out into the countryside. I'm emotionally exhausted from the sprint-final debacle, and having to deal with the disillusionment of not taking two gold medals. Steen's friendship is a rock that I steady myself on. The lush green countryside is now free from the clinging fog of the last week, and I feel my spirit soar into the blue sky.

The bike works its magic, carrying me out of disappointments and into the natural world. Also, the joy of sharing life with a friend makes the future look brighter. The Pan American Championships are coming up in Quito, Ecuador, and then the World Championships. I'm eager to take them on. I've given up a gold medal, but know that my worst enemy, self-doubt, has been vanquished.

I feel like a child, holding a burning match, waiting for the signal to light the rocket's fuse.

"Not yet, dear," I hear an adult say.

"Aww, c'mon. I want to see this thing go."

"Oh yes, dear," says a stranger, the face hidden. "It's your turn all right. Soon there's going to be quite a bang."

CHAPTER 14

ROCKET RIDE

rocket ride /rawket ryde/ *n*. **1** *slang*. for cyclists, a startling journey, often at a pace that cannot be sustained. **2** *see also:* legal jargon for a harsh sentence. Abrupt removal of the subject from society, followed by an explosion resembling a firework display. Return is unlikely.

—From the *Cyc.L.O.W.Ps*.

It's just a telephone message.

The weather's good, the training's going according to plan. But today, August 13 2002, the voice on the answering machine, the voice of my friend, Julie Multimaki, is frightening me.

"Lori-Ann," she says, her voice hesitating, "please call me as soon as you get this message."

From the tone of her voice I already know it's one of those calls—the nightmarish ones. I make the call.

"Brenda's dead," says Julie.

Brenda Miller, effervescent Brenda, so full of life that she gave off sparks. She was with a group of women riding in Jasper National Park when a van blew a tire and plowed into their midst. An accident like so many things that happen to us: like a watch on a track. A second later, and it's just another near miss, one to be forgotten in the forest of bewildering events that make up our lives.

Brenda's husband, Jack McCutcheon, shoulders his grief at the funeral on August 15. The memorial service is packed with people representing the fullness of Brenda's life. I'm there, wishing that I could praise her for her faith in me. "What you saw in me," I would say, "I found, too. The money got me to Sydney for a race; your belief will carry me forever."

Later, in January 2003, Jack will have Brenda's 1976 University of Alberta Department of Pharmacy Gold Medal award encased in silver. He will present it to me, as a memorial to Brenda. To this day, whenever I travel, it hangs from a chain around my neck, a tangible remembrance of her relentless commitment to excellence and her self-lessness.

Two days after the memorial service, Steen and I are on our annual wild goose chase.

Every year there is a goose chase, like 2001, the bike odyssey to Szczecin, laden with mix-ups and miscues, compounding one another like chimpanzees let loose in a toy store. After the initial frustrations, I put my hands behind my head and relax. Why not wait for the chimps to sort themselves out?

It's hard to be positive, though, when you've put one goose chase behind you, but it's clear that another is brewing.

"You'll have to pay excess baggage charges, ma'am," says the ticket agent, a dour woman, bored to be checking travellers in at 7 AM Saturday morning.

"Didn't you get the CCA letter?" I say.

"What letter?"

I show her the CCA letter asking airlines to waive excess-baggage charges. It's crucial to cyclists because we travel with bike boxes, separate wheel cases, as well as our clothing bags. Excess charges can run to $250 per rider.

That wouldn't be so bad, except this agent is charging Steen and me for the Edmonton to Calgary leg. There will be more charges thereafter.

"No, ma'am," she yawns. "Haven't seen this letter, and I'm not authorized to waive the charges. How are you going to pay? Cash, debit, or credit card?"

"Steen," I say, "let's forget it."

He convinces me to carry on. I plunk down my credit card, and foot the latest gouging by the airline industry. In Calgary, matters deteriorate further. Continental Airlines, the carrier arranged for by the CCA travel agent, has some bad news.

"Sorry, ma'am," says the Continental agent. "Security regulations prohibit travel to Ecuador with more than two bags." Steen and I have three bags each.

"We're going to the Pan American Championships," I say. "We're on the Canadian National Team, and need everything we're carrying."

"Sorry, ma'am, those are the rules."

"We've paid for these bags to get here. We can't race without this gear."

"I'm really sorry," he says, "but I'm not responsible for your agent not informing you."

His name tag reads "Bill Gates." If only he had Microsoft's Bill Gates's powers and influence.

"I'll be back," I say.

"Steen," I say, "call the CCA athlete-go-to guy, and see if he can do something. It's his fault."

Steen makes the call. The go-to guy is now the get-lost guy. He gives Steen a blast. How dare we disturb his Saturday morning him with our trivial difficulties?

"Let's rent a car," I say, "and go home."

"Be positive," says Steen. "Quito is at 10000 feet. You're on schedule to set new records."

"Ma'am?" It's Bill Gates. While Steen and I were conferring, he found a solution. He can re-route us through Miami and to our destination on LAN (Chilean) airlines. Fortunately, LAN has no fear of transporting more than two bags per person to Ecuador. It will mean an overnight stay in Miami, and extra cost, but we do it and arrive one day late in Quito.

Steen's right. Quito is where records are set.

But I'm here for more than setting records. I'm here to live out the trust Brenda placed in me. Her memory is at once painful and powerful. The best way for me to deal with her death is to ride my heart out. In the 200-metre qualifying round I clock the best time. It's a personal best and a Canadian record. I win the match sprints, and in the 500-metre I set another Canadian record. On the last day of racing, August 23 I win the Pan American Champion Keirin event.

However, medals are not the only things being picked up here. The athletes are billeted at the Quito University campus. We're eating at the dorm cafeteria, but avoid salads or anything touched by the local water. Still, by August 23, ten out of twelve athletes in our vicinity have come down with food poisoning. Victim number eleven, I think, feeling my stomach tie itself into hard knots, is me.

While the others line up for supper, I'm sitting outside on the steps of our dorm, hunched over. My stomach is churning, and my abdominal muscles are rock hard. Canada's Kilo rider, Travis Smith, is also an emergency medical technician. He is rubbing my back, and joking that the problem might be my appendix.

"Appendix?" I say, squeezing the tears out of my eyes. "Where is that?"

The pain doesn't relent, and I take an antibiotic, Cipro, in the hope it will kill what I think is a stomach bug. By the next day, the pain has subsided, and our team has a few hours for sightseeing. We stop by a giant statue of the Virgin Mary, and shop for alpaca sweaters. I stop at a McDonald's and risk a burger. It stays down. Maybe, I think, the eighteen-hour journey home won't be too bad. I'm wrong.

At the airport we're charged for excess baggage again. Also, I'm sweating like a tourist on the Las Vegas strip. Steen has to help me walk, and he's tired too. He's been up all night helping me to the toilet. I hung onto the bowl, heaving until I saw angry red stars.

At Dallas/Fort Worth International Airport we change planes. My pain threshold has been trained to exceed any normal limit, yet the pain is so intense that I think I'm going to die. My poor mind, desperate for relief, thinks that Gravol will help. Of course, even though we're waiting in an airport, there's none to be found. The journey to Edmonton is a nightmarish voyage. I'm half alive, sweating, and unable to move.

Two days later, at 9 AM, I am in the U of A hospital, lying on a gurney, staring at the gentle face of my physician.

"Good news and bad news," she says.

I nod, and don't know what to hope for first.

"Good news is we *think* it's your appendix. It's probably infected... don't know for how long."

I nod.

"It burst, and all that infected gunk was poisoning you. You haven't gone into total septic shock yet. You're strong—you'll make it."

I nod with more vigour.

"Bad news?" she says.

"Okay," I croak.

"You're going to miss the World Championships."

The tears streaming down my cheeks are cold, tiny rivers, carrying my hopes away. I can't cry out loud, though. It hurts too much.

Hours later, the surgery done, I'm lying in my bed, staring at the clock. The second hand sweeps around the dial, the minute hand follows, and the hour hand crawls after. Light from my window comes, goes, and night falls. I could watch the clock forever. It's good that the pain's gone. I tell my friends, as they visit me in the recovery room, "I don't hurt anymore." They nod. I repeat, as though they're deaf, "I don't hurt any more."

They humour me and say, "That's great."

It is, but it's even better to be alive.

Days later, Steen is in for another visit. "How you doing?"

"Okay, except for the bugs," I say, my fingers rubbing on my bare arm.

"Bugs?" he says, casting his eyes around the room for insects.

"The bugs under my skin. I am allergic to morphine. Makes me itch, like there are bugs crawling under my skin."

"I brought you this," he says, and hands me my Canadian Centre for Ethics and Sport Doping log.

Steen and I have voluntarily subjected ourselves to an anytime-anywhere agreement with the CCES to provide samples. As part of the agreement we provide a detailed schedule of our training and any medications that we're taking. We have to be where we say we will be and submit to drug testing.

"I'm asking the staff to record what they're putting in me," I say. "In case there's a random test."

"Planning to race tomorrow?"

I ignore the barb.

"You almost died," he says.

You watch, I say to myself. I'm coming back, and I'm going to need your help, but first I have to get out of this room and back on my bike.

Am I a little extreme in my attitude? I'm a rider.

This, to North Americans, doesn't explain much. Read Lance Armstrong's first biography, his tremendous account of his successful struggle with cancer. He accurately explains the winning rider's mentality. I'm not the only person who has faced personal difficulty and fought my way out. It's something a lot of non-cyclists do every day. For them, and for most riders, suffering is just a step along the way. However, riders train themselves to keep the pedals turning. No matter what.

Tommy Simpson, the only British rider to win a pro road racing World Championship, died on the pitiless slopes of Mount Ventoux in the 1967 Tour de France. The slopes of the mountain are rocky solar reflectors, and cooked the water out of the riders struggling up the dusty road. Simpson was dehydrated, collapsed, and near death. Still, he begged the roadside fans to put him back on his bike.

They understood, helped him back on, and he died.

It was nothing new to them.

Three weeks later, I'm shuffling down the street trying not to strain my severed abdominal muscles. My recovery is slow, and I appreciate my parents' help. They drove from Ontario, and stayed with me when I was discharged. A day later I collapsed after dislodging some hidden septic material, and had to be readmitted.

My diary, instead of recording the usual litany of stretching, weights, and then a bike workout, says, "Walk—thirty minutes." For weeks, a walk is all I can manage. Like many top athletes, I have no fat on my body, but in less than one week I lost fourteen pounds. During my ordeal, I had vomited so hard that I burst blood vessels in my eyes.

How long had the storm in my appendix been brewing? What effect had it had on my performance? It didn't matter. I still wanted my turn.

It would just have to be next year.

CHAPTER 15

WAITING FOR DIRNDL GIRL

waiting for dirndl girl /wat ng for dern dil gurl/ *phrase*. **1** a state of naive
anticipation: one that associates a beautiful setting with a happy ending, Hollywood style. **2** a period of distraction, wherein the harsh
sacrifices and brutal training for competitive cycling are avoided. (*See
also:* **off the back**)

—From the *Cyc.L.O.W.Ps.*

"Cheetah power," I mutter, and focus on my prey. Once more, I'm bear-
ing down on my quarry. "There is no escape for you." I pour on the
speed. The distance is closing, and I can feel the electric charge of
victory coursing through my body. This opponent is a bulky, but wily
veteran. If I defeat her, I will be champion.

A crack—a gaping chasm—appears in the sidewalk block ahead
of me.

Jump or shuffle? Those are my options. After all, in the South
Edmonton Sidewalk Speed Walking Championship, hazards are part of
the challenge. My opponent is a gigantic woman, clad in a gabardine
raincoat, trundling down these ancient and tilted sidewalks. In spite of
her bulk I can barely keep up.

If I jump, the scar tissue in my stomach muscles will not forgive me.
On the other hand, if I shuffle, I'll lose her before the stop sign—the finish line.

My jump, more like a tiny hop, makes me wince, but I beat her.

I lean on the stop sign, my forehead glistening. It's September 9,
2002. Lori-Ann Muenzer, Commonwealth Games double medallist, is

reduced to racing overweight people on her home sidewalk. I think of previous disasters:

1. Being twisted apart by Cuban strongmen.
2. Having my morale beaten like a rug.
3. Falling off cliffs onto jagged rocks.
4. Giving up a Commonwealth gold medal.
5. Having my guts explode.

Which was the hardest to accept?

I shuffle home, my head spinning. Which one made me cry the most? Number 5. Definitely number 5. As I lay in my hospital bed, it was the disaster that made the tears burn my skin. I had battled through self-doubt and had touched victory, the Commonwealth Sprint Gold, only to wave it goodbye. The race in Quito showed I was on track to win more World Championship medals.

In fact, Kerrie Meares, my antagonist in Manchester, had taken silver at the Worlds. Her performance was proof that I was a contender.

Was a contender, a somebody? And now I was a . . . ? I paused on the threshold of my doorway, and noticed that the woodwork on my house was peeling and rotting. It would need a lot of work.

So would I. I had three months to come back from the grave and get into the game. Three months from now I would be training with one of the world's greatest track sprinters, Frederick Magne. Steen had arranged for this opportunity. I would be training with other cyclists from around the world at the UCI indoor track in Aigle, Switzerland. The international cycling federation built and maintained the facility. At Aigle I would be coached, fed, taught French, and put up in dorms. The federation would even lend me a commuter bike to tool around on. It would be track-bike heaven.

I gritted my teeth, and hauled the door open.

I am not a *was*. I *am*. Don't ever write me off. Not until I say so. And not even then.

The prospect of track-bike heaven lifts me over the usual obstacles. I'm without a sponsor, and have the USD $2500 per-month cost of staying at Aigle to resolve. However, the chance to train with the world's best is what Steen and I know I need. I'll go, even if it means going into the hole.

Although Steen is optimistic about Aigle, I know that I'll have to battle the old demons of isolation and loneliness. I recruit Dr. Jean Cote, a sports psychologist in Kingston, Ontario, to help me learn how to deal with the prospect of being isolated from my friends and supporters. Over the next three months we spend hours on the phone, discussing ways for me to best the loneliness bug.

Efforts to develop my whole being continue. I'm taking my photography course and have been attending yoga classes. Less high flown are my efforts to get tickets to a live Chantal Kreviazuk performance. Her show was sold out, but I learned that a radio station had two tickets for the person willing to perform the wackiest stunt. I call the station, and offer to ride the rollers in their studio and sing a Christmas carol. They pass, probably because they're afraid I'll crash and wipe out their DJ. Twenty minutes later I call back, and offer to ride my mountain bike around my yard and sing (on live radio) one of Kreviazuk's songs. They agree.

I ride around the house singing into my cell phone, crashing into a drainpipe, trees, and the fence. I win and attend her performance. It's good, if only for an evening, to be normal.

Teaching spin classes, doing weights on Steen's program, and a return to riding help me regain my fitness. By December 14, my training diary is looking familiar. The entry for that day says, "Really good session with Steen. Thought I was gonna puke."

Things are back to normal.

Also, my parents and I have continued the reconciliation that began in 1998 when Mom invited me to a surprise party for Dad's retirement. This year, for the first time in over a decade, will be a full-scale Muenzer family Christmas.

What could be better? I'm spending Christmas with my family, and then I'm going to track heaven. It's like a movie, one of those hopeful '60s films where someone tries really hard, always plays fair, but then at the cruellest moment, gets hurt. As they recover, they get discovered (if they're actors) or get recruited (if they're athletes) and go on to fulfill their dreams. In fact, the idea of going to the Swiss Alps reminds me of one of those movies: *The Sound of Music.* One of my friends e-mails me and says I remind her of Julie Andrews, playing the character of Maria, running over the top of a hillock, lace dirndl waving in the breeze, singing and exulting. Maria is the epitome of good nature, happy endings, and, perhaps most memorably, dirndls. I am not a dress- or skirt-lover. However, if this persona meant a happy ending, I could overlook the dirndl.

At the time, I forgot what happens to poor Maria—Dirndl Girl—by movie's end.

It started well.

My diary says, "UCI objective: to win." The proclamation, made in red ink on January 13, 2003, fits my environment. It *is* track-rider heaven here. Even our sleeping location is meant to optimize our fitness. The day starts with a forty-five-minute train ride from our high-altitude lodgings to the track. Sleep at high elevations, and your body grows more red blood cells. When you travel to the lowlands, there's more available oxygen to power your muscles and improve the training effect.

After the train ride, it's French class from 8:30 to 10:00 AM, and then we're on the track for 10:30 AM. After the morning workout it's lunch, and then nap time. Or, more accurately, snoring time. A score of tired riders, flaked out under duvets, makes an impressive symphony of snorts, snorks, and snurgs. After our rest, it's back on the track, dinner in the cafeteria, and then the train ride up the hill to the dorms.

Not surprisingly, my riding is going well. Also, for the first time in years I have time to read. The only problem is that most of the available books are in French, and the only English bookstores are not open on Sunday, our day off.

Surprisingly, Fred is weaning me off my habit of scripting my races. He says that "the best actors improvise." He says that if I have formed a plan, but the unexpected happens, I'll be caught off guard. Instead, he says that if I lead, I block. If I follow, I force my opponent to keep the pace high and to wear themselves out. Simple, *n'est-ce-pas*? This advice is exactly what Steen and I had hoped he would offer.

However, there are a few worries intruding into track-rider heaven. My back is sore, and I'm having trouble finding the chiro or physio rehab I need. Also, I begin to have allergic reactions to something. My eyes become the size of raisins, and I have trouble breathing. Further, the renter of my house, Chuckie, is bouncing his rent cheques and not paying the utilities.

By February, Fred has a heart to heart with me. He is happy with my progress, and the leadership role I'm playing for the younger riders. He tells me to think about the upcoming three World Cups as tests for the

World Championships. More importantly, though, Fred reveals to me his secrets for warming up and what gear ratios to use.

The question of gearing is of absolute importance. A track bike has one gear—the one you select. Pick too small a gear and your legs are twirling like chopper blades, but you're going nowhere fast. Too big a gear, and your opponent will out-accelerate you and leave you, eyes popping and struggling, to get the big gear moving.

Having Fred, a multi-time World Champion, reveal this information is like having a master chef tell you their recipes. Not only have I gone to heaven, I feel like St. Peter has given me the keys to the place. One day, Laurent Jalabert, one of the stars from the Tour de France, pops into Fred's office.

Indeed, I am in a high and rarefied place.

The first test of the new program comes when we travel to Moscow for the first World Cup. I see Steen there, but we have little time to talk. My results are encouraging. I'm fourth in the 200-metre qualifying, and fifth in the 500-metre.

Fred reminds me, "The best actors give their top performances when they're improvising." I abandon my usual pre-race preparation. I read a novel while waiting for my heats, and don't complete my elaborate stretching routine. Fred has me try a new warm-up too.

I end up eighth. It's an acceptable result, I tell myself. My competitors have been on a track for months, and I've had just five weeks of board time.

According to my diary, I gave myself an A+ for my pre-race prep. Also, "My confidence in our daily training has been increasing each and every day...I was in control and confident."

So, I ask myself on the plane back to Aigle, "Why did Steen look worried?"

Two days later, the diary reads, in red ink: "Really, really tired. Couldn't stay with the women at all." Three days later: "Still have a cold, and feel tired." Two days after that: "I'm having a hard time right now." The stated objective, for the week of March 3, is "recover." Fred reduces my training, and by March 13, I feel my legs propel me to a series of starts and sprints that light the track on fire. I'm relieved and think I'm riding again at a World Championship pace.

Good thing too. Before I know it, I'm at the second World Cup, in Aguascalientes, Mexico. On arrival my diary records, "Racing starts tomorrow," and I jot a small happy face in the margin. Although Fred wants me to be completely spontaneous, I write out my blunt expectation and my simplified strategy: "WIN." What had taken pages of my notebook now occupies less than one small sheet.

The races occur. I place eleventh in the match sprints.

The happy face does not reappear. No results are entered in the diary. There is no detailed analysis of the kind I used to write. Why write that this is my worst result in three years?

It's like the disgrace in Cali. This time, I'm not crying in a cubicle, but talking with Steen. We're on the patio of the Fiesta Inn Hotel, on their wrought iron chairs. Steen is not asking me what's wrong. He's telling me.

He's facing me, his eyes blazing hotter than the furnace, like the air wafting around us. "Everything we've worked on for three years is being undone."

I look at the feet of the patio chairs.

"You're over-trained," he says.

That, I think, would explain the illness and fatigue. The training rides, easy road rides, had turned into death marches.

"What's Fred doing?" he says.

I shrug.

"Two weeks after you got there, I could tell you were in trouble."

What has Fred been doing?

We've drilled and drilled. There's been some specific work, but not as much as Steen would have laid on. Also there's none of the Steen patter, correcting the little errors that add up to speed-sucking habits. Fred doesn't have the time Steen can devote to me.

"Lori-Ann?" he says. "Did you hear me?"

"Eh?"

"Lori-Ann, you have to leave."

I look out over the pool. Waves of heat are warping the vista of the buildings and hills. Out of the shade it would be a hellish day.

"Lori-Ann? I think you should come home."

Aigle is cool, and the air, in the shade of the mountains, is frosty. How nice to be there, I think, trying to avoid the issue.

"I'm going back," I say.

"Good."

"To Aigle."

Steen shakes his head. I usually listen to him, but I yearn to become independent. "Even if I come home," I say, "you won't be there for long. As soon as I'm back, you're leaving for six weeks to train with the Aussies." It's true. He's going soon to train with the Aussie coach, ex-Quebecois rider, Martin Barras. "I'll talk to Fred," I say. "It'll work out."

I'm still waiting for Dirndl Girl to appear, a Swiss Miss, striding through a meadow of alpine flowers, bursting into song and lifting my spirits.

One week.

That's how long I wait for the Swiss Miss in Aigle. The training plan, handed to me on my return to the track, is a photocopy of the last one. All the riders are on the same plan. We're expected to be robotic riders churning out the program. In contrast, Steen's plan changes every month.

Fred sends me home after the latest laggardly road ride, and I sleep for two and a half hours. The next day, I'm so tired that I fall asleep on the train ride to the dorm. I crawl to my room and lapse into a near coma.

The next day my diary records, "Feel sad + blah." An unhappy face is recorded in the margin.

The next day is a repeat. My heart rate is soaring through the target zone. I call Steen.

"Fred wants me to go to South Africa for the next World Cup."

"Don't," says Steen.

"It's all paid for," I say, "and the CCA has come through with funding for my stay here."

"You're over-trained."

"All I have to do is ride."

"If you go," Steen says, "your whole season is ruined."

"I'll be okay."

"You haven't done so badly in five years."

"Three," I say, correcting him.

"Can't you see what's going on?" Steen is uncompromising, blunt, and right. That bugs me.

"I'll think about it," I say, and hang up.

At last, I'm in track-rider heaven, and I'm finally being supported by the CCA. How can I think about leaving? I'm wondering if Steen is giving me the advice of a guardian angel, or is he an unwitting deceiver? I review the careers of other sprinters who have been at the centre. Some have gone to the podium; others have lapsed into listlessness and burnout.

The next day, I'm in Fred's office, and he is angry. He thinks I should go to South Africa. I try to discuss Steen's concerns about my training and tactics. Fred, a three-time World Champion and holder of four other World Championship medals, bristles at my questions. I feel like I'm arguing with St. Peter. It's not easy to challenge a cycling icon. My voice is soft and uncertain.

I leave the office, feeling like a boxer who's taken too many hits to the jaw. The track, set in the base of a valley surrounded by towering mountains, had seemed like heaven. As I walk out of the complex and look back, I feel like an outcast.

At the end of the movie Maria has to flee to safety, with only the dirndl on her back. I could wait forever, but she's left and won't be coming back. Forget about her.

There's someone else I've got to find, and soon. Two people, actually, and Steen is one of them. It's now April 4 and the World Championships in Stuttgart, Germany, are in four months.

After giving my notice, the dorm superintendent, braided hair swirled on her head like Princess Leia, arrives and checks my room. I've cleaned the white-walled room, and am waiting for the results of her inspection. I half expect her, like a boot-camp sergeant major, to put on a white glove and run her finger along the top of the doorframe. She stoops to look under the bed, and stares into the room's corners, hunting for wild dust bunnies. I pass, and am given the haughty look reserved for those who have decided to check out of track-rider heaven.

I, on the other hand, give her the look reserved for those who think I should be ecstatic at paying the privilege of USD $2500 per month for living in a dorm. The inspection was the easiest part of leaving. I am carrying several bags, and over 100 kilograms of excess baggage. I have to take two trains to get to the Geneva airport. I get off one stop too early. My back is put out from wrestling with bikes, bags, and boxes.

At home, I note that my delinquent renter is gone. Steen provides me with a new training schedule. Field Law agrees to take me back, half days. I go to yoga. My diary says, in thick felt-tip blue letters: "BACK ON STEEN'S PROGRAM!!"

It's like being in heaven.

CHAPTER 16

BIKE MONSTER

bike monster /bik mon stur/ *phrase*. 1 throught to be mythical. Creature exists, but, because of its tendency to destroy other personality aspects, is often suppressed. Ironically, its absence leads to mediocrity. 2 *see also* ***Dirndl Girl vs. Godzilla***, Japanese science-fiction film. Metaphor for tension between opposite personality aspects. In cyclists, this conflict may lead to the devastation featured in film's final sequences.

—From the *Cyc.L.O.W.Ps.*

Although it's April in Edmonton, the flowers won't be blooming until mid-May. No matter to this sunflower.

On the other hand, maybe I'm a butterfly, broken free from the constraints of a tight wound Swiss cocoon. If Maria were here, I am sure she'd burst out in a song, something about sunshine, blue Alberta skies, and friends.

Most Canadians dread spring cleaning, but I'm so glad to be home that I plunge into a fit of home renewal. After all, I'm thirty-seven and want a home I can be proud of. I rake my front lawn and paint my bathroom. Even grotty tasks like sanding old plaster walls are a welcome change from the artificial existence I lived in Aigle.

The training progresses well, and I'm reassured by Steen's presence, brief though I know it will be. Also, it's good to see Brenda's widower, Jack. In one week, we have dinner together three times. Almost every night I'm making up for the boot camp isolation I suffered in Aigle.

By May 3, Steen has left for Adelaide, Australia. On my last motor-pace session at the track, the blue skies turn white, and a typical Alberta spring snowstorm blankets the city. Some of the leaves, electric-green shoots, have come out, and the snow is a white crust on the new growth. Even this weather setback can't quell my enthusiasm, and I'm looking forward to World Cup IV in Sydney, Australia.

In Sydney, I don't rely on improvising, but don't spend the time I used to either in planning my sprints. My new approach seems to work, and I'm third in the match sprints. My Manchester nemesis, Kerrie Meares, places eleventh. Only a few months ago she was riding the same qualifying times as I did. In spite of what happened in Manchester in 2002, I sympathize with her. I know how disheartening it is to be on the log chute, and sliding towards oblivion.

Occasionally, I call Steen. He's staying in Adelaide with a group of Aussies who, like most riders, are broke. They are not homeless, but phone-less. From our limited communication, I glean that he's having the same experience I had in Hyeres, France in 1994. I remember how draining it was to be living without the necessary support. Now, our roles are reversed, and the student is concerned for the master.

However, I don't tell Steen of the fantastic turn my social life has taken. Movies, dinner, and coffee meetings are interspersed with training. I go to Drumheller and Yellowknife, and play tourist. Training? No problem. I'm on the track with his brother Lars, and we're following Steen's program.

By June Steen has returned from Australia. However, I haven't seen him much: my thriving social life takes over when training ends. Also, I'm counting the days before the Worlds in Stuttgart. Our last pre-Worlds race is a flop. The CCA sends the Canadian Track Team to Colorado Springs for a meet. On arrival, USCF officials surprise us, and say that the race is a selection event for the US Team only, and we cannot be allowed to compete. There will be no last chance to dust off my tactical abilities.

Oh well, I think, and let my newfound social success distract me. It's so good not to be a Swiss Army robot carrying out tasks with grim precision. The social contact I had foresworn for over a decade tasted like honey and I was a butterfly wallowing in its sweetness. Camping, movies, and Shakespeare in Edmonton's outdoor river valley venue follow one another in quick succession. The diary shows as much activity on the social frontier as on the track.

I'm like a teenager during her first summer away from home. I don't bother to ask myself what Steen would think. I can't ask—he's in Aigle, training for the B World Championships. The B Worlds are the UCI's championships for countries that don't have the resources or the prior track results to qualify directly for the Olympics. The top two go through to the Olympics or World Championships. I hope he's doing all right.

It's so hard to focus without him.

"Lori-Ann?" It's Cyndi, Steen's wife, calling.

I am home on July 9, after dinner at a friend's. Yesterday I met a friend for breakfast, another one for coffee, and had dinner at another's. Today was the same. "This social stuff is sure draining," I say to myself, and hope Cyndi's got good news for me.

"Hi, how's Steen doing?"

"There was a crash."

I feel like a puppy who's chasing a cat, and forgot about the length of her leash.

"How bad?"

"He's being sent home tomorrow and they'll operate Friday."

"What happened?"

"He was third in the sprints, and just missed the silver."

This, by itself, was crushing. A first or second in the B Worlds means an automatic qualification for the 2004 Athens Olympics. It's been years since a Canadian man has qualified for the Olympics.

"Did he crash in the sprints?" I ask.

"Someone crashed him in the Keirin. His shoulder is separated. It's not good."

Not good is an understatement. A separation is worse than its cousin, a broken collarbone. At least a broken bone will heal; torn and tortured muscle and gristle languish for months and are never the same.

When Steen is discharged from hospital, he's in continual pain, but he still comes to the velodrome to supervise my workouts. His loyalty is touching. I know that it's hard to watch when you've have seen your own career halt in a crumpled heap of bodies and bikes.

Off track, I continue to celebrate my social success. I travel to a friend's family reunion in Saskatchewan, and take part in a family football game. I'm living a dual life: world-class athlete and average citizen. I think I can have it all.

I'm right. I do get it all.

In the midst of the football frolic I miss a pass, but catch an injury—a pulled calf muscle. The greatest source of sport injuries are recreational sports. Out-of-shape adults overtax their bodies, and limp to the emergency rooms. Or, in my case, a highly trained track cyclist unused to field sports is as vulnerable as a flabby office worker.

I wanted it all; I never thought about the definition of *all*.

Nine days later I'm at the World Championships in Stuttgart.

The pages in my diary for the Worlds are blank as if I hadn't been there at all. Unfortunately, my results confirmed this impression.

In the match sprints I plummeted to eleventh place. I had never placed lower than third at a previous Worlds. The diary's silence speaks also of my failure to prepare. There are no scripted plans. The blank pages don't record the excuses: my allergic reaction to some peanut butter, the lack of grocery stores in our area, and infighting among Canadian Team members. Of course, the early season overtraining in Aigle isn't recorded either. Neither was my late-season gadfly impersonation. I didn't have to write out the reasons for my disgraceful performance.

And the performance *was* disgraceful, so disappointing that I don't dare call Steen between heats. I went through the motions, hoping for Lady Luck. Of course, she's another woman you can wait on forever. From the first heat to the last I knew I was in trouble.

The call home to Steen scared me more than anything in a long while. I remember sitting in my room, staring at the bland fixtures and fittings—mass-produced, without character. Life without my dreams, schemes and accomplishments—the ones that set me on fire—was no better than this production-line room. Failure could relegate me to a mass-produced life. It would be the death of my individuality.

No. It would be worse: it was extinction. I would end up as a footnote to history, one of those names on the UCI list of World Championship medallists. I'd be an obscure medallist, but never a champion.

What price had I paid to come this far, only to flop? The usual milestones of a thirty-seven-year-old life—relationships, careers, family—had been sacrificed for this failure. All the suffering, made harder every year by age, the workouts more demanding and my body less resilient, had been placed on this altar of mediocrity.

The thoughts chilled me. The phone seemed a million miles away. Eventually, I made the call.

"Well," Steen says, his voice quiet, like an old man hearing a wayward child, "come on home."

He didn't criticize me. It made the pain worse.

I had been hoping to cheer him through his ordeal, a shredded shoulder that wasn't healing. Steen had coached me to my successes, all the while nurturing his own career. All of this he had done without receiving a dime. And now, when his career was shattered, he needed payback, validation—thanks.

Instead? Instead of a hit, I delivered a miss—a Swiss Miss—a marshmallow-topped mediocrity of a ride.

What else could you expect from the last three months? Domestic happiness? Maybe, but never a World Championship.

The dizzy singer in the skirt had to be controlled. Somebody more calculating, less needy, and uncompromising had to be located. Even the original Dirndl Girl, Maria, had to locate an iron core of courage in order to save herself. This year the recipe for my competitive life was clear. Take one bike, add Dirndl Girl (a.k.a. Swiss Miss) with a busy social calendar. Bake for one season, and taste mediocrity.

What would new formula look like? It wouldn't be wearing a dirndl. It would have to be powerful and fiery.

Change the recipe. Take one bike and substitute one Monster for the social songstress. Combine the two and you had Bike Monster, or simply the Muenster. That sounded better.

But even if I found this Godzilla of the velodrome, how could the beast and the beauty co-exist? Dirndl Girl had been the death of me, but I didn't want to see her stomped *completely* out of existence by a rampaging beast. Similarly, I didn't want the fire-spewing terror lizard to be subdued by a nursery song-warbling governess.

In the midst of my shame I struggled to see a path.

At the time I had a sense, an inkling, like an image seen in the corner of your vision, something like a momentary flicker that dances in and out of visibility. The answer is on the periphery, but I'm squinting, trying to see it clearly.

Why do I want to keep trying? What kind of person, faced with the fallout from this failure, would continue? Maybe not a person, but a monster.

Like an animal turning its back on a summer pasture, I have to head to the mountain. Can't I see what will this lead to? Maybe I should stop trying to see what's happening in the future. Maybe I should make the future happen.

After all, what would Godzilla do?

CHAPTER 17

PLAYING WITH FIRE

on fire /on fie er/ *n. phrase* **1** to ride beyond expectations. **2** *Related to:* **playing with fire.** Common ignition source is the Olympic torch—it has incinerated more riders than matches have forests. **3** *See also, (in the sense of playing with fire)*: punishment first identified with mythical Prometheus who stole fire from the gods. He was staked to a rock. Crows ate his liver. Coaches may suffer similar fates. (*See entry* for **El Toro.**) (*See also,* **ambition-success-disaster cycle.** In this process, madness and quarrelling overcome participants. Flames consume their dreams.)

—From the *Cyc.L.O.W.Ps.*

The question was an ember, sizzling in the back of my psyche.

I knew I had to come back. How, was one question. Before answering that, though, there was another question: why?

The dragon was well-fed and well-entertained. She had watched me burn up my adult life, toast relationships, singe my psyche, and incinerate hundreds of thousands of dollars, all in a quest for—what?

My ambition-fuelled monster was starving, its ribs showing. Why keep going? I couldn't let the poor thing starve to death. A more insightful answer would have to wait.

In the meantime, there were two matters to take care of before the 2003 season could be consigned to the scrapheap of athletic disasters. The first was the Canadian National Championships in Bromont, Quebec. Throughout the Championships, though, the question burned in my bruised psyche, and I sleep-rode to another three National Titles. A bonus was Jack McCutcheon's attendance at the Championships. The day after the meet we attend a local golf club, and our roles are reversed.

He's the champ, burning up the course, while I loll in the cart, my legs and mind totally exhausted.

The second essential—my vacation—arrives. David and Monica Nelson, the mountain-biking couple, invite me to their new home in Kelowna. I arrive in time for the worst forest-fire season in decades. Houses are exploding like firecrackers. No sooner do I appear than we're packing pictures and paintings in blankets. I remembered making an idle joke, upon arrival, about the fires glowing in the hills.

"I guess you can play that old dating game," I said.

"What?"

"If your house was on fire and you had only ten minutes to choose, what would you try to save?"

Hours later, it's no joke. Their house survives, but we spend the next few days at their relatives' home in Salmon Arm.

As I travel home, I think of my season and the fires in Kelowna. I had seen the flames sweep down the hill and lunge at homes, consuming them like a starving beast. The house next door would stand untouched. One burns, the other survives. Even out of the smoke and fire, people were carrying on. The survivors of the Kelowna fires were hopeful and grateful for a chance to recover and rebuild.

So was I.

I still didn't have the answers, but the images of fire—of destruction and renewal—monopolized my consciousness. By the end of October I'm at my desk in my South Edmonton home, the late summer light pouring in through the windows. At this time of year the light is like warm honey, drenching everything in gold. But I'm not admiring the quality of the atmosphere.

I'm typing out my goals. Ever the fastidious legal secretary, I laminate the declaration in plastic and bind it in my diary. The paper I choose is yellow, the colour of gold. As the keyboard clacks away, I know this is my last chance.

Goal one? "Gold medal at Athens," I type.

Also, I've expanded my vision. I add, "It's not just about winning Gold, but about understanding the process (training programs), focus (mental training), and my dedication and commitment."

Goals two, three, and four? Yes, I have other goals. Many riders and athletes don't, and are high, dry, and washed up at the end of their careers. I learned, when I had abandoned the sport in the 1994, to broaden my focus. Hence, "Take time out for photography courses, public speaking, meditation, yoga, and reflect on past, present and future." Also, I tap, "Give back to the community through public speaking with kids in school and various community groups."

Next, I type out my vow to search each week for sponsors.

Lastly, I type out the most neglected part of my vision—my life with other people. It is, typically, the shortest. Ironically, hopping from party to party, from house to house, left me no time for the people who would always be with me.

I push myself back from the keyboard. I want this—all of this—to happen. I don't know how. I don't know why I'm so wildly ambitious, but I want it *all*. Amidst the ashes of 2003, and through the bitter film that played over my eyes in the hotel room in Stuttgart, I still can't see the how. But I can feel the now. The now is different. The me is different. I don't know who, or what I am.

I thought of my own experience, only a year ago, when the hot flame of infection had burned my body. I had stumbled through the 2003 pre-season, only to overtax myself in paradise. The rest of the season had gone up in the smoke of self-ignition.

Fire is strange. It breaks down what is temporary, but refines what is lasting. Have I been transformed? Or have I perished in the flames?

Grrrrr. I can hear heavy footsteps.

Where's Picasso? This painting's not finished.

I'm desperate to get to Athens, the city of my dreams.

In October Steen gave me a basic program. The chance to reignite my career fills me with an intense enthusiasm. It's like hurling a bucket of gas on a fire. No, that's not strong enough—it's like driving the gas truck onto the fire.

Yet, it's only part of what I'm training for. I've got to prepare for my post-racing future. However, the future depends on who you are. Out of the ashes of last year, a new being has arisen, but I can't describe or name her. I have a track coach, and know I could use a career coach. Metro Community College's Web site outlines a course called "Career Changes and Choices."

I scroll down to a course that seems made for me. The summary reads, "You want to change your career but don't know how or where to start."

"Yeah, right," I mutter.

It continues, "This intensive, interactive program will assist you with your career planning." No time like the present. After all, I'm approaching thirty-eight.

"The self-scoring version of the Myers-Briggs Type Indicator will provide immediate feedback on how you relate to others and make decisions."

I wonder if the Myers-Briggs has a Dirndl Girl or a Godzilla scale.

Later, I'm in the Metro College classroom, reviewing my test results with instructor Julie Milne. My personality type is clearly...unclear. Years ago, I had taken the same test, and had scored as an extrovert. Now, I'm on the borderline of introversion.

One thing that stands out is my satisfaction with my current life. I am a full-time cyclist and am often alone, away from my office mates. On the other hand, I like being in the office and reconnecting with my team there. Then Milne comes to the final results. The ambiguity continues. The results say I should focus on marketing, sales, public relations, and communications. Focus: a funny word for someone going in four different directions.

I drive home through the late-October darkness, and ponder the results. I spent $175 and four weeks to find out that I am four different people: A seller, a huckster, a glad-hander, and a talker. All this, and an introvert, too. An introverted huckster? A introspective saleswoman? A reluctant meeter-and-greeter? A shy public speaker? Ludicrous. But true.

For example, public speaking is something I have always been drawn to. As a child I entered public-speaking competitions, and faced off against other children—often competing in the post-meal program at Legion dinners. The food-sated vets would pat their stomachs, light up a cigarette, and sit back, waiting to be bored. Up to the podium would come Lori-Ann, preparing to give a discourse on magic. "Abracadabra!" she would shout, and then stamp her foot, proclaiming, "Alakazam, you're a monkey!" Tableware would rattle, and vets would sit up, blinking.

Years later, was I still on stage, putting my foot down and trying to get attention? "Leave with a course of action for planning your future," the course outline said. Good advice. The future does depend on who you are, but which "who" was I?

There was only one "I" that was beyond doubt, and I didn't need Myers-Briggs to tell me.

"Olympic gold medal?" asked Steen.

On this night, in late October, we're sitting on the clapped-out couch in the velodrome clubhouse. The clacking of the aspens' thin branches, waving in the bitter wind, is a warning of the coming winter. Summer is not, in this season, anything more than a hopeful fantasy.

Yet, hopefulness is on the menu. Steen is frowning, squinting at my draft 2004 goals planning sheet. It is, I hope, the final draft.

"Yeah," I say, trying to read his face. Maybe summer is not the only fantasy here.

"Olympic medallist?" he asks.

"That's right."

"Whoa."

Steen's never doubted me before. Why now? The Olympics is just another race.

"You mean after last year?" I guess.

Steen's staring at me.

"Last year was just a blip," I say. "Two thousand, 2001, I was on track. Two thousand and two also, and then my body blew up."

He turns to his notebook. Steen's clicking his pen, the point going back and forth into the barrel. Is he listening?

"Last year?" I say, and shrug, "We're starting from a clean slate."

He's staring at the pages.

"I won't let this end with my failure in Stuttgart," I say.

He hasn't moved.

Maybe I sound irrational. After nearly seventeen years of struggle, after near-death experiences and near daily torment, why keep going? I've been so close, but I've been so close so often. Why would things change?

A worse thought, a chilling thought, clamps my heart. Have I asked for too long, for too much? Have I worn out my welcome with Steen? He's spent years coaching, prompting, hand-holding. Good results, but never what we swore we would achieve.

To look at the price of your dreams, to see the cost, in a concrete-block bunker, with an iron-hard wind scratching at the windows, is like seeing an X-ray of your life. All the flesh, all the pretence, is gone. There's only bone and what's inside is instinctive. Everything else is gone.

I saw the stark outline of my life, the bleached-white framework of my being, now in the autumn gloom and the winter of my career.

Do I like the looks of it? No. Not yet.

Does Steen? The silence is killing me.

Steen looks up from the sheet. "If," he says, staring out the west window into the late fall sky twilight, "you want a gold medal."

"I do."

He holds his hand up: silence in the class. "You will have to work harder than you thought was possible."

"You've worked me hard for four years. This is just another..."

The hand goes up.

His pen clicks, the tiny noise echoing in the empty clubhouse. Steen makes a note in his coach's journal. "I will find out how badly you want it," he says. Steen looks up. "How much time do you have?"

"You tell me how much time I need to do this."

Steen makes a series of precise, carefully drawn notes.

"There will be two peaks this year," he says, inscribing his plan. "One will be the World Championships in Melbourne, Australia."[1]

Steen doesn't have to tell me what the second peak will be. He's agreed, and that's all that matters.

It's the toughest workout I've had in a year.

See, I tell myself, as we sweat our way through days of pushing iron amidst the clank and clang of the gym, it *is* just another year.

Steen's returned me to the basics, and it seems to be a continuation from 2002. I'm in the squat cage, eyes popping out, sweat bursting from my face, and he's behind me, spotting. I'm so exhausted that I'm hallucinating. My legs are quivering, and he says, "There's a World Cup in two weeks. How bad do you want it?" The weights grow fifty pounds lighter, and I nearly send them through the roof.

The Aussies and the Europeans have money, machines and teams of coaches. Their organizations exist to minimize the stress and maximize the results for their riders. I have a part-time job, an old bike, and a hole in my disc wheel. I ride my handmade tires until the sidewalls fray. Other countries have several riders qualifying for the Athens Olympics. Canada has one rider. And that rider doesn't have a coach.

She has something better: Picasso.

Post-Olympus Footnote: Confidential Commentary by Steen Madsen

1. Months later, at the end of 2004, in the quiet of my house, being interviewed by Karl Wilberg, I can say what had to be unsaid, or at least *understated*.

Yes, Lori-Ann asked me for an Olympic gold medal. I never said she couldn't do it.

I was wondering *how* she could do it.

She told me she wanted the Olympic match sprint gold medal. This goal was like no other. Every gambler and nut case would throw their lot in with the true contenders. People would risk their money, lives, and minds on reaching this goal. I recalled the well-known 1997 *Sports Illustrated* survey. Aspiring Olympic athletes were asked if they would take a drug that would guarantee victory for five years. Also guaranteed was a nasty side effect—death after the big winning streak. The result? Not withstanding the grim cost, half the surveyed athletes would clamour for the stuff.

In addition to the kamikaze approach of our competitors, we would be facing, as usual, well-equipped teams. The Canadian National Olympic Track Cycling Team was likely to consist of one person: Lori-Ann.

After telling me of her goal, I stared at the year's training outline. I knew that there could be only one peak. The Worlds would be a warm-up, a chance for us to springboard to Mount Olympus, and a chance for our competitors to show their hand, boast, and then let down for the Olympics. I saw this as an opportunity, but one I kept to myself.

Lori-Ann assumed that there would be two full peaks; there wouldn't be. How do you tell an athlete, "Don't go for the World Championship, gamble on an Olympic gold"? On the other hand, how do you not tell them?

Another problem was looming—a bigger, basic problem: how? There's nothing specific in a coaching manual on winning an Olympic gold.

"If," I thought, "I was to get to the Olympics, how would I train for it?"

My injury last year had scotched my chances of qualifying. But still, how *would* I do it? My theoretical plan, the Steen Madsen-win-a-gold plan, would be a guide for the design of Lori-Ann's. I let the pen drop to the paper, but it didn't write.

The pen was fine. The plan wasn't.

Usually, when designing her program, I would write it for me, and then detune it. When it comes to strength events, women, compared to men, have a built-in physiological disadvantage. Their bodies attempt to preserve a higher percentage of body fat. The net result is an inherently lower power-to-weight ratio.

Why not do the usual? Just add in more training and increase the intensity. That approach had worked before. The results of my program in 2000, 2001, and 2002 had demonstrated her world-beating potential, but this was an Olympic year. And, last year, the quality of women's sprinting had seen an enormous improvement.

Here is why she saw me hesitate.

Here is why I had no speedy answer to her request: I was about to do something unheard of, something dangerous, and something that runs against the principles espoused in any coaching manual.

It is not something I would ordinarily recommend, not a conclusion to come to lightly or quickly.

"I will no longer detune your training," I said to myself. "I will train you the same way I would train myself. There will be *no* modification." I clicked the pen, and started to write.

What was I doing?

First, to wager everything on the maelstrom of the match sprint? And what about slipping past her the reality that there would be only one peak—the Olympics? The Worlds would be no Championship, but a full-dress scrimmage.

Second, what about the training plan? It would have taken me to the limit and probably beyond. Lori-Ann was going to be thirty-eight and had a bad back. How could she last?

Was I nuts? No. Was it a risk, a huge risk? Was I hoping for a bit of luck? Yes, yes, and yes.

Days later, when we started the program, I had trouble keeping up with her. "So far Madsen," I said to myself, "you've done well. Next is the hard part—the mental training."

Luck? Actually, Picasso didn't need luck. We needed El Toro, the Muenster, whatever you call it—the fierce competitor that lies within any true sprinter—to come to the fore. Our worst enemies were the forces that combined, like picadors, to pick, probe and stab at Lori-Ann's psyche. The stresses of being unsupported were the real enemies.

Every jab would drain blood from the rampaging competitive beast. And, I knew that there would be no money to send me. I wouldn't be there to protect her from the slings and arrows of a disinterested sports system.

We all face situations where victory is elusive, but responsibility for defeat is not. I wouldn't be racing, but coaching an Olympic athlete puts you in the ring just the same. Earlier that year I saw a bullfight in all its gory glory. I know the odds of survival for the bull.

If I guessed wrong, and she came home from Athens empty-handed, I'd be ready for the expected conclusion to the bullfight. In the true bull-fighting tradition, there is only one ending: the bull is killed. If he is lucky, he takes one or two of his tormentors with him, but the end is always the same. Still, it had never stopped a beast worthy of the name "El Toro" before. So why now?

CHAPTER 17 ½

EL TORO

el Toro /ell to roe/ *n. Spanish*/ **1** the Bull. Epitomises the winning cyclist's irrational need to meet the opponent head-on. **2** users of this guise are often ignorant of the typical career arc of the persona. **3** Spanish for **bike monster.** *(See related entry).* **4** Steen Madsen.

—From the *Cyc.L.O.W.Ps.*

Picasso or El Toro? Who is he today?

Today, December 7, 2003, at the Burnaby velodrome, it's El Toro.

Steen's recovery from his shoulder separation had involved his own version of art therapy. He had painted a mural-sized canvas. The scene, done in the style of Picasso, features a bull, a matador, and his horse. The three figures have coalesced in a struggle to the death. The horse's guts are spilling out. The bull is a killer. The matador is in limbo. Clearly, Steen is the rampaging bull that has destroyed his tormentors.

Today, El Toro is looking at me from under his dark brows. We have been sprinting, and El Toro has just beaten me by a huge margin.

"I caught you napping," he says. Steen had taken advantage my inattention. He dove for the pole line—the inside of the track—and crushed me. I was so far behind I quit. "And you gave up," he says. "Never give up. Never."

I'm staring at the track, soaking up the bombastic word blast. I'm grinding my teeth. It's bad enough he's beat me, but there's more to it. Steen's talking, but I'm not minding the words. Something else is catalysing my anger. It's his pointed finger. Everyone has a sound or gesture that, for them, is like a red flag to a bull. For me, it's the pointed finger. If I had wide nostrils, they'd be flaring and there would be steam pouring forth.

"Go to the stairwell," he had said before the verbal whipping, and now we're standing by an empty stairwell. It's like being taken out to the woodshed.

"What you're doing is wrong," he says, shaking his head.

"I've gotten to this point by doing what's right."

"You tighten up."

"You're always telling me to tighten it up!" I say.

"You have to loosen up," Steen says.

I am ready to hurl my helmet to the track. "Make up your mind."

"You need to be more social."

"This is match sprinting, not a tea party."

"Be nice," he says. "Tanya (Dubnicoff) was nice."

He's right. Duba was expert at socializing between rides. Still, the mention of my old rival makes the hair rise higher off the back of my neck.

"Be . . . social?" I say.

"When you get on the bike—that's when you turn it on."

My head slumps down. I've imagined my fierce inner beast, my inner Godzilla—the Muenster—rampaging around the track. And now Steen he wants her arch-nemesis, the Swiss Miss—Dirndl Girl—to appear between rides and dispense small talk on the infield.

Muenster on the track, Dirndl Girl off.

I've achieved everything by single-minded determination. Flicking from one extreme to another is foreign to me. But Steen wants me to morph from the Muenster to DG, then return to the Muenster in a matter of minutes. Even poor Dr. Jekyll took more time to transform into the wild Mr. Hyde.

"Okay," I say, and do up my straps. "Let's go."

The straps are so tight they bite my flesh.

How do you be social at an indoor velodrome when the only other inhabitants, on a Tuesday morning, are a handful of vets? The vets, mostly retirees, are tooling around the track, their legs barely turning. At the beginning of the four-day camp, I had lectured them on track etiquette. Since then they've kept their distance.

I close my eyes, and conjure up the image of Dirndl Girl.

"Hi," I call to one surprised vet.

"Huh?" he says. I've never spoken to him before. Actually, I have, but only to warn him to get out of my way.

"How ya doin'?" I ask. He's looking around, wondering if I'm going to sock him. He looks guilty.

"Okay," he says.

I smile, like he's said the most clever thing imaginable, and I ride up to the next straggler. I repeat the performance, my glued-on smile now becoming a beacon of goodwill. I advance to another dawdling vet, and this time I even joke.

"You get in my way again," I say to the astonished vet, "and..." His eyebrows leap up, and he starts to decelerate. "You owe me a coffee."

He smiles, and agrees.

They all seem relieved. It's as if Godzilla, instead of ripping their heads off, gave them a hug.

Steen is at the line. I roll up, adjust my helmet, snug my gloves over my fingers, and beam at Steen. Like a switch, *click*, I turn off DG, and summon up the Muenster. Watch out, El Toro.

Of course it worked, and I hit the line well ahead of Steen.

Steen's advice was at once ironic and masterful. It ran against a lifetime of habit to smile at spectators and jest with teammates before an event. Like many women, I was always afraid to look stupid. My solution was to stay coiled up at all times. As a consequence my overactive adrenal gland kept pumping out the juice and burning up my energies, leaving me flat for the final 200 metres.

Steen had probably planned the confrontation. He's deliberately surprising me, so I can learn to respond to the unexpected.

On the track he's trying to exploit my weaknesses, and using the small 200-metre track to concentrate the effect of my mistakes. With short straights between each 180-degree turn, there's little chance to recover.

Off the track, he's taught me the lesson of the year: stay loose, and be open to learning. Look around at the surroundings, talk to your competitors. On the track, flick the switch. Save the Muenster's powers for the race. In the race, make your responses automatic, and trust that you'll make the right move.

All of this is possible if you've got belief. All of this is possible if you've got someone to paint the picture for you. With a good coach, like Desmond, I'd be able to hit the top ten. The last 5 percent, that's what Steen said I had to find. We thought it was in Aigle.

Wrong. It was here all along—in the painting Steen was working on. The broad strokes had been made. The final touches, the critical strokes that distinguish a masterpiece from the masterful, were being applied.

The camp ends, and the next day I'm reminded that this is not any year. I fly to Victoria to attend a Canadian Olympic Committee information session. The participants receive media training, the latest on the current anti-doping rules, and wrap up with a gala dinner. The day after, I'm home and meet Jack for a steak dinner. Later we attend Handel's *Messiah* at the Winspear Centre for Music.

For a few days, from Christmas to New Year, Dirndl Girl is back in town. In fact, on New Year's Eve, she's dancing for six hours at a club, and ends up swapping her Jones of New York suit jacket with a friend whose shirt is too small. The dancing continues until my knees are swollen.

When I come home, I look at the clock and realize two things. First, it's 5 AM on January 1, 2004. The first race in Burnaby is ten days away. Finally, after years of lobbying, I'll be allowed to race against the men. The Canadian men are as fast as the world's top five women. Secondly, in a week and a half I'll know what number really comes before 2004. Is it 2002, the year of the rocket? Or, 2003, the year of Dirndl Girl. The Muenster is scared. Good scared.

My diary entry about track training for January 9 reads: "Scared myself with just how fast I got going. NEVER have gone this fast. WOW!"

My new speed is a result of Steen's insistence on roller training in an extraordinarily big gear, and lifting massive amounts of weight. On January 10, the combination catapults me to a new women's track record for the 200-metre. Steen, too, sets a new track record for the 200 metre

I qualify third out of fifteen, the only woman of the bunch. The racing is ruthless, and I fight my way to fourth place. For days after, my legs feel like they've been injected with cement.

The next Burnaby camp is one week later. I'm rubbing my hands, excited to see what new speeds I'll hit. Before I leave, I make a series of money calls, and not for me. Steen's been struggling to make ends meet. Also, it's clear that he's coming to these Burnaby camps for my benefit, not his. I call Sport Canada, and beg them to issue Steen an injury card.

These cards are limited in number, and are designed to help athletes through their recovery. I complete the process by convincing Steen to have his physician fill out the forms. For once, the system comes through for Steen and he gets the card. Surely this is one good omen.

A doctor's office is a doctor's office.

Low-backed chairs, *Reader's Digest* magazines, issues of *Macleans* with tattered covers—they're all the same, and so are back injuries. They always reappear at the worst time. On January 19, I'm in an office in Burnaby waiting for Dr. Irving, the chiropractor, to repair my back. Two hours earlier I was lined up on the velodrome home straight to do a seated start. This was to be a major effort in a big gear.

Unfortunately, it was too big. The blossoming strength of my legs overcame the frailty of my back. Starting a bike is no different than weight lifting. Every muscle of your body is uncoiling, and if your form is off, you risk an injury.

Steen and his dad carried me into Dr. Irving's office. After he treats me I can walk, although it's like my post–appendix-surgery shuffle.

No one knows more than I how much is at stake this season. The winner in Athens will be the one who trains best, rides smartest, and negotiates the usual traps and hazards. Many competitors will hazard their health, hoping to keep it together long enough to hit the medal podium. Some of the gamblers will peak before the Olympics, and fizzle in Athens. A few of them might make it.

No one's going to make it with a bad back.

After a month of therapy, I'm relieved to see progress. This year, the National Team camp will be in Ft. Lauderdale from February 20 to March 7. Everything is good on the home front too. I'm staying in contact with my sister Jennifer, Mom and Dad, and, of course, having my Monday night dinners with Jack. When we leave, I feel whole, healthy, and ready for the camp.

Sometimes the travel arrangements at these camps have been chaotic, so I've arranged for a rental car for Steen, his brother Lars, and myself. I don't want to be dependent on anyone. The last thing I need is a surprise.

I've never seen Steen like this.

We've been in Ft. Lauderdale for days, and he's been on edge and distant. Several times, he and Lars step out of earshot, shaking their heads, and frowning. They're being torn apart, but they won't share it for fear of distracting me.

The riding is not going well. The CCA has put us up in the middle of an urban war zone, and the hotel air conditioner is a mould-infested machine spewing spores into our room. My breath is rasping, and my track performance suffers. In addition to Steen's undisclosed problem, the demands of sprinting are chiselling at his vulnerable shoulder and his morale. Our minivan is giving us problems. It's owned by Rent-a-Wreck, and lives up to its name. The timed trials come. I do not distinguish myself.

Finally, we move to a decent hotel suite, and I can breathe. The food is good, too.

The news from Steen is not.

His wife's best friend, Jill, is also Lars's ex-wife. Shortly after we arrived, Steen and Lars learned that she was attacked, raped, and butchered. She stumbled from her apartment in Edmonton, covered in blood and near death. Jill is a tall, blond and athletic Venus. She's smart—a high school vice-principal—friendly, and courageous. Her assailant was a neighbour. He asked for help moving some furniture. Jill's reward was to be confined, degraded, and nearly murdered. She fought her attacker, but bare hands stand little chance against a meat cleaver.

Jill's innate kindness made her vulnerable. Her strength and courage kept her alive.

No wonder Steen and Lars were in emotional agony. No wonder they didn't want to tell me. Of course, nothing we're going through can compare to Jill's ordeal. For days she teetered on the edge of life, and still suffers from paralysing and persistent terrors.

Steen's wife, Cyndi, is frightened. But she's telling Steen to stay at the camp. We wander through our daily routine as though we're walking in a fog. Steen's shoulder is killing him, and his mind is tortured by divided duties. He wants to be home, but he knows he has to compete. Also, I know he feels obliged to help me.

Is this quest worthwhile? Like a horse, I keep my head down and pull against the harness.

Don't think. Just ride. Things will be better in Mexico.

"You lost it, Lori-Ann."

It's Steen, rummaging through his luggage, muttering about a nylon pull strap. Because of his tender shoulder, he can't lift the wheel case, and needs to pull it. "What did you do with my strap?" he asks.

"I saw it at Houston International," I say, and look at the luggage carousel at Aguascalientes airport. As usual we have more luggage than Jackie O.

"You lost it," he says, and shakes his head. He's acting like a parent who's suffered at the hands of a forgetful child. Earlier, in Ft. Lauderdale, we had fought over who had used up the laundry soap.

"It'll show up." I stare at the revolving carousel.

"I need it now," he says, and reaches for the wheel case. It's a heavy plastic container, designed to protect our wheels, and is as awkward to carry as a truck tire.

"Steen, don't," I say.

He grabs the wheel case, winces, and stalks to the taxi zone.

We don't talk until we get to the Fiesta Inn Hotel, and even then we don't speak; we argue. Eventually, Steen fishes out his credit card, and gets his own room. The deskman's eyebrows rise, but he's seen this before—travellers at the ends of their ropes, bickering and biting, arriving at the place of their dreams, only to let everyday conflicts overwhelm their good spirits.

The room is quiet. No TV, no Steen. He keeps the TV on as a kind of background sound, like a white noise that he finds soothing. I'm glad to be rid of this noise and the other soundtrack: the sound of Steen and me butting heads. Since leaving Edmonton we haven't had five minutes to ourselves. The pressures of trying to make time standards, and the pall cast by Jill's ordeal, have pitted us against one another. The problem isn't who used up the soap or who lost the strap. The problem is us.

The old thoughts, the bewilderment at the high cost of this adventure, and the slim prospect of rewards return. I need someone to talk to, but I don't relish another go with El Toro.

I pick up the phone and dial Edmonton.

"Jack," I say, "it's Lori-Ann." We talk for an hour.

I don't know what the training plan is for tomorrow, but I quit. Worrying, that is.

"Hello, Ms. Muenzer," says the waiter.

I'm alone, ordering breakfast on the hotel patio. The breakfast is a leisurely and genteel affair. In Edmonton, drifts of tired snow will carpet the landscape for another two months, but here? I inhale the scent of tropical flowers, and let the warm morning breeze play over my face.

I return to my room. There's a knock at the door: it's Steen. He apologizes, and we are on good terms again. I could dance him around the room.

At the track, my qualifying ride in the 200-metre is my best in years. I'm second, only five hundredths of a second out of first. A good qualifying time in the event means an easier ride in the initial rounds. I meet the eleventh-place qualifier, Italy's Elisa Frisoni, in the first round. I've got plenty of speed on her, so I don't give any thought to a tactical plan.

She beats me in the first round.

And why wouldn't she? I towed her to the finish. Muenzer had the legs, but Frisoni had the brains. I don't have time to solve my tactical weakness and fight my way back in, but end up sixth, trapped again in the fifth through eighth place finals.

During my warm down, I unzip the top of my skinsuit and slide it over my undershirt. The top is no longer a tight fit. I started track racing wearing a size large, but I've been trimming down. I make a note to request a smaller suit.

The next day, during the 500-metre event, I'm thrusting forward, standing on the pedals and accelerating off the start line. After rounding the turn, I'm at full speed, and trying to sit down on the back of the saddle.

I'm stuck!

My skinsuit's baggy crotch is snagged over the saddle tip. I'm trapped on the front of the saddle, and plowing through the air like a human air brake. Finally, the Lycra gives, and I don't crash. My time is good—only two-tenths of a second slower than my best—but I keep silent. I imagine the headlines in the Canadian Cyclist Webzine: "Rider crashed by skinsuit."

Steen and I pack up for the return to Edmonton. As I fold my threadbare suit into my bag, its played-out carcass reminds me that I need some new tires too.

I've lined up some Dugast tires, beautiful handmade tires that weigh 140 grams and cost $350 each. I can hardly wait to glue them onto my race rims. I should delay the happy day, though. The tires have a limited life span. As a result, other teams change them after so many rides. Not this rider. At $350 apiece, I'll have to guess how much life they have left.

Better guess right, I tell myself, and zip the bag. You never know when they'll blow up.

From March to April, my diary details the steps and strategies Steen laid before me. There's only a month before the next World Cup in Manchester. I'm slaving in the weight room, sweating on the track, and at night, staring at the TV. No, I'm not watching *Friends*: I'm watching my track enemies.

Steen has provided me with videotape of previous World Cups. I'm analyzing the world's best and becoming a student of the game, no longer just a blunt-force rider. I'm working on the weakest link: my inability to find tactics to match my strength.

Also, several times a week, I'm visualizing my successful races. I'm imagining the rides I had in Burnaby, and looking at them from the first-, second-, and third-person points of view. I'm looking at them the way visitors to an art museum stand back, tilt their heads, and examine a painting.

All of this and, on March 2, shovelling snow off the track.

One week later we're motorpacing. As the motor whirrs, I feel the speed capability of my legs increase. Having Jack watch my session is a boost. As I warm down on the Argyll Velodrome's apron, I see the other good-luck Jack: a large hare, his white winter fur giving way to his brown summer coat.

Speed, two Jacks, and a Steen: I'm certain they'll send me to the top.

Sure enough, while warming up in Manchester I can feel the speed pouring out of my legs. Steen's training plan is being followed to the closest of tolerances. I'm like a finely made painting, every stroke, every shade and colour, every line, drawn out by Steen's steady hand. Also, he has me return to scripting my goals.

My notes for April 7: "First goal: qualify first in the 200-metre. Second goal: one race at a time. Race just as well as during today's tactical training with Steen."

The next day, I take in a movie, *Under the Tuscan Sun*. I'm trying to relax, and save my energy for tomorrow's race. I write the movie's message—to live boldly and to act unselfconsciously—into my diary. A day later, when I hit the finish line for the 200-metre, I look up to the scoreboard. My time is the fastest. It's all going like clockwork.

Unfortunately, when a clock is wound too tightly, its cleverly fashioned wheels and levers have a way of springing apart.

In spite of all the cue words, I rode the match sprints like a half-witted training partner for my opponents. I would have been last had it not been for a rider from the Netherlands chopping me down to the pole line and being disqualified. My tactics were prepared, but I wasn't prepared to use them. Once the whistle went, so too did my brain.

Dirndl Girl, the Swiss Miss, had hijacked my brain.[1]

The next day, I'm on the rollers warming up for the last event, the standing 500-metre. This should be a good day because there are no tactics in the 500-metre: it's a raw test of speed. All I have to do is warm-up, and let my legs crack off a medal-winning time. Steen's in the stands, and I want to put on a good show for him.

"Lori-Ann."

It's Steen. He's materialized in the pits, and is anxious. Like El Toro, he's bulling his way towards me. For such a young guy, he's like the father of a wayward teenager.

"I'm about to do the warm-up," I say, "I feel good."

"We've got to change it," he says.

"It was great for the 200-metre."

He insists, and I make the changes like a confused robot trying to adjust to a new task.

I ride to my slowest time in over a year.

Post-Olympus Footnote: Confidential Commentary by Steen Madsen

1. Good thing I have thick hair, and lots of it. Between Burnaby and Manchester a trail of black hair that I've pulled from my head marks our travels. Lori-Ann was making and remaking the same tactical mistakes.

Years ago, before the competition deepened, she could make an error, but use her tremendous strength to make up the difference. It had worked at all but the highest level—the top of the podium. Since then, the sport had transcended a mere speed competition. Tactics were indispensable.

I knew it. She knew it. We had worked on it, in video review, sparring on the track, and even using word association. "Tanya Dubnicoff," was all you had to say, and she would get a spark in her eye. Say, "Kerrie Meares," and the normally present smile would vanish.

In Burnaby, I said, "Dubinicoff was social, she knew how to turn off the switch." Dubinicoff was also a masterful tactician. I invoked her name, hoping to see Lori-Ann rise to the challenge: be as wily and as adaptable as Dubinicoff—social off the track, and a terror on the boards. There, it worked.

By the time we got to Mexico, our mutual frustration overwhelmed my ability to coach her. I was exhausted, trying to be athlete, Lori-Ann's coach, and absentee husband to my wife Cyndi. Lori-Ann got schooled by a beginner, Italian rider Elisa Frisoni. I chewed Lori-Ann out, hoping to spark some fighting spirit; the lecture backfired, and she turned the anger on herself.

At the velodrome in Aguascalientes I knew she was going to lose. So did Lori-Ann. She was riding the rollers, and telling me she wanted to throw up. She could taste bile; I could smell fear.

At Manchester, I decided that I could be athlete and coach no longer: I went along, not to race, but to coach Lori-Ann. We got some World Cup points, but that was all. At the end of the day it was up to Lori-Ann. She had to decide to be a racer—a ruthless competitor.

Instead? She fizzled like a waterlogged rocket. At this point, my gamble wasn't looking good.

I felt like I was one of my ancestors' fictional countrymen—Hamlet, a man fated for disaster. And I knew that like the Prince of Denmark, I had to brood and brainstorm a way out of this quagmire.

As the airliner drones over Greenland, I stare out the window, biting my lower lip, wondering how the fastest qualifier can finish so poorly. Another rider, German Matthias John, is a rippling rocket of a sprinter, routinely qualifying in first place. His 200-metre time is the envy of the track world. Although he'll power his way out of the first round, he's often eliminated in the eighths. Matthias has all the speed in the world, yet he can't use it to his advantage. Perhaps he and I can form a sprinters' support group.

Sympathy, however, will not solve this problem. The problem isn't speed, but preparation. I need to ensure the Muenster, and not the Dirdle Girl, appears for the sprints. I also need to avoid distractions. Whether the source is from friends inviting me out, or a last-minute change to my warm-up, my concentration can be fragile. I need Steen, but I do not need distractions.

I sit upright in my chair.

The apprentice does not challenge the master. Not unless they have...graduated? Somewhere, in all the turmoil and turbulence of the last four years, I had moved up. Not to master, not by a long shot, but perhaps to freshman or sophomore.

In one month, the last World Cup will take place in Sydney, Australia. Two weeks later the World Championships are in Melbourne.

A thought blasts through my mind: "I HATE TO LOSE WHEN I KNOW I CAN WIN." My tortured ambitions can't take it any longer.

The Muenster will consult with Picasso.

The Muenster will return.

I look around, wondering if anyone noticed my mental shouting. My seat mates are still, some dozing, others distracted by the in-flight entertainment. For me, there will be no distractions. My ride will be coming to an end in Athens.

If I had hoofs, I'd be pawing the ground.

CHAPTER 18

SCHOOL AND THE SEVENTH SENSE

school /skool/ *n.& v.* **1** *In the sense of*: "I schooled him/her." Imposition of a lesson, reminiscent of unpleasant public school experiences.

seventh sense /sev enth senz/ *n.& phrase* **1** obscure perceptual ability shared by successful riders, downhill ski racers, motorsports athletes, and fighter pilots. Located in the narrow information band that precedes a catastrophic **rocket ride**. *(See related entry).*

—From the *Cyc.L.O.W.Ps.*

Two days after I return home, on April 14, the clouds dissolve into billowing grey waves of snow. The wet flakes swirl around the trees, and pile onto the ground. The roads fill with slush, and the trees groan. The bikes stay inside. Even a mountain bike would be stranded in the drifts. Just as well, I think, looking out my window.

These were rare days, free from demands, when I can consider what has happened, and what might be. I've got the speed, but I'm making tactical mistakes. They're not huge errors, but at this level, they need not be. One miscue, one look left when I should look right, and my opponent claims the win. I regroup for the next round, but the price has been paid, and the ultimate reward is now bronze or silver, not gold.

The phone has been silent too. I had been expecting a new program from Steen. He said to take the day off because of the weather, but there was no mention of future training. I hope he doesn't think I blame him for my letdown in Manchester. Snow has coated the trees, and in my heart I feel the cold grip of guilt. Steen's the last person in the world I would want to hurt. He's the reason I've come this far, but it goes deeper than that.

I would trust him with my life, and for five years now, I have.

Two days later, I hear from him. It's as if he's been plotting, planning, in a secret laboratory. When we meet, he sends me to school.

"When you go to the Burnaby camp," says Steen, "I want you to write."

Today is April 22 and we're in the velodrome clubhouse, surrounded by bikes, trophies, and souvenirs of past races. He and I are about to start a motorpace workout, and are sitting on the threadbare sofa, its exhausted springs creaking under our weight.

"Write? I say.

"With a pen and paper."

"Write what?

"What's happening in the races."

"Am I a reporter?"

There is no smile. In fact the face says: "Don't ask questions, comrade." He says, "Write down who you're up against, and their qualifying time."

"Why?"

"And," he says, "write down your plan for each race, leading and following."

It's Picasso again. He has that faraway look, as though he's staring at someone behind me. Steen points to the imaginary person and says, "When the race is over, I want you to write down what actually happened."

"It's like I'm back in school," I say. "You want me to write lines, don't you?"

He's already heading to the door, his motorcycle helmet in hand. I don't get an explanation.

After all, Picasso is as Picasso does.

Today it's a two-hour workout. Steen's in full artist form today as he pilots the powerful road-racing motorbike around the track. I'm whirling around the track, fighting to stay in the bubble of quiet air behind the motor's rear wheel.

Jumps, twenty-metre sprints, flying half laps, all of these I'm doing in an effort to hunt down the motor. I'm breathless and raspy voiced, hurling my bike after my quarry. The motor is tormentor and ulti-mately—because it's never caught—a teaser. But what a tease.

Steen's piloting is dead on. He smoothly advances the throttle, antic-ipating my accelerations, keeping one, maybe two inches ahead of me, all the while maintaining the perfect line through the turns. I have no idea how fast we're going. My concentration is total; at these speeds—close to eighty kilometres per hour—there is no room for distraction. Normally, we have five senses, maybe six.

I've found the seventh. All I know is the sense of speed: my mind has been stripped of any thought, save one—go faster.

The sense, as I warm down, of fulfilment is profound. It's better than the feeling I've had after yoga, or any other form of meditation. It's speed therapy. I highly recommend it.

So, too, do I recommend playing hooky.

For me this means going into work. Much of my training is solitary, and by April 28, I have had enough isolation. Steen has decreed today to be a rest day. However, my inner Dirndl Girl needs human contact, and I head in to work at Field Law. Steen is also a part-timer at the firm, and works in the library. This day, he is strides past my cubicle, and almost drops his cargo of books.

"Lori-Ann?"

"Yesss," I say, and keep typing—*clickety-clickety-clack*.

Steen glares. I smile and shrug.

Days later, I'm forgiven and Steen hands me the plan for May. There is an inscription at the head of the page. Steen's not styling us as animals, but as warriors. He quotes Sun Tzu, the fourth-century BCE Chinese statesman and general: "...therefore, when capable, feign incapacity; when active, inactivity. When near, make it appear that you are far away, when far away, that you are near. Offer the enemy bait to lure him in; feign disorder and strike him."

Masterful and insidious, I think as I hold the plan. Who else would take a 2400-year-old treatise on war and politics and turn it into a train-ing plan?

No need to fake it, I think. My competitors have plenty of reason to think my incapacity is quite genuine. This year, I'm a symbol of unful-filled potential, qualifying well, and racing poorly. To my competitors I'm not a contender; I'm a roadside marker. Steen's suggesting I use my past performance as bait to lure them in, to have them underestimate my abilities. The audacity of the plan is astonishing.

Of course, if he's wrong, it's also the height of hubris. If his lessons don't take, I'll be just another post-Olympic has-been. If he's wrong, seventeen years, countless miles, gallons of sweat, an entire landscape of sacrifice and pain, will be for nought. Nearly a generation will have passed, from start to finish, without me reaching my goal.

A little chilling, that thought. It was quite a gamble. And I did not know the half of it.

"Haul it back in, girl," I gasp.

The front wheel is shuddering under the turn's g-force, and I'm wrestling my bike back to the pole line on the Burnaby track. I launch myself out of the curve and over the finish line.

I'm still panting when the timekeeper says, "You're the fastest."

I'm up against the men at this Western Canada track meet on April 30. I never expected to qualify first, but no one bests my time—another new track record for women. Like a good student, I write my plan for the sprints, and record the actual-versus-planned ride. I don't win, but place third. The men are astonished. So am I.

Not so surprising is the weather that greets me on my return to Edmonton. On May 5, when most other world-class riders are training somewhere warm, I'm riding in an eye-watering spring snowstorm. My riding gear is plastered with translucent slush, and I write in my diary: "What the...?"

The day after, Steen drops by my work station at Field Law. We go through the plan for Sydney.

"It's really important to write out your tactical plan—the plan and the actual," he says.

"It worked in Burnaby," I say.

"This is a World Cup," he says.

"I beat the guys."

"They're not the ones I'm worrying about. It's the last race before the World Championships. You're coming up to a peak."

"For the Worlds?"

He stares at the written plan. Eventually, he says, "It's going to be hard—you're training through this race."

"I feel good."

"I'm going to train you, hard, right up to the race."

He's never done this to me before. Steen's watching, looking for my emotional response, as if I'm a subject in a psychological experiment.

"No problem," I say

"It's going to be a fight, Lori-Ann," he says.

"Okay."

"No, not okay," he says, and shakes his head like I'm a slow pupil. "It's going to be a fight—like never before—of how much you want it."

"All right."

Steen makes a small note in his coach's journal. I imagine him, carrying a clipboard in a lab, checking up on his newest creation—something laid out on the slab, wires and electrodes trailing off to computers. In a couple days I'll get a hint if it's Franken Muenster or the Creature from the Swiss Lagoon.

The plane drones on to Sydney, over a blank expanse of ocean. I'm rubbing my legs, trying to keep them loose. I'm still rubbing them the next day after spending the morning in Sydney's Gold's Gym boosting weights. The next day I'm on the Dunc Grey Velodrome, trying to dissapate the lactic acid from my overtaxed legs.

Two days later, I note in my diary: "Legs still feeling a bit thick." I am not given, prior to a race, to any negative thoughts. What I really wanted to write was, "Legs totally trashed. What is Steen doing?" After the 200-metre qualifying, the morning of May 14, I'm asking the same question. I've qualified sixth. In Manchester I had been first.

After qualifying, I ride my rollers, trying to revive my legs for the sprints. Maybe this is what Sun Tzu would do. Don't qualify first—feign weakness. The weakness is not feigned, I discover, as my first-round opponent, England's Victoria Pendleton, lays down a textbook example of how to school your opponent. She takes advantage of my sluggishness to relegate me to the repechage.

Now there's one ride left. I'm in a three-up race, and only the winner rejoins the meet. I'm either in or out.

Off track, I had remembered to stay loose, jovial. On the bus to the track today I read a book, and the reading helped me stay relaxed. That's fine until you hit the line. I remember Steen's pronouncement. "It's going to be a fight."

Too soon, it's time for the repechage. Yvonne Hijgenaar of the

Netherlands—the fastest qualifier—and Rosalee Hubbard of Australia line up on the track. I'm not on the line, though. I'm watching from the pits, my rear wheel in pieces. The *rider whip*, the official responsible for organizing the riders and ensuring they're ready, is staring at me.

"Ms. Muenzer," he says, holding a clipboard and reading my name, "it's time."

"I'll be right there," I say, and close my eyes.

"Please, I whisper, "Jeremy, hurry up." My Canadian National Teammate is changing my gear to a higher ratio. Please forgive me, Steen. I have not had the time to do a plan for this race.

At least I have remembered to fight.

"Okay, LaLa," says Jeremy, calling me by my team nickname, and rolls the bike to me. The official looks relieved. Eric is waiting, and he waves me forward.

I do not rush. I *do* feel hungry.

I feel my eyes open, not wider, but as if they're stronger. My breathing is deeper, and the air pouring into my lungs is like a rush of air onto a fire. On the line, I feel the handlebars, as if my hands have been skinned. I sense every ridge and bump of the grip tape.

The race starts, and Eric Van den Eynde gives me a weak push.

No plan. No push. Just desire, and a refusal to let it all pass by.

On the final lap, and coming out of turn three, Hijgenaar and I are side by side. I'm storming past, keeping the upper body loose. I blow past her, and there is no sign of Hubbard. The fastest qualifier has lost. I have won.

I go on to the quarters. First, though, I have to do my homework. I write: "Each race is going to be a fight. A fight of how much you want it. You're training through this World Cup, so bite the bullet. Fight for it."

And I do, taking France's Clara Sanchez, the second-fastest qualifier, and move on to the semis. In the semis I go against Anna Meares. She and I take it to three races, but I'm defeated in a photo finish, and head to the bronze medal round. There is no time for recrimination because the World Cup Sprints are a one-day event. The fight continues, and I write: "You're in the boxing ring. How bad do you want it?"

Perhaps my opponent, Venezuela's Daniela Larreal, wanted it too, but I wanted it more. After the race, the bronze medal is hung around my head.

The day after, in the 500-metre, I take a cue from the sprints and my newfound fighting spirit. I decide to ride without gloves. It's verboten, in the track world. It you fall, the first thing to hit the track is the heel of your hand. On a wood track, you'll collect splinters and lose skin. On a concrete track you'll lose skin and more.

I wanted to feel every bump on the track, and to have, all the pain and effort catalyse my whole being. It worked: the raw sensations aroused the inner Muenster, and spurred me to a silver medal.

The gloves have indeed come off, I think, and glance at the top of the podium where Hijgenaar, the gold medallist, waves to the crowd. The World Championships, two weeks from now, are in Melbourne. What could I do if I was rested?

When I pack up for Melbourne, I review Steen's plan, and the huge amount of training in the next two weeks. Eventually, I hope, the training intensity will subside and my legs will become supercharged. Steen promised a peak.

A jersey, a Rainbow Jersey, could be my pot of gold.

Two things happened at the Worlds. A Rainbow Jersey was not one of them.

First, Steen's still working me hard. So hard, that on May 22, less than a week before the Championships, I call home for help.

"I'm struggling."

"Shut it down," he says. "But write out your tactical plan, tonight, and call me."

The night before the racing starts, I write in my diary, "Legs felt heavy, like I was pedalling squares."

Second, I continued my schoolwork.

For three hours a night, four days out of the five preceding the racing, I'm in my room, writing, and reviewing my tactical plans with Eric, and then with Steen long distance.

The work pays off, and I advance to the semis. Once more, I face Anna Meares.

My notes say, "How bad do you want it? Find the open door, and bust through."

I sense the door is ajar, and am shouldering it like I'm escaping a burning house. The semi-finals are best of three rides. After the first two, Meares and I are tied. Before the last ride I'm sitting on deck, wondering why my focus has blurred, wondering why my morale has gone flat. The race starts, but the monster stays home, locked within my psyche. I'm edged out, and diverted to the bronze medal ride.

This time I'm against Pendleton, who schooled me in Sydney. After all the training, after all the planning, this was to be my last chance at the Rainbow Jersey. The Muenster vented her dissatisfaction, and the schooler is schooled, two straight. Later, in the gold medal round, Meares is beaten by Svetlana Grankovskaia of Russia.

I'm glad to be on the podium, wearing a World Championship medal, but still longing to be at the top. The final results, with their listing of times for the last 200-metre, don't interest me: the only result that matters are the placings. Steen, why didn't I peak? Franken Muenster, why did you leave?

In Sydney I was schooled. In Melbourne, I was Picassoed.[1]

Perhaps the 200-metre time for my last semi-final ride against Meares should have cheered me. It was the fastest ride of the finals. Had I a chance to reflect, I could have seen something more to it than a handful of seconds, tenths, and hundredths.

Possibly I could have seen the future, but I was too busy looking ahead to notice that.

Post-Olympus Footnote: Confidential Commentary by Steen Madsen

1. Yes, she was Picasso-ed, and heaven help me if it did not pay off in Athens.

I can say this now. I never expected her to do so well at the Worlds. Although I hadn't given her a chance to fully recover, she fought and claimed a bronze medal. Only a fraction of an inch in the semi-final with Anna Meares stopped her from heading for a Rainbow Jersey.

"So far, so good," I thought, so long as what we had sacrificed would be redeemed in Athens. Otherwise? I had made the biggest Canadian coaching miscalculation since Team Canada underestimated the USSR at the '72 hockey summit.

Between the World Championships and the Olympics was twelve weeks. The gap would give us time to make final preparations. It would also give fate plenty of time to fine-tune its surprises.

Of these, there would be some; that much I was sure of.

CHAPTER 19

HERE BE DRAGONS

here be dragons /heer bee dra gunz/ *archaic phrase* **1** on ancient maps, signifying a region of great peril for the explorer. "Dragons" was a comprehensive term for dangers, imagined and real. (*See entry for* **dragons.**)

—From the *Cyc.L.O.W.Ps.*

The bumpy secondary highway unreels beneath my wheels.

It's June 7, and the aspens lining the road are leafed out, their teardrop leaves an electric green. At 8 AM in Northern Alberta the sun's been up for four hours, but the air carries the cool memory of the brief night.

Brad Remenda, my training partner from Juventus, and I whirr down a modest grade. I relax, breathing in the sweet air. A capable feeling, like a boxer who feels the weight of the muscles, but no effort in moving them, fills my limbs. The Olympics is a distant land, too far away to overshadow this peaceful morning. The countryside, a patchwork of hay fields, and aspen stands, waits for the sun, wind and rain to do their work. The daisies by the roadside nod at me, and wild roses, a tentative magenta, dot the deep green brambles.

For a moment, the photographer in me says, "Take a picture of this beauty." However, I'm on a training ride, not a tour.

Later that day I cart my 2004 World Championship bronze medal to work. My colleagues exclaim, and hold it carefully. For them it's a novelty, but a bronze medal is a sight I've seen before. It's been two years since the rocket blew, and I've clawed my way back to the World's podium. This may be my last medal, and the moment is one that makes my eyes burn.

The days stretch out, and the sun burns above the horizon from 4 AM to nearly 11 PM. The grass climbs to the sky and ants scurry in the green profusion. On June 9, after cutting my grass, and dousing the anthills with a home-brewed potion, I sit on my back step, and ponder the contrasts in my life. One day, I'm racing to be the fastest woman in the world, and the next I'm exterminating ants.

It's good to have an ordinary life: work, house, and friends. However, in ten weeks the Athens Olympic Games will be finished, and so will the seventeen-year odyssey, a span of half my life. I rise, my perennially tired legs complaining as I head in the back door. What's on the schedule for tomorrow?

It's a question I ask to distract me from the obvious question: is there a life after this one? In ten weeks my extraordinary, competitive life will be over: No more World Championships. No more travel. No more heart-busting workouts. No more insanely confident feeling as I tear around the track, chasing the motorbike.

"Go to sleep, Muenzer." I say, and ignore these thoughts. Morning is only eight hours away, and in the next few weeks there will be little time for sleep.

The days follow, and the diary records, in neat blue script, an increase in media attention: two interviews with CBC and one with the print media. Why, I wonder, are they paying attention? It's an ordinary season, and I've got ordinary problems.

For example, I have, (like most Canadians), equipment that is wearing out, and a full set of plans, but a half-empty wallet. My tires are bald, and my five-spoke front wheel has a hole, plus I have major travel expenses looming. Two races in Victoria and three weeks later I'll fly to Hyeres, France, for Steen's final pre-Olympic camp. Only one Victoria race is sponsored by the National Team, and the COA provided only half my Olympic prep budget.

I can't skimp. These events, in the six weeks prior to the Olympics, are critical to maintain my physical and mental abilities. Although the press is excited about my chances in Athens, sponsors are not. Two likely prospects have just turned me down. The Investors Group and the Dairy Council were sponsoring athletes who were dedicated to their sport and the community. With my many years of speaking to schools and World Championship results, I figured I would qualify. I figured wrong.

The problems are like dragons. Pressure, lack of money, old equipment, no official support, travel screw-ups—these were the ordinary dragons. On track there were all the others, the extraordinary ones. Steen had promised that what had happened in Melbourne would carry over to the Olympics. All I have to do is get there healthy and happy.

Even Field Law has turned down a sponsorship request. It's too much. I sit at my computer and smack the keys, tapping out a one-page make-or-break memo. I'll either get the sponsorship or lose my job. The memo goes to the partners. I wait, half expecting to be fired. One week later there is still no answer. How am I going to pay for the camps?

A chance meeting with Bob Waterman, the chief financial officer of Field Law, occurs.

"What's going on?" I ask.

"Haven't you checked your e-mail?" he says.

My mouth opens, but no sound emerges. I race to my desk, and open up my e-mail. I nearly fall out of my chair. Field Law has come through. Relief and gratitude turn me into a noodle. One day torture, and the next the golden apples.

At least the training is going well. Steen's been focussing on motor-pacing, and I'm feeling the speed sense revive. I don't ask how fast I'm going. I don't have to. I don't want to.

All I need is the pressure of my expectations and the public's to set me up for another heartbreak like the one in 2002. I just want to ride. Fast. The seventh sense tells me that I'm going like a rocket. My sixth sense tells me to watch out for dragons. Dragons are for slaying, and something inside me wants to kill them—all of them—before I'm done.

Kill dragons? With pleasure. I wonder, for a second, what kind of person loves to cut the lawn and slay dragons.

The Juan de Fuca Velodrome, in Victoria, British Columbia, is set amidst the pines and rock hummocks that characterize the south end of Vancouver Island. On a clear day the white volcanic mountains of Washington's Olympic Peninsula are visible across the Strait of Juan de Fuca. It's an exotic setting and when I arrive on July 9, I feel charged with a zeal that's bursting to be released.

Dragons, watch out.

I ride the 200-metre qualifier for the men's sprints. I'm third, and smash Dubnicoff's 1994 games record. In the 500-metre I best Aussie rider Michelle Ferris's 1998 record. Also, I take the one-lap record from my old friend, Jennie Reed.

The men are not immune either. I'm allowed to ride with them in the sprints, and end up in a six-up race for fourth place. As I walk my bike to the line, I pass one of my competitors, a young man, all of nineteen years. He grins and says, "Let's go, Grandma."

A thin smile appears and vanishes. It never pays to tip off your victims.

Tanya Dubnicoff is here as a coach. She and other spectators gather round me. "Watch this," I say, and fill them in on my plan. We line up, and I'm in the top position, hugging the rail. When the whistle blows, I accelerate like it's the start of the 500-metre. The men hesitate. "You chase her," they say to one another.

I chop down the bank, and surge to top speed. The crowd is on its feet, and their roar is like a wave chasing me down the track. I hit the finish line forty metres ahead of the first man. I roll around the infield, letting my burning legs cool down. I pass the nineteen-year-old. He's not looking at me. Can't blame him—Grandma just gave him a hiding.

For the balance of July, my seventh sense is flaring like a blowtorch. During training on July 17, Steen and I are practising our jumps. I dive off the banking, and glance over my shoulder, expecting to see Steen storm past me. He doesn't. We finish the workout behind the motor, and this time I learn my actual speed. Suffice to say, if I had been on city roads, the police would have taken my license away.

The Nationals are taking place in Victoria, in the middle of my peak training cycle before the Olympics. Unfortunately, the CCA is insisting I ride. The Championships, starting on August 4, are like a lumpy rock island sucking my boat into a reef. Something may be salvaged from this, I hope, and plan to ask the CCA if I can ride against the men.

In Victoria, the local organizers agree, but the CCA executives shake their heads.

I win all my events, and Steen wins the One-Kilometre Time Trial Championship. After the racing we have only an hour to pack for the flight to Edmonton. A twelve-hour stopover, and we're on our way to Hyeres. The medal ceremonies will take place when I'm in the air to Edmonton.

"Please move up the medal ceremonies," I ask the CCA officials.

"Nope."

"The local organizers are okay with it," I say, "I'd like to receive my Championship jersey and medals now. I've got to get onto a plane."

They bend their heads together, and whisper among themselves. A moment later, the announcement: "Nope."

I'm disappointed, but not surprised.

"Come on, Lori-Ann," says Steen.

The locals had made me a poster, wishing me good luck in Athens, and had hung it in the stands. The poster is pressed into my hands. Steen and I, looking like overloaded porters, trundle to the exit. Still, this could be my last Championships, and I'm reluctant to leave. I pause at the threshold and take one last glimpse at the velodrome.

An announcement startles me. I take a closer look. The stands are blotted out by the spectators: they're standing, clapping, and cheering me. No official pat on the back could inspire me as much as the standing ovation. I wave, feeling as though another dragon has bit the dust.

Fourteen hours later, I'm on the plane to France. Steen and his wife Cyndi are travelling with me. Steen had wanted a camp in the south of France. Two weeks ago he said, "Make it an outdoor 250-metre track, and make it hot. Outdoor track wood is weathered. It will be the same in Athens."

Picasso has spoken again. Fine. I know just the velodrome: one complete with a dragon.

I made the arrangements, in my rusty French, with the velodrome director, Monsieur Garnier. He has assured me that everything will be in order.

We're going to Hyeres.

Ten years ago I left Hyeres with a broken heart and shattered knees. It took me a year and a half to recover. The little dragons, the ordinary ones, are behind me now. The big ones, the ones that nearly killed my career, are waiting on the other side of the ocean. I left them there ten years ago, and I've decided to return for a showdown. What kind of person, after everything I've been through in seventeen years, would seek out the setting of a humiliating defeat?

And what do the media expect? A gold medal—the interviews made that clear. I humour them, saying I'm shooting for the gold, but inside I know I'm gunning for a medal—any medal. More than that will set me up for another soul-twisting finale.

What of the CCA? Do I have their unqualified support? There is an error on the official results sheet for the Canadian National Championship 200-metre qualifying ride. According to it, the rider with bib number one—the first-place finisher—is "*unknown.*" I'm the National Champion, and the only Canadian track rider to qualify for the Olympics, but my association doesn't know who I am. Neither do I.

I'm on the edge of the seat, staring out the window like so many times before and wondering what am I doing—sailing out into the void? Why have I picked Hyeres? Must I slay this dragon too?

I stretch out my perennially sore legs. There's no time to wonder why my life has attracted these beasts. A relationship between ambition and adversity? I shake my head. It would take a book to come up with an answer.

It's a hard climb through groves of cypress.

It's just as I remembered. The road to the Velodrome Hyeres Toulon-Var is a heart-thumping, height-grabbing hike. Daniel Morelon, local resident and multi-time World Sprint Champion, has lent Steen his road bike.

We climb, silently, past hay fields and the houses lining the flanks of the mountains along the coast of southern France. The road winds up the mountain, and the track, surrounded by cypress, nestles on a rocky ledge, perched like a balcony overlooking the Mediterranean.

I push my bike onto the apron, and tap the wood of the track, a hardwood imported from Cameroon. The wood is a deep walnut brown, as hard as teak, and offers no resistance to my high-pressure tires.

For a moment I pause and gaze around the deserted track. Nineteen ninety-four seems like another country, a place where a younger, vulnerable Lori-Ann was beaten on the anvil of international competition. Now, the bad memories are like thin ghosts, and in the idyllic setting, I sense that there will be a reckoning. This time, *I* plan to be the hammer.

My helmet is strapped on, and the memories are left behind. Today, August 10, is a day to practice my neck turns, the swivel joint a track rider needs to be able to ride forward, but look back at one's opponent. On the track, Steen and I spar lightly like cautious boxers before a big bout.

The next day is a rest day. Yet my mind is awhirl with remembrances of past events, and anxiety about life after the Olympics: my mind is whirling with these thoughts. Steen senses my distraction, and suspects my competitive instincts are blunted. He has me review a video of the Manchester World Cup. I replay, in my mind's eye, the race I should have ridden. Tactics have always been my weakness. The next day proves it.

"You were napping," says Steen. We're rolling around the apron. Steen rode me up, down, fast and slow, making Kerrie Meares' Commonwealth Games rodeo ride seem like a folk dance.

"Sorry," I say.

"Don't be sorry," he says, "just don't fall asleep."

I stare at my handlebars.

"Know at *all* times," he says, "where your opponent is."

"I was watching."

"You were daydreaming."

Now he's pointing, going on a bona fide El Toro rant.

"And another thing: watch for your opponent pushing you—the speed will increase. Don't let them push you."

I start to explain. He cuts me off.

"If you're behind, your jump has to be explosive, not like it was today."

"But..."

"Never hesitate when passing on the bank—never give up the attack."

"I didn't."

He shakes his head like a father whose child has brought home a poor report card. "You gave up," he says.

It's true. The worst dragon, I think, is the one inside.

"Fight it," he says, and points at me. "All the way to the line."

"I..."

"All the way."

Our bikes are coasting. The tires make a low hissing on the apron. Steen looks ahead, his voice is unfocussed, as though speaking to himself:

"Lori-Ann, everything you've worked for in the past ten years comes down to three laps. Give it your all."

"Okay," I say, and look at him.

Okay is a thin word, incapable of communicating how much I wanted to do well for Steen, to somehow repay what could never be fully paid. Okay? Okay.[1]

Post-Olympus Footnote: Confidential Commentary by Steen Madsen

1. I warned her.

"Here, in this corner," I said before we started the match, "You'll get your ass kicked."

"Oookay," she says, and lolls on her bike. Even though I warned her, she was too stupefied, too complacent to respond. Lori-Ann was not in the mood for sprinting. Most unfortunate.

Mood is for cattle, lovers, or choosing what CD to play. It is not for match sprinting, so I kicked her butt. Several times. I used my body to block, biff, and side-swipe her. The finale was spearing her with my helmet. I put her through another 2002 Commonwealth Games Roller Derby ride.

"Lori-Ann," I say when we finished, and were rolling on the apron. "You lost because you made some errors."

"Yes, Steen," she says, staring at her pedals.

"Worse than that, you didn't win before you got on the bike."

"Huh?"

"Walk onto the track like you're a winner. Do the warm-up confidently, lace up your shoes, get onto the bike, and then boom, flick the switch."

Her head slumped further. "Okay".

"You weren't willing to race. People are willing to die to win this race. They are willing to crash, knock you out, and break bones."

"Okay."

Could she understand the lesson? Yes. Did she have the courage to see her faults? Yes. Could she put it all together in Athens?

Tomorrow, Cyndi and I would head home. Lori-Ann would be on her own. The last question, the final answer, would be up to her. It would take only one of those unexpected and isolating events to throw Lori-Ann off.

And there would be nothing I could do about it.

There was no money for the Canadian Team to have her coach in Athens. When I left her in Paris, cheeks glistening with tears, I wondered if she could tough it out. I knew from past experience not to count on help from anyone. At least Bell Communications had spotted us a cell phone. I had a feeling it was going to get a workout.

Ten years ago, a roasting like that would have crushed me.

But ten years is a cyclist's lifetime. Instead of cringing I resolved to put paid to another dragon—the sleepy-eyed dragon of carelessness and mediocrity. After the lecture is over, Steen broods, knowing that soon he will be a mere spectator. I know how badly he wanted to be at these games. The crash last year robbed him of that chance, and he's at Hyeres only because of me.

I carry part of him when I head to the Olympics.

The value of this camp appears the next day when Steen mounts the motorbike, and begins the rubber band drill. Steen roars out of turn two with me in pursuit. He guns it—opens a gap, stretching the imaginary rubber band that joins us—and I drop down the bank and try to snap back to the motor.

The drill comes at the end of a three-hour session. My seventh sense is flaring, and there is no escape for the bike.

After the warm down, Steen is waiting, his helmet on his lap, sitting on the motor.

"Maybe seventy-nine," he says.

"Huh?"

"That's how fast."

I nod, and wipe the sweat out of my eyes. "Is that good?"

He doesn't comment, save to send me home. [2]

The wheel of my track career has come full circle. The only thing familiar about the Hyeres track as I pack my gear and swing my leg over my road bike is the face of the director, M. Garnier. He's been ill, but has left the hospital to see me off. I'm touched that a near stranger has risked his comfort to wish me well. Steen and I thank him for the use of the track. As I fly down the hill, my bike tires singing, I'm thinking about the dragon of isolation and loneliness that sent me packing ten years ago. Today, I know the dragon is cast aside on the track, mortally wounded while my wheels sped on the sun-torched wood of the track.

Post-Olympus Footnote: Confidential Commentary by Steen Madsen

2. This day I knew.

The speed! I had never seen anything like it. After all the years, all the gut-wrenching, muscle-shredding effort, after all the oxygen debt, and exhaustion, not to mention the personal cost, she had been transformed. Lori-Ann was not just strong. Not just tactically smart. She was a fully formed sprinter, a competitive machine constructed with one purpose and one purpose only—to unleash a storm of speed, to win, and win big. In other words, I thought as I put the motorcycle away, if she could just get to the games without any last-minute insults, humiliations, or snubs, she was going to be an Olympic medallist.

Of course I didn't tell her. She had enough to worry about.

CHAPTER 20

ATHENA

archetype /ark uh typ/ *n.* **1** for cyclists, as much an entity to become, as to be.

athena /a thee na/ *proper noun.* **1** goddess (Greek) of war, wisdom, justice and skill, who would never accept defeat or injustice. The champion of those on an odyssey. **2** Athens is her city, Mount Olympus her home. **3** an archetype. Most riders are unaware of them. Others become them. **4** speaker of an obscure language, the language of Champions.

—From the *Cyc.L.O.W.Ps.*

Could it be?

The 2004 Athens Olympics are the biggest in modern history. Hundreds of millions of people around the globe will tune in, log on, or attend. Yet, as I set out my gear in my room in the Athletes' Village, I feel the tranquillity of a homecoming.

I remember the welcoming hug from the first person to meet me at the village gate: Anna Meares.

For now, the other athletes in my unit are at their events. The house is quiet, and I can focus on my job: ride the bike and kill the dragons.

The first order of business, though, is to find the most important features in any athlete's village: laundry, food, and Internet.

The second order of business takes place the next morning. At 8 AM Eric Van den Eynde drives me to the velodrome. It's a pleasant trip. Gone is the harried apprentice, head bowed with anxiety, and mind blinded by self-consciousness. I walk into the Athens velodrome and stop on the threshold.

The lens in my mind is open and the lens cap is off.

I'm scanning the velodrome. It's not indoor or outdoor. It's got a roof, but the sides are open, the better to admit the breeze. Banners and flags hang over the open sides. Like a theatre prior to a performance, there are no spectators; only workers and the actors—the athletes—in warm-up clothes, fidgeting and fussing.

My trip to the pits like a return to a stage. The other players in the show—Desmond, Jennie Reed, and the other athletes—look up from their tasks and greet me. I have a good feeling, like an actor who knows her lines. It's hard not to let on that I'm charged with a newfound strength.

I meander to the track and examine the bank angle. The wisdom of Steen's choice is apparent: the track configuration is near identical to the Hyeres velodrome. Also, Hyeres has similar weather. In fact, during the course of the games, the notorious Athens summer heat never matches the scorching temperatures of Cote D'Azure, Hyeres.

The first workout and the times kept by the Canadian team staff confirm two things: the track is fast and so am I.

At the village there's no rushing to find food, lodging, physio, or chiro. The relaxed setting is one reason to remember this village, but I have other reasons for imprinting this place on my mind. Possibly, this is my last race.

Every time I dare to imagine the possibilities, a wave of emotions threatens to sweep over me. I have to stop, close my eyes, and concentrate on a simple task.

"It's just another race," I say at the track, on the ride home, and in my room. "It's just another ride." I repeat my mantra while the wave flexes over my head. The work Steen and I have done allows me to believe that I can make it happen. I hold back the wave, and enjoy the games. The wave is not obscured; it's just not a factor—yet.

I wander throughout the village, greeting other athletes, and booking appointments for chiro, massage, and physio. Usually, the night before serious training I'm tense, pushing to make all the preparations. Tomorrow, August 18, I've got a two-hour workout, and need only one person to time me. What's to worry about?

My tortuous history—the hooks thrown at me on and off the track—had proven that ambition attracts adversity like cat hair to a black wool suit. Life is complex, and the more you push the boundaries of the bell curve—fighting against the averages—the greater the forces pushing back. Life is a gamble and the odds favour the casino.

Finally, after seventeen years, everything was happening the way it was supposed to. Who says the house always wins?

August 18, 2004, 7:00 AM, Olympic Village, Meeting with Team Officials

"Just one person."

I'm pleading for help.

"I need one person to time me," I say. "Steen can't be here, and he needs to know my times."

"Sorry," says the Canadian team representative. He checks his watch.

"I only have a two-hour block on the track—11 AM to 1 PM."

"That's when we're going to the road time trial," says the official.

"*All* of you?"

He shrugs.

"I'm on my own?"

There's no answer. I'm the only Canadian to qualify for the track, and no one will help me.

"We've got to go," he says, and waves to his ride.

"Please," I say, hoping for just one person to help.

Nothing changes.[1]

Post-Olympus Footnote: Confidential Commentary by Steen Madsen

1. I knew this would happen. It always happens.

This year, Lori-Ann is the *entire* Canadian Olympic track team. She travels with five bags weighing hundreds of pounds. In spite of this, no one met her at the Athens airport.

What happened this day was more of the same. In fact, I planned on it. Past experience told us that she would be abandoned. Prepared or not, it's still an insult, and can throw an athlete's psyche into a tailspin. Developments like this were not making my gamble any easier.

August 18, 2004, 11:00 AM Athens Olympic Velodrome, Velodrome Track Apron

According to my watch, it's 11:02 AM. Good thing I'm a creature of habit. Seventeen years of training take over, and I realize that recycling the hurt won't get this workout done. I lift the bike onto the track. It seems to weigh 100 pounds. The other teams, support staff bustling and teammates chattering to each other, are busy, energized.

I fasten my helmet. The muscles in my jaw tighten and I push my bike, dawdling like a kid already late for school, afraid to meet the principal. My legs are like a doll's stiff limbs.

How long did I stand there?

A familiar face from the past appears.

"Hi, Desmond," I say, and wave at my old coach. He gives me a face-splitting smile.

"Lori-Ann?" Now, it's Martin Barras, the Aussie coach. We greet one another.

"If there's anything you need," he says, "just ask."

"Martin, can you time me?" The words are automatic, and seem to come from outside me.

"No problem."

I roll out onto the track, and see the Aussie and American men whiz by. By the next lap I'm on the train, and spinning away. The speed of the *train*, a pace line in track terminology, is perfect. We circle the track, each half lap the leader pulling up, and dropping onto the back of the train. The familiar payoff—the feeling of flight and freedom—returns. We're minding each other's space, but sharing it too, making adjustments so fine that a track-side observer would think the riders chained to one another.

Like a train approaching a terminus, the line slows, and I coast on the apron.

In spite of my disillusionment, I remember to look around, to soak up the setting. The big-screen scoreboard at the end of the track is playing a video about previous Olympic Champions. My neck is straining as I look over my shoulder at the screen. These were athletes who fought, struggled, and forged their way to these games. No one had it given to them. They sacrificed everything for their ambitions and made it happen. These past champions were athletes like...me.

So what? They are what. I am what. We are what.

My head slumps, and I feel a burning in the corners of my eyes. This is not just a track. This is not just a velodrome. This is where I belong. Ambitions bring adversity, but I will not be defeated.

Damn you, wherever dragons be. I will *not* be cheated.

The hairs on my arms are tingling. I feel an inner being wake, and its hot blood flow. This beast refuses to go quietly. Go quietly? Only if I'm killed first.

I faced the dragon of Hyeres, and I'll face the dragon of indifference, too. I'll not slump around in the village like a Mr. Snuffleofagus. I want to make Steen proud of me. The weathervane has turned for the last time.

The only question is: how can I beat this system?

Martin is standing by the track. Martin, the coach of my rivals. Martin, the man paid to defeat me. Martin, my helper.

"Ready?" he says.

"Ready."

I not just survived this spiritual crisis, but gained an unexplainable benefit: my eyesight improved. As I sped over the boards, I could see everything in a sharper focus. The lens of my mind and my eyes had been jolted into a new capability.

Later in the evening I call Steen. (After the games, I'll check my phone bills. They record eighteen hours Steen spent coaching me by cell phone from Edmonton.)

"I can't believe it," he says. "What were they doing leaving you alone?"

"I don't know."

"They all went to the time trial?"

"Everyone."

"The rules say only one of them could help," says Steen. "What a waste. Did someone time you?"

"Martin."[2]

He snorts. My chief rival's coach got a first-hand chance to read my form. I tell Steen the times, and describe the workout.

"How do you feel?" he says, after noting my observations.

"Good."

"Really?"

"This place is so cool," I say. "I'm glad to be here."

"Sure?"

"I knew if I got through today, that I'd be all right. I was looking around like you told me to. There was this video."

"Video?"

"An Olympic history. It helped me to get through."

I don't mention the strange improvement to my eyesight that also occurred today. I say, "You got me to a new level at Hyeres. I beat the demons there. I'll beat them here too."

Another silence.

I say, "That's good, but there's more."

"Okay," says Steen.

"It's like something is waiting."

"Eh?"

"I don't really know, but I'm not sure I can hold it together." I am fumbling, stumbling with my words, trying to express what I am feeling. "Sometimes I feel like it's all going to crush me."

There's another pause. It's evening here, and morning in Edmonton. Have I called him too early in the day?

"Lori-Ann?" He sounds awake.

"Yes."

"It's just another race."

Post-Olympus Footnote: Confidential Commentary by Steen Madsen

2. This day she was really cross. Her abandonment had the potential to hurt, but she had the strength of character to turn it around. There was no way anyone was going to cheat her of her run at a medal. She rebuilt her confidence. Of course, baseless confidence has killed more people than roller skates left on driveways.

Yet, the times Martin recorded told me that there was a foundation to her belief and mine. I felt like a gambler at the horse track who sees his steed surging to the front. After she rode the 500-metre, I felt like the horse had rounded the last turn and was on the inside, pushing to the front. Still, there was plenty of time to step on a stray roller skate.

I've killed every dragon thus far. "Trust yourself, and fight," I think. It's something I've been believing in since the Sydney World Cup in May. As I stroll to my room, I remember this morning: I left the village feeling like a kid whose friends had abandoned her for a new school. Now I'm coming home knowing a couple of them were still with me.

The thought of home reminds me to call Mom and Dad. "We love you, and you're doing a good job," they say. Their validation boosts my spirits, and I feel like the latest dragon is thrashing around in a Hollywood imitation of the last gasp.

Encouragement continues.

After the next day's workout, I walk to the velodrome bike lockers. The walk is interrupted by other riders and team staff wishing me well. En route, Mark Connolly of CBC TV collars me. He has Canadian Olympic speed skating gold medallist Catriona LeMay Doan and Curt Harnett in tow. Connolly wants us to pretend it's a chance encounter. It's an honour to be in their presence, and I'm nervous, but play along like an improv actor. It helps me stay loose.

But there's more to it. After, LeMay Doan and I discuss the mental aspect of competition. She says that during an event, she has hypersensitive sight and hearing. Every noise and sight floods over her.

"Not me," I say, and tell her that I develop a sensory tunnel: I'm aware of only me and my opponent.

She is tiny, much more so than the image of her plastered on her sponsors' moving vans. Yet, LeMay Doan has the presence of a giant. She and I are quietly trading our thoughts and observations about sport. Before we part, she says, "You deserve to be here."

It's the last blow for the sneering dragon of indifference. *Hissss*, goes her dying breath.

Just in time too. Tomorrow, August 20, is the 500-metre race.

I feel like a panther, ready for some exercise. "What about a 500-metre race?" I ask myself. "Just for a little appetizer."

During the warm-up, my seventh sense tells me, "You're ready." My legs are crackling with energy. "Steen, Steen, Steen," I chuckle to myself, knowing this was the result he intended.

As I'm called to the line, the notes I reviewed the night before play out in my mind. I grip the handlebars, and start the countdown:

"Fifteen seconds to go, hands into locked position, arms cocked, strong, looking at clock until five seconds," say the notes.

"Four seconds, three seconds, slide back, two seconds, one second, Blast out! Look down black line, and hammer the Beast..."

The notes and the ride meld, merge, and I'm feeling the air rip at my skinsuit as I bore into turn one. Out of the turn I'm leaping down the line, repeating Steen's dicta: "Smoothness is control. Control is speed. Speed is power."

And, speed is fun. Mind-blasting, mind-roasting fun.

I thrust my bike over the line, and look up at the results board. It's my best time ever—34.628 seconds and a Canadian record. Even so, the time puts me in seventh place. Meares wins in an Olympic and World record time. The four spots from fourth to seventh are separated by .3 seconds. Pendleton, sixth, is .003 seconds ahead. This is the most competitive field I've ever seen.

The line up for the doping control, mandatory for the medallists and also for me—the random choice—is a chance for me to congratulate Meares. She's vibrating with happiness, and lets me hold her gold medal. I'm so proud of her that she's smashed two records in one ride. Today is her day, and I'm pleased for her.

As I hold the medal, a Canadian Team official recoils in horror.

"Don't," he says, and pushes forward.

I step back, wondering if I've broken a rule.

"You'll jinx your ride in the sprints," he says, and looks at me as though I've burped in church.

Meares and I shrug, and I continue to admire her medal.

Later, I call Steen, and read him the split times of the other riders. Picasso needs the information to finish his painting. If Steen says, "Worry," then I'll worry. But he doesn't. He says, "Stay on the plan."[3]

Post-Olympus Footnote: Confidential Commentary by Steen Madsen

3. Her result in the 500-metre told me everything I wanted to know: she was on form for a medal, hence, "Stay on plan." However, results in major events are determined by an athlete's ability to manage the mental aspect. She was living, breathing and acting like a winner, but the tournament was three days long. Lori-Ann had never sustained the prize-fighter attitude for two days straight, let alone three. It takes tremendous energy to sustain this level of rabid determination. Sooner or later she would crack.

It was the same for the other contenders, though. The question would be, who could recuperate in time for the next round?

August 22, 7:00 AM, Athletes' Village, Medal (M)-minus Sixty-one Hours

I continue the fiction that it's just another day.

Breakfast, a call to Steen, laundry, and then answering e-mails. Eric drives me to the track, and I ponder the decision to use disk wheels front and back. The wind has been up, and a front disk wheel can be like a sail leading you off course. Inside the velodrome, it's dead calm, so I put on both disks, and prepare for the 200-metre qualifying ride. We are starting in reverse order of the World Championships. Therefore, I'm third last to go.

I ride well, and place fourth.

I can tell, during the post-ride interview with CBC, that I'm not fully peaked, but a pattern is coming clear. I've climbed from seventh in the 500-metre to this morning's fourth place. "Steen," I say to myself, "this smacks of one of your plans. Don't peak me for the Worlds, don't peak me for the 500-metre. By a process of elimination, this means...?"

I'm in an ideal position. The early ride will not be too taxing, yet not too easy. Meares, Natalia Tsylinskaya, and Tamara Abassova qualified ahead of me, but I'm not surprised. They've been in the top three for months. On the other hand, I can read the stares my competitors are giving me. The looks say, "Where did she come from?"

The one eighth final is at 4:30 PM, so it's back to the village, and writing out key words for this afternoon's race:

"Race it as if it's the FINAL...watch out for Jennie."

And, as I sit on my bed, I pen the final statements: "How bad do you want it? I have everything to gain. My legs are there...Enjoy the PEAK WEEK."

I review my plan and nap. As I drift off, the warm breeze coursing into my windows, I think, "Keep track of Jennie...she can be unpredictable."

Olympic Velodrome, 4:30 PM, M-minus Fifty-one Hours

I'm leading, watching over my left shoulder, keeping watch on Reed. No sign of affection between us now. We both want what only one can have. Second lap, I'm still watching, using my new-found visual ability to track her as she shuttles up and down the bank. Approaching the turn, an old habit overtakes me: I glance forward.

It's all she needs.

Sssss, go the smooth tread of her tires on the wood, and I glance back at an empty space once occupied by Jennie Reed. Don't panic, I say, and latch onto her trail. "Wait, wait, wait," I murmur, as we rumble into the final lap.

The pitch of the bell changes as we pass. Turn two arrives, and I punch it. In the corner of my eye, I can sense Reed springing out of the saddle, hunched over the bars, head jiggling and tossing. Then she's gone, and I fight it to the line.

The win puts me into the quarters.

Before I'm off the bike, I'm predicting what Steen will say. Later that night he says it:

"Why didn't you have your eye on her?"

"I..."

"You didn't you know where she was."

"I did, but..."

"Your head turned," says Steen.

"For just..."

"Boom, she was gone and you lost control of the race."

"I didn't panic," I say, and hold the phone away from my head. Steen's voice is jabbing out of the tiny phone speaker.

"You can't lose sight again. You can't daydream," he says.

"I know."

"That's not good enough. Who are you up against in the quarters?"

"Larreal, from Venezuela."

"You let *her* get away, and there's no catching her. You know her time in the last 100."

The info I've passed on to Steen confirms that over the last 100 metres, Larreal and I are even. She has the reckless Latin American rider attitude: do what it takes to win. I beat her in the quarters at the Worlds, but it wasn't an easy ride.

"Lori-Ann?"

"Yes."

"Seventeen years, and all those miles. It's all coming down to three laps."

"I know," I say.

"Remember, it's just another race."

It's the strange dichotomy I've been living with for days.

After the call, I have a massage and fall into bed. There will be no socializing, no sightseeing. I'm here for one thing only.

Dragon killing, maybe a medal.

August 23, Athletes' Village, 8:30 AM, M-minus Thirty-two Hours.

I'm back in bed after doing rollers, mental prep and stretching. The quarter-final is at 4:30 PM. The day stretches on, a pleasant routine of logging onto the Net, answering e-mails, and buying stamps for post-cards. By 2:00 PM I'm collecting my gear and heading to the track.

Olympic Velodrome, 4:00 AM, M-minus Twenty-four Hours

"What a fantastic job to have," I say to myself as I pump up my tires. The well-ridden Dugast tire, hand-sewn like a tailored suit, rests on my race wheel like a sack. *Whoosh, whoosh*, sighs the pump. The tire carcass stiffens and fills. I watch the pressure gauge settle on 220 pounds per square inch. Amazing—this tire weighs less than one third of a pound, yet it can support me and contain highly pressurized air. I put the wheel into its protective bag, designed to prevent nicks to its rock-hard sidewall.

Time to go. The once-empty track is clogged with riders fighting to warm up before the upcoming events. A few final jumps on the track, and I'll be ready for Larreal.

Boom! Tools fall to the concrete floor, and heads swivel. My ears are ringing. Whose tire exploded? Who's going down? A rider on a blown tire that's turned to Jell-o is destined to crash.
No one's fallen. Whose tire?

My tire.

I put my hands to my head. Why now? The Dugast, its supple, exquisite casing, had had enough. This tired tire had taken me through the 500-metre and the 200-metre, as well as World Cups and the World Championships.

Shards of shredded pink rubber and silk are plastered against the inside of the tire bag.

Jean, the French team mechanic trots over with a new five-spoke wheel. It's an immaculate creation of carbon fibre, with a pristine tire. Jean is a favourite of mine. I've brought him jugs of maple syrup, souvenirs of Canada, and he's worked on my bike, and lent Steen parts.

"*Merci*, M. Jean," I say, taking the hands away from my head.

"*Pas de problem*," he says.

His generosity is not just a sign of sporting ethics: it's a sign of acceptance. It's like being at home, and having your lawn mower break. Without even a call for help, your neighbour comes over and sets up a replacement. Plus, it's a Honda mower, too.

After the wheel change, I'm making final jumps—hard accelerations—that will awaken my legs for the race. It's a free-for-all of curving and carving riders, hurtling at over seventy kilometres per hour.

Back in the pits, I review my notes for Larreal. "Deliverance," the header of my notes say, "starts with attitude." Tire blown? Don't panic, let someone help. Pre-race nerves? Joke, stay loose. Today is just another day: another day where I know that I belong here, that I'm not just watching an Olympian, I *am* an Olympian.

The result is a level-headed clarity of thought that makes me eager for the race. I walk to the chairs at track side. Larreal and I have to draw numbers, scraps of paper laid face down on a board, to determine start order. The commissaire, grim faced, as though bringing a choice of weapons to a duellist, holds the board before me. I draw the paper up, glance at it, and raise an eyebrow.

He looks at me, the face says, "Pistols or swords?"

I hold the paper to my chest, and stare at him.

He blinks

I stare.

"Well?" he says.

"If I tell you," I say, squinting at him, "I'll have to...keel you."

The slip of paper decreed that I would lead. On this track, it's clear that the leader has the advantage. Today, I know, is going to be my day.

The commissaire blows the whistle, and I cruise out onto the banking. I'm sweeping across the bank, ensuring Larreal is on the tactical defensive. Second lap, and I'm mid-bank, controlling the race. I turn forward, an instinctive response to get my bearings.

Shh, shh, shh. It's the sound of someone's tires accelerating as they work their bike side to side. It's not coming from my bike.

Larreal chops down, a white-suited vulture plunging down the bank, and surges ahead of me.

No time to groan or curse. I latch onto her wheel, but keep some distance. I know that she will take me to the rail and beyond the instant my front wheel overlaps her rear wheel. "Patience, Muenzer, patience," I say, reacting more than thinking. We hit the bell lap, and enter the turn.

As my notes ordered, I smash the pedals and hammer around her. There will be no drag race; I must seize the lead and crush her. I've found my Steen-given speed, and my front wheel is whining as it tears through the air. A white blur in the corner of my eye tells me Larreal is unleashing her finishing kick.

The blur fades, and I'm speeding to the finish. The line sweeps beneath me.

I've won.

Steen? Hope you didn't see that one.

The second ride I'm following and stalking Larreal. She's carving and arcing across the track. Larreal's using the entire surface, denying my jump, making it clear that she's going to cut me off. Up, down, up, down.

She's following a pattern—just what I'm looking for. Up goes Larreal. Down I dive.

Larreal is vigilant, and stares at me over her left shoulder as she bores down, ready to hook me and head me into the apron.

And up I go, my right-hand climbing turn intersecting with her left-hand dive.

The hook's intended victim becomes hook victor. I'm using my size, and no one's seen this from me before. Larreal is startled, and hoists her handlebars up and back, straining against the pedals to avoid smashing into my rear wheel.

She's stopping... and I'm going.

I open a gap and make a false start of the sprint. Larreal takes the bait and guns it. I wait until she's overtaking and then put the hammer down, this time with feeling. She fades. I don't, and I've made it through the quarters.

I jump on the rollers to let the lactic spin out of my legs, and beam at the CBC crew that humps it across the infield to video me. I'm grinning and give them the thumbs-up.

"Steen?" I say to myself, "Is this loose enough?"

While I warm down, I watch the remaining races. Germany's Katrin Meinke has fought her way through the repechage and has a tough draw—she's riding against Meares. Meinke, a sophisticated and clever rider, has been struggling for the past year to come back. It's a fight I can relate to. Also, in 2000 she was among the first to congratulate me on my first World Championship medal.

Meares leads Meinke, and the score is 1–0 in the Aussie's favour. Meares is on the bank, watching over her shoulder like a barn owl with a swivel neck.

Meinke plummets down the track and zooms ahead of Meares. Meares follows, but Meinke's veering back up the bank, and Meares is on the defensive. It's a bold manoeuver. At one stroke—a chop—she has taken the initiative and the ride. Meinke forces the 2004 World Championship silver medallist to a third ride. Meares wins, but she's had a scare.

The move is etched in my mind. The eyes of the apprentice have been replaced, and I'm watching these races, like an eager graduate student, watching the dynamics of my upcoming opponents.

Back home, I watch the DVD that Steen made me from this year's Manchester World Cup. I'm playing it on my laptop, and trying to gauge the tactics of my opponents. The DVD is helpful, but nothing I saw matched Meinke's move this afternoon. Meares had the speed, but Meinke's chop was a tactic that spoke of control. It was *the* move of the games thus far.

"I'm feeling good," I say to Steen. It's the usual evening call. I'm lolling on my bed, letting Steen lecture me.

"You got caught again," he says. "Larreal almost took one from you."

"I pulled it back."

"That's not good enough," he says. "Tomorrow the racing starts."

"I've been racing for two days."

"The *real* racing," he says, "starts tomorrow."

"I let Larreal have it in the second ride. I can do it tomorrow too."

"Anna won't let you have any chances," he says. "If you're sleeping, you won't get a chance to let her *have* it." He drags "have," out like it's a long exhalation.

I pause.

"And neither will Martin," Steen says, "He'll play games. You watch."

"Okay."

"Lori-Ann, it's all about who wants it the most—who can fight it to the line."

"I want it."

"That's not enough. You have to put it together. There's no room for error."

"Okay."

"None."

"Right," I say, and sit up on the bed.

"Today was a dress rehearsal for tomorrow."

"I watched what happened today," I say, wanting the master to be impressed. "I thought I'd be up against the Russians in the semis, but

I'm up against Anna." I pause. We both know this is turning into a replay of the World Championships.

"I've done this before," I say. "I took a ride from Anna at the Worlds." Steen and I know she's taken more from me than I from her.

"I saw Katrin open the door," I say, and relate her masterful ride. "I want to go through it, Steen."

"You can do it Lori-Ann." The words are clear, certain, as though it's part of a formula. "But remember," he says, "It's just another race."

Before I sleep, I review, one more time, my notes about Meares. They say: "I beat her in Melbourne...how bad do I want it? Don't get caught napping. Gonna be rough. Scrap. Fight."

August 24, Athletes' Village, 7:00 AM, M-minus Nine Hours

At 7:00 AM, it's rollers, stretching, and then mental rehearsal. It's the mental part that I know I have to wrestle to the ground. My last ride against Larreal was the fastest ride of the quarters. A trail of dragon blood has followed me to Athens. I'm ready for more, but know I have to keep a lid on my excitement. Solution?

I immerse myself in my daily routine. A trip to the laundry, chiro, and it's time for the track. The routine, the just-another-day-at-the-village sequence, has protected me from the pressure cooker of the games, a stress cook pot that can steam you to death.

Olympic Village, 3:00 PM, M-minus Three Hours

So many of my days had been extraordinary days, emotionally draining, but rewarding. Days when I had been tasked to the utmost by the demands of world-class competition. Yes, today was no exception.

As I watched Aussie Sean Eadie run Meares into the rail, I thought, "How nice of them to put on this dramatic reconstruction of the Muenzer versus Meares Meltdown in Manchester." Eadie and Meares performed a full-contact scrimmage. *Biff, bam, and swoosh,* they're flipping and flicking each other. Meares is demonstrating that she's sharpening her hooks.

For whom? Dirndl Girl? A mewling songstress cowering and biting her nails? Ha.

It's not for nothing that one of my notes for this match says: "Be prepared to BUMP."

Knock yourself out, kids. I have a warm-up to do.

I ready my bike and voyage onto the track.

Click...click...click. I'm riding, one eye on the track and one ear cocked to the rear quadrant, trying to identify the sound. A cardinal rule of cycling is to never ignore a strange sound. On a properly functioning bike each part moves without conflict. The only sound should be a soft hiss as the high-pressure tires skim over the wood planking. I stop and let the other riders whirr past me. I check the tires, the chain, and the cranks, the usual trouble spots.

Nothing. I shrug and shove off.

The sound is continuing, but not continual. I don't have a mechanic or a spare bike. Nor do I have more time, so I ignore the rule and launch into my last efforts—short sprints at over sixty kilometres per hour.

As I ride along the rail, preparing for my final sprint, I see my mom. For a moment my breathing stops and then as I approach, the face shifts and it's not her. I'm shaking my head, trying to refocus. The railing looms towards me, and I swerve.

"Pay attention, Muenzer," I say, and begin the last effort.

The bank is two storeys high, and I use its vertical drop to accelerate. My speed sense tells me we're going well over the target speed. The next bank is coming, everything is looking...

Kaboom! No wondering this time. It's my rear wheel. Again.

The shredded tire slaps and flaps. The back end squirms and fishtails. The bank is rushing towards me. I know the odds. A puncture on the straight? Probably make it. On the bank? Good luck.

I pray that no one's coming behind me, letting their speed from a big effort carry them into a slow-moving vehicle—me. A collision will be catastrophic. The tortured tire is whacking the frame. Damn, will this bike ever slow down?

Finally, the speed bleeds off. No one has creamed me. I let limp onto the apron and loosen my toe straps. My heart is thumping, and it's not from the physical effort.

"Scared the shit out of you, eh mate?"

It's Eadie. He's laughing as he coasts past me. He's a schoolteacher by profession, and one of the most profanely humorous riders on the planet. This time his joke is nearly accurate.

Eric helps me off the bike, and I walk to the pits.

Martin meets Eric and me. The Australian coach has a wheel in his hand. It's a new race wheel, with a fresh-out-of-the-box handmade Italian tire. He's offering it to me.

"Thanks," I say, marvelling at his kindness. The fact that I am due to race Martin's athlete, Meares, is not lost on me. Also, I see Jean, the French team mechanic; striding over. He, too, is standing by, a loaner wheel in hand. Once again, the generosity of my competitors is profoundly moving. It's acceptance that makes me never want to leave this place and this time. On the track they'll take me to the limit. Off the track?

I couldn't have better friends.

While Eric changes the wheel, I head to the washroom. En route, Daniel Morelon passes by. Morelon, a sprint legend, won two Olympic golds and eight World Championship titles.

"*Bonne chance*," he says, and nods.

"*Merci*," I say, and stand, dumbfounded, interrupting my quest for comfort. The legend actually recognized me. It's another sign that I've finally made it. Will this be like any other day, but the last of so many?

I don't like the sound of the phrase, but I have a race to ride.

Olympic Velodrome, 2:30 PM, Minus 1.5 Hours

"Sharp, and in control...don't get caught napping," say the notes. So what happened in the first ride against Anna Meares?

The draw dictates I lead. Meares is using the track, swerving and swooping, her course reminiscent of the Manchester 2002 debacle. I'm calm—too calm. I turn my head forward. It's a casual gesture, one the dopey dragon would approve of.

Quick as a barracuda, Meares is down the slope and leading. I try to overhaul her. We're side by side, charging for the line, and she drifts up to the edge of the red line. One more millimetre and she's literally over the line. Her right elbow comes out, and she fends me off. Close to the line, but clean. She's the winner, and I'm heading to the pits.

There are only five minutes between heats. Five minutes to flick the switch and wake up. I'm staring at the boards of the track, looking but not seeing.

What happened? I need to get the Muenster going, the same confident and capable beast that took Larreal. Steen's right, I will not get a
chance to let Meares have it. She'll take it first. She'll annihilate me.

Annihilate? That's the word she used in the interview forwarded by
my Edmonton housemate, Matthew Sweet. "She annihilated me,"
Meares had said of our ride in 2002. Again, a reference to the
Meltdown in Manchester. An innocent reference, or was it part of the
psych campaign that culminated in today's Meares and Eadie demoli-
tion derby?

Do they think I can be intimidated? Apparently, yes.

Katrin Meinke wanders by. She swats me on the backside, and
says, "Remember the move I made yesterday?" Meinke wags a finger
at me.

Time's nearly up. I hop on my road bike, and circle the small warm-
up track, the piranha tank we call it. I'm circling, facing the prospect of
another last-minute lapse extinguishing my roll. The prospect is a barb,
an abrasive thought that strikes the flint of my desire.

A spark, then a flicker. "They think you are beaten," I say to myself.

The flicker leads to a flame. "They think you're beaten before the
race starts."

The flame leads to a blaze. "Don't think about all the training, the
years and the miles. Stop thinking. Just take charge."

The blaze is crackling, flaring and roaring. Dammit, I want to win.
Defeat will not be permitted.

I slip off the bike, and walk to the deck area. I feel bigger, stronger,
and confident again.

Annihilate. I like that word.

I'm flexing my hands, clenching and reclenching.

Meares? This one is mine.

I follow, keeping my distance, and watching for Meares to look forward, for her vigilance to lapse, for a small crack in the doorway. I'm
following, trying to ride in her blind spot. I'm roaming the bank, up,
down, up, down, and rattling her chain. She's staying mid-bank, mini-
mizing the angle she has to cover. Finally, I'm up on the rail, my
potential energy at its peak.

Her head turns, not fully forward, but rotates, the profile changing
slightly.

Now.

I'm chopping down on the bank. She's seen the move, and she's plummeting down on me. I veer up the bank, and lean, bracing myself for a crash. It's legal; she's got room to avoid the crash—if she wants to. And she wants to.

Like Larreal, she pulls back, but cuts it close. She's thwarted, and I head for the pole line. A gap opens. We're given the bell. I sense her passing on the outside. I drift up the bank, taking Meares up. It throws her off, and I head into the final turn. I don't ease off.

The match is one all.

Now it's the photo finish, the one handed to me in Melbourne, that taunts me. I want to extinguish any chance of a World Championship replay. We redraw, and I'm given the lead.

"You're the biggest woman here," said Steen and Eric. "Use it. Get into their personal zone, and force them off their line. Control the pace." Their words are now mine. Their words, my notes, will be my actions.

We sit on the chairs, waiting for the signal to walk to the line. We're like two kids, pulled out of a schoolyard fight, sitting in the principal's office. No talking. No smiling. Just waiting. Someone's going to get it, and I know who.

The large screen above the scoreboard flickers, and for a moment my adrenaline-fused mind is distracted. It's the Olympic history video.

So what? To all of you who ever said, "So what?" This is what. I am what.

Don't ever stop me, don't anyone get in my way, or you will go *down*.

Barbaric? Uncivilized? Crazed? Only as much as needed.

I rise from my seat, and try to contain my heart. Can people see it pounding beneath my skinsuit? "Slow breaths," I say, and will the heart to stop its thumping. Take the heart rate down, Muenzer, and bring the Muenster out.

We walk to the line. There was only Meares and me. Nothing else existed. Nothing but control and confidence.

The ride is on, and I'm leading. The dopey dragon's lying on the side of the track, with the imprint of my riding shoe on her ample butt.

Meares is yo-yo-ing up and down the track—four moves to one of mine. She's frantic, trying to throw me off.

Go ahead, girl, but I'm in charge.

The bell is ringing, but I don't hear it. All the officials are standing, immobile, their mouths open, but no sound issuing forth. The stadium is full, but all I hear is the insistent voice in my head: watch her, don't lose track. She's on the move, leaving my field of vision, entering the blind spot.

My head turns, a mere nod to the rear quarter. Meares is leaning forward over her bike, like a jaguar leaping for its prey, except she's moving in slow motion, and I can see everything clearly—her helmet, the lines around her mouth as she strains on the bars. She's dropping and closing on me.

I'm waiting. Still watching.

Meares is like a locomotive, churning and burning.

She's moving to the pole.

I'm hung up, above the sprinter's line.

It's not indecision. It's not uncertainty.

It's my perch, and I'm dropping down now, settling like a boulder thumping to the ground, and shutting the door on her. She's got to come around, and the final sprint is on.

Meares is a fighter, and in the last turn she's charging around me. I can feel the air pushing off her, buffeting me as we reel in the last metres. The finish line, a black line on a white bar, sweeps beneath my wheels.

For a second, I could have been anywhere, any time, any one of a thousand races I'd won. Your guts are filled with lava, your muscles like iron ropes, your mind aflame with victory lust.

For a moment.

Edmonton, Sydney, LA, Ipoh, Bromont, Manchester, Burnaby, Antwerp...

Athens.

My shoulders are thrown back, my head rises, and I gulp huge lungfuls of air. I know what this means. My tactical ability had caught up with my strength. My ability to mobilize my potential had peaked.[4]

The last dragon is dead, and not a moment too soon. One day, one hour, one minute, twelve seconds later, and it would have been too late, the last chance fleeing forever.

Beside me is Meares, her eyes tired, dull with fatigue. I grasp her hand, and thrust it into the air, her hand raised with mine. To ride against a tough, determined competitor, but one who respects the rules and her opponents, is a privilege. I was as proud of her as I was of my own ride.

Eric is pleased, and he helps me off the bike. I've got one hour before the final—the gold medal final. The last dragon is dead, but the looming wave of possibilities is still poised overhead. On the one hand, I've fought a terrific battle, need to shuck off the too-tight skinsuit, and celebrate. On the other hand, I'll be up against Abassova, one of the fastest women on the planet. Careful, sophisticated, cat-like Abassova, the victor over reigning World Champion Grankovskaia.

It's all coming together, but fast—too fast. I can't afford a last-minute revival of the last dragon, the distractible, destructive one. I finish my warm down on the rollers, and give CBC the thumbs-up. A silver medal is not what I've slaved for. The notebook is pulled out, and I leave the velodrome. The noise inside was tremendous, and the cell-phone reception was poor. I need space, and I need help.

Call Steen. Get my bearings. Reassure the Muenster.

Post-Olympus Footnote: Confidential Commentary by Steen Madsen

4. We both knew that the round against Anna Meares was the critical event. I told her: "You win against Anna, and you're into the gold-medal round. You know what that means."

Lori-Ann's focus had lapsed in the first ride, but she recuperated. Every other athlete had their coach *there* to jolly them out of the Death Valley of low morale. I was thousands of miles away, and she had to fight her way out, unaided. All I could do was watch the big screen in the Rose and Crown (a pub in my law firm's office building). The noise was overwhelming. Everyone wanted to sling their arms around me.

I couldn't hear a thing.

Parking Lot of Olympic Velodrome, 3:20 PM, M-minus Forty Minutes

Where is he?

I check the number. It's right, but there's no answer.

I dial again. "The customer you have called is out of the service area, or is not available. Please try again," says the smug computer voice. Try again? What, after the gold-medal ride?

Jack, I'll call Jack. Jack will know.

The phone rings. Jack answers.

"Jack, it's Lori-Ann."

"Ha, ha, ha," he says. It sounds like he's in a bar.

"Jack, it's me."

"Who?" he says and starts chuckling again.

"Jack, it's Lori-Ann. Find Steen, call Steen."

"We're watching at the Rose and Crown pub."

"Jack, call Steen."

"Can't hear you..."

It's like a horror movie, where the about-to-be-massacred victim is on the phone, begging for help, and their friend thinks the call is a prank.

I hang up.

When in doubt, use reason.

I will my pressure-plagued brain to think. Steen, I remind myself, works with me at Field Law. Today, in Edmonton, it's a workday. In any law firm, there's one person who knows where everyone is.

I snap the phone open and dial.

"Connie," I say to our faithful receptionist. "It's Lori-Ann."

She's surprised, needless to say, to hear from me. "Everyone's at the Rose and Crown," she says. Connie is tickled by the irony.

"This is not the time to be funny," I say. "I need help. Find Steen. Tell him to get where I can call him."

"Okay."

"I've only got a few minutes."

"You're on your own, Muenzer," I say.

Eric, our Canadian team manager, has been steadfast, wise and helpful. But Steen and I have been on this journey for years, and it's his reassurance I crave.

Plan, I think, make a plan. You have to do it yourself. Even now, at the end of the line, it's still your journey. I focus on my notes for a ride against the Russian. Leading? Following? I calculate the best attack and make a plan.

A call. An answer.

"Lori-Ann?" Steen says.

"Steen, I've got a plan."

"You scared me. That first ride with Anna," he says, over the background street noise, "just about killed me. What were you doing?"

"Steen, I only have a minute."

"Okay"

"Here's my plan," I explain the strategy.

"Spot on," he says, and then relates what I really need to hear. "Everything we've worked for, everything we've sacrificed, comes down to three laps. All the plyos, all the roller training, all the weights, all the miles. Seventeen years. It all comes down to three laps."

"Right."

"Don't think that it's an Olympic ride."

"Okay," I say, and check my watch.

"It's just another race."[5]

Just another race, I say to myself. A mix of the ordinary and the extraordinary. It's just another race, and it's the Olympic final. So, too, is it a blend of the extraordinary (standing outside the venue talking on your cell phone to a coach a million miles away) and the uber-extraordinary— making it into the Olympic gold-medal final. All this could crush my confidence, and leave me a shaky, shaken rider. The wave could curl overtop, and squeeze me out in a banzai pipeline of stress. *Fooom!* Wipeout.

Some other time. Not today because after all, it's just another day and just another race: I've had plenty of those.

I walk into the velodrome and remember why I'm here. It is, as Steen says, just another ride. Two rides in fact. Not three. There will not be three rides; it's not part of the plan.

Post-Olympus Footnote: Confidential Commentary by Steen Madsen

5. Not only had Lori-Ann ridden out of the Death Valley of mental letdown, but she had cut through the post-ride excitement to construct a feasible plan for the gold-medal ride. Amazing.

Almost as amazing as standing in the entrance doors of an office tower, couriers and business people passing by, while you press a cell phone to your ear and coach someone on the gold-medal ride. Not just amazing, but surreal.

Olympic Velodrome, 3:46 PM, M-minus Fourteen Minutes.

The notes said that Abassova stays low, and relies on speed, not tactics.

The first ride is just like the book said. There's no posturing, no posing, or pretending. Abassova's leading, and I'm doing an Anna Meares, forcing the pace, keeping her wondering where I am. Coming out of the last turn into the bell lap, I drop like a vulture, overtake her, and overwhelm her.

Ride one—Muenzer.

The second ride, Abassova is following, and I'm staying low, but flicking up and down, letting her know that an attempt to overtake will be a ride into danger.

On the bell lap Abassova tries to lure me up. She's going where she's never gone before, and I don't take the bait. The bell clangs in my ears, and I'm only now looking forward. For the entire ride I knew where she was: behind me.

Her final 200-metre kick is good, but Steen has prepped me perfectly. I wind up the gear, the bike moving effortlessly. Again, there's no sound—nothing but me and the speed. I can see the lines between the boards, the finish line approaching, the whole scene is in hard-edged focus.

Abassova is left behind like a silent, stationary sentinel.

I fight it to the line, but when I hit the mark, I do two things: One, I raise my hand and point. It's a salute to me *and* to everyone who helped. The gesture is, "*We* are number one." Second, I smile. A big smile. A relieved smile.

I've come home, and I've got an Olympic gold medal.

Olympic Velodrome 4:00 PM, M-plus Three Minutes

Eric takes me off the bike. All through the match he's been a reliable, unflappable manager. I notice he's got tears in his eyes. So do I.[6]

I want to warm down, but the press rushes forward. The CBC interviewer holds the mike, and the thoughts tumble out, the images and remembrances blurring.

"How does it sound," he says, "Lori-Ann Muenzer, Olympic gold medallist?"

"It's so cool," I say, my eyes glistening, "it's the pot of gold at the end of the rainbow."

But it's about a lot more. I sweep the medallion—Brenda's medallion—to my lips. "I got so much inspiration from Brenda," I say, and explain how she helped, and how she died. "This is for Brenda, who isn't here." I hold the medallion out, to let Brenda know. "This is for you."

The interviewer is gazing at me. I think of my journey and everyone who helped fill the sails. The camera's still on, the crew is grinning. They want more? All right.

"It's been ten years, and five years with Steen Madsen, someone who was crazy enough to believe I would do it. It's because of Steen, Jack, Brenda..."

My voice trails off. I remember the dragons too—the different faces of my multi-faceted inner opponent.

"I put it together with all the tools Steen gave me. We're extremists, Steen and I, and we took it to the limit. At the camp at Hyeres, there were some demons I had to face. The camp was amazing—it was the race rehearsal for Athens—250 metres, hot, same time zone. It set everything up."

The interviewer is nodding. He wants more? No problem.

"Steen told me to take a look through your lens—open up your eyes."

He's still nodding. After so many superficial interviews, I've finally got someone's attention.

"Nothing," I say, "is impossible..."

I pause and remember. I see myself, naive and hopeful, walking into the TD Bank, seventeen years ago. I remember crashing in Cuba, Edmonton, and the near-death experience in Quito. I remember my grandmother, and Brenda's cheque in my boots. I remember my family's renewed love, and the family of athletes who voyaged with me. I remember Steen and his artistry. I remember so much, feel so much. The words have to be chosen like the right tactic: make them count, and make them win.

"It's up to *you* to decide what your limits are."

He nods, as though I've said something important.

Post-Olympus Footnote: Confidential Commentary by Steen Madsen

6. There had been a lot of tears on this voyage; fortunately, now there were some happy ones. I was glad the last ride wasn't a contest. It gave her a chance to enjoy hitting the finish line.

So, what do I think about the medal? There is no bigger honour to an athlete or her coach. Although the gold medal is not an end in itself, it brought its tremendous honour and charisma to our journey. Her life and mine will never be the same. I'm building a career as a stockbroker, family man, and maintaining my other life as a coach, but a day doesn't pass without a thought of that gold medal.

Edmonton, Alberta, Canada, December 2004, M-plus Four Months

"I've finally figured out who you are," says Karl, the writer and author of my story.

Usually he doesn't tell me anything. He's forever pestering me with questions. He examines and cross-examines me, using his trial-lawyer skills to draw the answers out.

We sit in his study. The session begins, and I leave the day behind. The memories return, and I can see the places, the people and the races. Underneath and lurking are the levers and wheels, the reasons why, and the rationales. I answer a question, then Karl stops me. The answer is explained, and the explanation is analysed.

It's taken months.

The story is mine, the answers were all there. Some needed to be teased out, others sprang out, others yet were chiselled out from the mass of beliefs, habits, strengths, and frailties that make up our personalities. Some organizing themes and motifs were obvious. Others not so: the origin and transforming role of ambition, the relationship between ambition, adversity, and persistence. All these themes had to be unearthed, one event at a time.

Today, for a change, Karl has something to say. "I've figured it out," he says, adjusting his glasses. He's an ex-track rider and downhill ski racer. Maybe he's figured something out about athletes in these sports.

"Okay," I say.

"You're an archetype. She is the protector of cities, arts, and industry. She is the guardian of justice and skill. She bestows command, skill and courage—victory for the just—destruction for the violent and unjust. She prefers diplomacy to warfare, but when angered, will fight to the death. She loves the domestic arts, like weaving, but wields a sword and the charmed armour, the Aegis. She's an unlikely blend."

I'm squinting, tilting my head. What's he on about now?

"She will never permit defeat."

I can relate to that, but who's he talking about? Karl pauses, and looks up from his notes.

"It's Athena," he says, "the goddess of wisdom, justice, and the domestic arts."

"Athena?"

"It's you."

Flattering. But me?

"She's an archetype. The word archetype originally denoted a process as much as a result."

"Me?"

"Athena fights. She has to. When you have ambitions, you have adversity. The battle defines you—is you. And your city is..."

"Athens?"

He nods. "Your namesake. At first it seemed to be a coincidence," he says, shaking his head like he's discovered the law of gravity. "But everything fit. I don't know where I first got the idea, but it's you. I'm not the first one to write your story either," Karl says, looking away, like he's seen something beautiful and true, something that we're not used to taking in everyday. "For a joke, one of my partners dredged up a list of other Karl Wilbergs in history. Most of them are dog show judges, music composers, and so on." He shudders and says, "But there was one..."

He tosses me a printout of an antiquarian bookseller's page. One of the books listed is a Baedeker travel guide from 1871. It's titled *Athens, and its Environs*. The author? Karl Wilberg.

The modern Karl Wilberg shrugs and changes the topic.

"You know how you say that you're not a good leader?"

I nod.

"Sorry," he says. "I don't agree. Look at all your speaking at public schools. Look at all the kids you've reached. And then there are the other speaking engagements too."

"So?" I say, sitting up in the recliner.

"What about the total strangers, the people in the stores, on the plane, everywhere?"

What's he getting at?

"Their eyes are shining, their faces beaming, especially the older women," he says.

He's right. I can't go into the grocery store without someone congratulating me, thanking me.

"You *are* something—something important," he says. "What do you think you're teaching them?"

Before I can answer, he says, "It's part of the archetype too. Athena bestows not only command and favour, but guidance too. She is the one who guided Ulysses during his Odyssey." He's talking as though he's doing no more than forecasting the weather. "It's your job, you know— giving adventurers advice for their own journeys. Something else for you to do. Ambition is good, it helps form us, but it's done its job. You've proven yourself. Now it's time for the new role."

I'm sitting in the chair, wondering what could happen next. Then again, maybe I've discovered the answer.

EPILOGUE

epilogue /epi log/ *n.* **1.** latin for last word. **2** a message, delivered from
the delirium of fatigue, but with an insight gained by surviving the
adversities that ambition brings. **3** invariably optimistic. See related
entry for *post script*: P.S.

—From the *Cyc.L.O.Ps.*

One gear, no breaks (brakes).

The phrase describes a track bike, the pace of a champion's quest for
the summit, and now a book and documentary film of the same title.
The phrase describes my journey before Athens, but also post–gold
medal. And why wouldn't it?

A gold medal, with all its charisma, prestige, and mythical status,
confers many things. The medal brought a cascade of other honours,
and I am grateful for them all. Among them, I was named 2004
Canadian Female Athlete of the Year, put on the Canadian Association
for Advancement of Women and Sport's list of Most Influential Women
in Sport, and awarded the Alberta Centennial Medal. Also, my Olympic
ride placed fourth on *Canadian Cyclist*'s list of the top ten Canadian
cycling accomplishments.

For me it validated my voyage, honoured my supporters—Steen, my
family, Brenda—and redeemed my sacrifices. A gold medal guarantees
many responsibilities, and foremost is the responsibility to be an example. Also, a gold medal is a catalyst, the signal that a chapter has
finished, and there is a new episode to write.

A few details illustrate the point. Two weeks after Athens, I resumed
training. I wanted to be the second woman to win the World
Championships and an Olympic gold medal in one year. Unfortunately,

the UCI scheduled the 2005 World Championships for Los Angeles in March. I would have less than seven months to do what would ordinarily be done in twelve.

Although my competitors and I all shared the same compressed season, Father Winter does not put his plans on hold—not even for a reigning Olympic champion. As usual, snow filled the Argyll Velodrome, and I spent a week every month living in Burnaby, training in Canada's only indoor velodrome.

Also, Steen landed a career in the financial industry, and he and Cyndi began a family. I was happy for him. He had helped me win an Olympic gold medal, but workaday realities meant he could no longer be a constant presence.

My life, too, was transforming. Karl Wilberg's prediction of a new role was coming true. Schools, businesses, and national institutions invited me to speak and pass on my message: "See it. Believe it. Achieve it." Although I tried to control the demands, I made over seventy appearances. Of course these had to be fit into a full-time schedule of training and travel.

The toll of public commitments, the ongoing lack of financial support, and not least of all, no coach and no track, turned the voyage into an ordeal. Want to know more? Watch *1GNB (One Gear, No Breaks)*, Chris Wilberg's award-winning documentary film of my short 2005 season, where the details of this voyage are laid out in their gory glory.

Regrets? Not one. A gold medal does not guarantee a pleasure cruise into a sunset of material success and nor should it. A champion may not win the title, or gain a rent-paying sponsorship. Breaks, or no breaks, a champion's spirit is always *undefeated*. I don't wear the gold medal around my neck; I wear it on my heart.

After the Worlds in March 2005, I let the sweet Alberta spring rejuvenate my soul. Transformations continued: my career as a legal assistant abruptly ended. I had, like many other top Canadian athletes, worn through the bottom of the resources barrel. I would have to regroup, and attempt to find an answer to this perennial problem.

In the meantime, EPCOR, one of Canada's top 100 employers, invited me to become part of their Road to Champions program. The company believed that a parade of champions (Kyle Shewfelt, Simon Whitfield, Adam Van Koeverden, Silken Laumann, and I) could bring our stories to Canadians. Also, audience proceeds would be plowed directly into amateur sport. EPCOR, which invests in energy and water production, realized that Olympic success requires an investment in athletes.

The Road to Champions program was a clue. One more ingredient was needed before the solution became apparent. *1GNB* provided the last hint. Chris' camera was in my face, detailing every nuance of the '05 season, but it wasn't until I'd seen his final cut that it struck me. At the 2005 World Championships I didn't win the title, but watching the film led to an invaluable insight. *1GNB* illustrates the stark realities of elite sport—you can't win a world title on your own.

I could see how fortunate my ride to Athens had been: fortunate for the ordinary citizens who chipped in, for the people like Steen, for the patrons like Brenda. Even when it seemed I was in the teeth of misfortune, an undercurrent of good people and good breaks had led to an Olympic gold medal.

On the eve of the 2006 season, I held a press conference and announced that I would continue to speak to audiences. I would use the film and this book as touchstones to deliver my message. And I would continue to train. However, I would take a one year sabbatical from competition. The press asked, "Why?" I didn't want to emphasize it, but they got my grudging confirmation about the lack of material support.

Immediately after, I cringed. My journey is not about criticizing those who didn't help; it is about celebrating those who did.

I needn't have worried.

The public understood the realities. Olympic success must not be left to fortune. There's only one gear on an ambitious athlete's bike, but, ironically, they need a break. Fortune plays a large enough role as it is. Why give it the steering wheel?

They say it takes a village to raise a child. So, too, does it take a community to support a champion. Want more gold medals, more athletes standing at the top of the podium?

Here's the formula: take fiercely dedicated athletes, their band of friends and family, and add a patron—a business-world partner like EPCOR. The athletes provide the idealism, the suffering and the sweat. The companies provide material support. The national organizing bodies organize the bodies. Result? Athletes win medals, inspire thousands of children, and the companies enhance their reputations as responsible citizens.

Still, the entire process requires faith. Corporate citizens are willing to support our athletes. What about the private citizenry? The spontaneous greetings, hugs, and congratulations I receive every day speak for themselves.

But are they empty gestures? I think not.

This year, I established a speaker's network for women, Pure Momentum Inc. In a matter of months, prominent Canadian female athletes, artists, and performers joined my roster. The media has supported my journey, and EPCOR has continued to take the initiative. They are now the sponsor of the Lori-Ann Muenzer Program (LAMP) for children's cycling, modelled on the Nancy Greene ski program. Thousands of people have seen *1GNB*, and my publisher, Key Porter Books, believed enough in this story to put it in your hands. Later this spring, EPCOR will co-sponsor my book and speaking tour.

At the end of the day, Athena has learned this much. We all get breaks, good and bad. The question is how you use them. In the end, the journey is about dreaming your dreams, and struggling to reach the stars. It is about self-belief and setting your own limits. And, this country and its people are with me all the way.

I couldn't have better companions for the journey.

LORI-ANN MUENZER'S ACKNOWLEDGEMENTS

Jennifer: You have always been there for me and you always believed in what I was doing. There isn't one word that says it all, but there is a phrase that does: "You are the wings beneath my feet." I love you.

Jack McCutcheon: Who would have known that our friendship would grow over two years and beyond? It has been an incredible journey getting to know you, but the best part has been spending time with you and for this I am truly grateful. Thank you for your patience, your wisdom, your insights, your stories, and, of course, the Monday night steak dinners! But most of all always being there, no matter what, and believing in what Steen and I were doing.

Brenda Miller: Part of the journey would not have been possible without you. You were a great help and instrumental in getting me to the Sydney World Cup to qualify for the World Championships in May 2002. Thinking of you inspired me many times, from August 2002 to August 2004, when the going got really tough and I wondered, sometimes, how I would be able to continue. Since Jack gave me your University of Alberta medal, in February 2003, it accompanies me whenever I travel. Many times on my journeys your medal gave me the strength to continue to turn the pedals. Together we were on the podium in Athens and I will always dedicate part of my Olympic gold medal to you. You are greatly missed but never forgotten.

Mom and Dad: Your teachings made me tough—tough enough to want to take on the world. The best part would start to come after the 1998 Commonwealth Games when you wished me luck, told me to ride like the wind, and told me to go out and to do my best. In Athens you said, "Go out and knock 'em dead." It was hearing your love and knowing that you were behind me that made all the difference in the world.

Grandma (Annie Rosena Abernethy): Your love was unconditional and you were always there for me no matter what. It didn't matter if I told you about a race that I was only able to finish or if I showed you the medal I had won. Oh, how I miss you since you've gone and I wish that I could show you one more gold medal.

Jim "Mr. Guinness" Horner: To the velodrome "gatekeeper," my mechanic, and friend. You were a part of my journey when I arrived in Edmonton and at the Juventus Cycling Club. You were always there with your stopwatch, a big smile, told a ton of stories with your thick Irish accent, and always there to give a great big hug when the going got really tough. You're never far away, Mr. Guinness.

Sue Wilberg: Peppermint tea will always remind me of coming over to the Wilberg house and working on the book. Thank you for all of your support and being the "balance" of this project when Karl and I would get off track with our crazy ideas and ramblings!

Karl Wilberg: Working with you on this book I never dreamt that I would re-open and re-visit my journey. In looking back, a lot of the evenings were hard work because of what we were unravelling, but never once did I ever doubt the direction that you were steering us towards. For many years I ran onto the next goal and objective without having had the time to digest that year's happenings. Without working on this story with you I would never have been able to understand and see all that happened. There were so many hidden golden treasures that you managed to uncover. Thank you for all of the revelations and insights that you have given me.

Steen Madsen: Who would have thought this would actually happen? We both had a dream of going to the Olympics and chasing a gold medal. You started off first as an athlete, then became both my coach and the best training partner anyone could ever have. I wanted to make you proud of our work. As a result, I have never worked so hard at anything before, nor had I ever wanted anything so badly that I was willing to put everything on the line. The bonus was that we got to show the world what all of our hard training was about! Thank you for your patience, for keeping me on track when it got tough, and for always answering my many questions. I consider you one of my closest friends and this amazing journey would not have been possible without you.

KARL WILBERG'S ACKNOWLEDGEMENTS

Any author will confess that a book starts as an idea and ends as an odyssey.

And, any odyssey requires a crew. Strong arms haul on the oars, nimble hands set the sails, and a wise presence presides at the helm. My crew includes my sons Daniel, Nicholas, and Matthew. The full complement includes my brother Curtis, and parents Robert and Barbara. I will leave it to each of them to determine which role they occupy on this ship.

So, too, must I thank my brother Chris, and his wife Monique, who have consistently supported me on this voyage, and have encouraged the venturing spirit that leads to fulfillment. Without their help, this boat would be trapped in the doldrums.

Also, I must thank my law practice partners, whose good natures have been taxed by the absences occasioned on this voyage.

An odyssey requires faith, and I thank our publisher, Jordan Fenn, of Key Porter Books, for his faith in Lori-Ann's story. So, too, do I thank our editor, Michael Mouland, and his able editorial crew, for fashioning a sleek, and purposeful craft from my draft.

Finally, I thank the archetypes. Foremost is my mentor, R.J. Childerhose. His willingness to share a half century of writing wisdom laid the keel of this ship. Second, is the artist, Steen Madsen, whose faith in me led to the book you hold in your hands. Third, is my wife Susan. Every odyssey has it's Odysseus, and every Odysseus, his Penelope. I am sorry to have kept her waiting so long. Last, is a champion that redeems and validates the dreamer in all of us.

A champion, like Lori-Ann will show you the way to the stars.

GLOSSARY

Match sprint
A head-to-head competition, usually consisting of three laps. Seeding is determined by a 200-metre qualifying ride. The riders compete in an elimination series. Early rounds are one ride, the medal rounds are best of three. After the initial round, a second chance is sometimes given—this is termed the repechage. Riders are then streamed into the medal rounds. Those who are eliminated from the semi-finals are grouped into a ride off of up to four riders. Most other rides are one versus one.

Pole line
Officially called the measuring line, it is the black line at the base of the track that is the shortest, legal, way around the track. Once a rider has dropped to the pole line, and is committed to the sprint (in the opinion of the commissaires) they must not rise above the sprinter's line—a red line ninety centimetres to the right of the pole line. Also, in the final 200 metres, once a rider has dropped below this line, they may not rise above it.

Apron
The transition from the infield to the track competitive surface. The inside of the pole line.

Velodrome
A purpose-built cycling track. Typically, from 250 metres to 333 metres in distance, measured on the pole line. Surfaces are usually wood, cement, or asphalt.

Track bike
The purest form of bicycle—one gear, no brakes. The gear is fixed, and no free-wheeling is possible. There are only three ways to slow down: apply

back pressure to pedals, ride up the bank (uphill), or crash into something. Often made of carbon fibre and other aerospace materials.

Track wheels
Like the bike, simple, sophisticated carbon-fibre construction, and expensive. May have a handful of spokes, or be a solid disk.